Green Advertising and the Reluctant Consumer

T0341046

This edited collection presents cutting edge research into the topic of green messages and subsequent consumer responses. The research studies draw on a rich tradition of communication, psychological and sociological theories that examine consumer responses in a nuanced way. At the same time, the studies present important implications for advertising practitioners and academics alike. Written by communications scholars from North America, Europe and Asia, the studies encompass a range of research techniques including experiments, surveys, content analyses and depth interviews. The book provides important insights into current practice as well as directions for future research.

This book was originally published as a special issue of the *Journal of Advertising*.

Kim Sheehan is Professor at the School of Journalism & Communication at the University of Oregon, USA. She recieved her PhD from the University of Tennessee, USA.

Lucy Atkinson is Assistant Professor in the Department of Advertising and Public Relations at the University of Texas-Austin, USA. She recieved her PhD from the University of Wisconsin, USA.

Green Advertising and the Reluctant Consumer

Edited by
Kim Sheehan and Lucy Atkinson

Routledge
Taylor & Francis Group

LONDON AND NEW YORK

First published in paperback 2024

First published 2015
by Routledge
4 Park Square, Milton Park, Abingdon, Oxon OX14 4RN

and by Routledge
605 Third Avenue, New York, NY 10158

Routledge is an imprint of the Taylor & Francis Group, an informa business

Publisher's Note
The publisher accepts responsibility for any inconsistencies that may have arisen during the conversion of this book from journal articles to book chapters, namely the possible inclusion of journal terminology.

Disclaimer
Every effort has been made to contact copyright holders for their permission to reprint material in this book. The publishers would be grateful to hear from any copyright holder who is not here acknowledged and will undertake to rectify any errors or omissions in future editions of this book.

British Library Cataloguing in Publication Data
A catalogue record for this book is available from the British Library

ISBN: 978-1-138-01654-5 (hbk)
ISBN: 978-1-03-293014-5 (pbk)
ISBN: 978-1-315-77963-8 (ebk)

DOI: 10.4324/9781315779638

Typeset in Garamond
by Taylor & Francis Books

Contents

Citation Information   vii
Notes on Contributors   ix

1. Introduction: Revisiting Green Advertising and the Reluctant Consumer
   Kim Sheehan and Lucy Atkinson   1

2. Consumer Receptivity to Green Ads: A Test of Green Claim Types and the Role of Individual Consumer Characteristics for Green Ad Response
   Elizabeth M. Tucker, Nora J. Rifon, Eun Mi Lee, and Bonnie B. Reece   4

3. The Role of Regulatory Focus and Self-View in "Green" Advertising Message Framing
   Ioannis Kareklas, Jeffrey R. Carlson, and Darrel D. Muehling   19

4. Communicating Green Marketing Appeals Effectively: The Role of Consumers' Motivational Orientation to Promotion Versus Prevention
   Hsuan-Hsuan Ku, Chien-Chih Kuo, Ching-Luen Wu, and Chih-Ying Wu   34

5. Green Eco-Seals and Advertising Persuasion
   Barbara A. Bickart and Julie A. Ruth   44

6. Sustainable Marketing and Social Media: A Cross-Country Analysis of Motives for Sustainable Behaviors
   Elizabeth Minton, Christopher Lee, Ulrich Orth, Chung-Hyun Kim, and Lynn Kahle   61

7. The Effectiveness of Benefit Type and Price Endings in Green Advertising
   Marla B. Royne, Jennifer Martinez, Jared Oakley, and Alexa K. Fox   77

8. Is the Devil in the Details? The Signaling Effect of Numerical Precision in Environmental Advertising Claims
   Guang-Xin Xie and Ann Kronrod   95

9. Victoria's *Dirty* Secrets: Effectiveness of Green Not-for-Profit Messages Targeting Brands
   Marie-Cécile Cervellon   110

10. Factors Affecting Skepticism toward Green Advertising
    Arminda Maria Finisterra do Paço and Rosa Reis   123

Index   132

Citation Information

The chapters in this book were originally published in the *Journal of Advertising*, volume 41, issue 4 (November–December 2012). When citing this material, please use the original page numbering for each article, as follows:

Chapter 1
Special Issue on Green Advertising: Revisiting Green Advertising and the Reluctant Consumer
Kim Sheehan and Lucy Atkinson
Journal of Advertising, volume 41, issue 4 (November–December 2012) pp. 5-7

Chapter 2
Consumer Receptivity to Green Ads: A Test of Green Claim Types and the Role of Individual Consumer Characteristics for Green Ad Response
Elizabeth M. Tucker, Nora J. Rifon, Eun Mi Lee, and Bonnie B. Reece
Journal of Advertising, volume 41, issue 4 (November–December 2012) pp. 9-23

Chapter 3
The Role of Regulatory Focus and Self-View in "Green" Advertising Message Framing
Ioannis Kareklas, Jeffrey R. Carlson, and Darrel D. Muehling
Journal of Advertising, volume 41, issue 4 (November–December 2012) pp. 25-39

Chapter 4
Communicating Green Marketing Appeals Effectively: The Role of Consumers' Motivational Orientation to Promotion Versus Prevention
Hsuan-Hsuan Ku, Chien-Chih Kuo, Ching-Luen Wu, and Chih-Ying Wu
Journal of Advertising, volume 41, issue 4 (November–December 2012) pp. 41-50

Chapter 5
Green Eco-Seals and Advertising Persuasion
Barbara A. Bickart and Julie A. Ruth
Journal of Advertising, volume 41, issue 4 (November–December 2012) pp. 51-67

Chapter 6
Sustainable Marketing and Social Media: A Cross-Country Analysis of Motives for Sustainable Behaviors
Elizabeth Minton, Christopher Lee, Ulrich Orth, Chung-Hyun Kim, and Lynn Kahle
Journal of Advertising, volume 41, issue 4 (November–December 2012) pp. 69-84

Chapter 7
The Effectiveness of Benefit Type and Price Endings in Green Advertising
Marla B. Royne, Jennifer Martinez, Jared Oakley, and Alexa K. Fox
Journal of Advertising, volume 41, issue 4 (November–December 2012) pp. 85-102

Chapter 8
Is the Devil in the Details? The Signaling Effect of Numerical Precision in Environmental Advertising Claims
Guang-Xin Xie and Ann Kronrod
Journal of Advertising, volume 41, issue 4 (November–December 2012) pp. 103-117

Chapter 9

Victoria's Dirty *Secrets: Effectiveness of Green Not-for-Profit Messages Targeting Brands*
Marie-Cécile Cervellon
Journal of Advertising, volume 41, issue 4 (November–December 2012) pp. 133-145

Chapter 10

Factors Affecting Skepticism toward Green Advertising
Arminda Maria Finisterra do Paço and Rosa Reis
Journal of Advertising, volume 41, issue 4 (November–December 2012) pp. 147-155

Please direct any queries you may have about the citations to clsuk.permissions@cengage.com

Notes on Contributors

Lucy Atkinson (Ph.D., University of Wisconsin, USA) is Assistant Professor in the Department of Advertising and Public Relations at the University of Texas-Austin, USA.

Barbara A. Bickart (Ph.D., University of Illinois at Urbana, USA) is an Associate Professor of marketing, School of Management, Boston University, USA.

Jeffrey R. Carlson (M.A., Purdue University, USA) is a Ph.D. candidate in marketing, School of Business, University of Connecticut, USA.

Marie-Cécile Cervellon (Ph.D., McGill University, Canada) is an Associate Professor of marketing, International University of Monaco, Monaco.

Arminda Maria Finisterra do Paço (Ph.D., University of Beira Interior, Portugal) is a Professor of marketing, Department of Business and Economics–Research Unit NECE, University of Beira Interior, Covilhã, Portugal.

Alexa K. Fox (M.B.A., The University of Akron, USA) is a Ph.D. student, Department of Marketing and Supply Chain Management, Fogelman College of Business and Economics, The University of Memphis, USA.

Lynn Kahle (Ph.D., University of Nebraska, USA) is Ehrman Giustina Professor of Marketing and department head, Lundquist College of Business, University of Oregon, Eugene, USA.

Ioannis Kareklas (Ph.D., University of Connecticut, USA) is an Assistant Professor of marketing, College of Business, Washington State University, USA.

Chung-Hyun Kim (Ph.D., University of Oregon, USA) is Dean, School of Mass Communication, Sogang University, Seoul, South Korea.

Ann Kronrod (Ph.D., Tel Aviv University, Israel) is an Assistant Professor of advertising, College of Communication Arts and Sciences, Faculty Affiliate, Cognitive Science, Michigan State University, USA.

Hsuan-Hsuan Ku (Ph.D., National Taiwan University, Taipei, Taiwan) is a Professor of marketing, Department of International Business, Soochow University, Taipei, Taiwan.

Chien-Chih Kuo (Ph.D., National Taiwan University, Taipei, Taiwan) is an Associate Professor of psychology, Department of Psychology, National Chengchi University, Taipei, Taiwan.

Christopher Lee (M.B.A., Arizona State University, USA) is a doctoral student, Lundquist College of Business, University of Oregon, Eugene, USA.

Eun Mi Lee (Ph.D., Ewha Womans University, South Korea) is a Research Scholar, Department of Advertising, Michigan State University, USA.

Jennifer Martinez (M.B.A., The University of St. Thomas, USA) is a Ph.D. candidate, Department of Marketing and Supply Chain Management, Fogelman College of Business and Economics, The University of Memphis, USA.

Elizabeth Minton (M.B.A., Idaho State University, USA) is a doctoral student, Lundquist College of Business, University of Oregon, Eugene, USA.

Darrel D. Muehling (Ph.D., University of Nebraska–Lincoln, USA) is a Professor of marketing, College of Business, Washington State University, USA.

Jared Oakley (M.B.A., The University of Memphis, USA) is a Ph.D. candidate, Department of Marketing and Supply Chain Management, Fogelman College of Business and Economics, The University of Memphis, USA.

Ulrich Orth (Ph.D., Munich University of Technology, Germany) is a Professor and Chair, A&F Marketing, Christian-Albrechts-Universität zu Kiel, Kiel, Germany.

Bonnie B. Reece (Ph.D., University of Michigan, USA) is a Professor and Chairperson Emerita, Department of Advertising, Michigan State University, USA.

Rosa Reis (M.S., University of Beira Interior, Portugal) is the secretary to the director, Polytechnic Institute of Guarda, Guarda, Portugal.

Nora J. Rifon (Ph.D., The Graduate Center at the City University of New York, USA) is a Professor, Department of Advertising, Michigan State University, USA.

Marla B. Royne (Ph.D., The University of Georgia, USA) is First Tennessee Professor of Marketing and Chair, Department of Marketing and Supply Chain Management, Fogelman College of Business and Economics, The University of Memphis, USA.

Julie A. Ruth (Ph.D., University of Michigan, USA) is an Associate Professor of marketing, School of Business, Rutgers University, USA.

Kim Sheehan (Ph.D., University of Tennessee, USA) is Professor at the School of Journalism and Communication at the University of Oregon, USA.

Elizabeth M. Tucker (Ph.D., Michigan State University, USA). Deceased.

Chih-Ying Wu (M.B.A., Soochow University, Taipei, Taiwan) is a Ph.D. student, Institute of Work, Health and Organisations, University of Nottingham, Nottingham, United Kingdom.

Ching-Luen Wu (M.B.A., Soochow University, Taipei, Taiwan) is an import-export executive, Elca, Taipei, Taiwan.

Guang-Xin Xie (Ph.D. University of Oregon, USA) is an Assistant Professor of marketing, College of Management, University of Massachusetts Boston, USA.

INTRODUCTION

Revisiting Green Advertising and the Reluctant Consumer

Kim Sheehan and Lucy Atkinson

The *Journal of Advertising* first devoted a special issue to green advertising in the summer of 1995. The guest editor of that issue, Easwar Iyer, indicated that the use of the word "green" in describing this particular type of advertising was meant to connote pro-environmental behaviors on behalf of both companies and consumers. Green advertising was further defined as a message promoting environmentally oriented consumption behavior (Kilbourne 1995); as a promotional message that may appeal to the needs and desires of environmentally concerned consumers (Zinkhan and Carlson 1995); and as a message that features an environmental attribute for a product or service (Schuhwerk and Lefkoff-Hagius 1995).

That issue, consisting of six papers, covered a range of topics that created what might be considered the first comprehensive framework around environmental messages, addressing the complex relationship between attitudes, behaviors, consumers, and advertising. Most notable in this issue was the framework proposed by Kilbourne (1995) that explicated the political and human relational elements of green attitudes. The political aspect of the framework was further explicated in papers addressing policy issues and agency management. To address the human relational element, other papers addressed the interplay of strategy and consumers, looking at how different positioning appeals (sick baby versus well baby) affected consumers.

In the nearly two decades since that special issue, the environment has become even more of a hot button topic among consumers, corporations, and policymakers. Federal Trade Commission (FTC) chairman Jon Leibowitz noted, "In recent years, businesses have increasingly used 'green' marketing to capture consumers' attention and move Americans toward a more environmentally friendly future." A 2010 study of advertising practitioners indicated that more than three-quarters of surveyed practitioners planned to increase their advertising

and marketing spending on green messages in the future. That increase is due to numerous polls showing that many U.S. consumers are willing to pay more for "green" products (e.g., GfK Roper Public Affairs & Media and the Yale School of Forestry & Environmental Studies 2008; Integer Group and M/A/R/C Research 2011; Mintel 2010). This trend holds true around the world, with recent polls showing that consumers in China (Ogilvy Mather 2011), Japan (McKinsey 2010), and Europe (FoodDrinkEurope 2011) are looking for ways to integrate sustainability into their lifestyles.

This trend is complex, however, with studies showing that consumers' green intent does not always translate into actual green purchase behaviors (Grail Research 2009; Lindqvist 2011). For example, a 2011 study by Nielsen reports that half of Americans say they prefer eco-friendly products, but only 12% of consumers are willing to pay more for them. The patterns are similar in other countries. This attitude–behavior gap reveals a discrepancy between consumers' environmentally friendly, socially desirable orientations and their real-world marketplace choices. The green advertising landscape is further complicated by questions of ethics and the numerous contradictory and sometimes misleading messages in green advertising. At the forefront are concerns about greenwashing, where messages overstate the environmental benefits of products and services.

Since that first special issue in 1995, green advertising has gained considerable academic attention in the marketing and advertising fields. Evidence of this now-widespread interest can be seen in the breadth and depth of the papers in this issue. The 1995 special issue laid the framework for the role of "green" messaging in advertising, and this issue builds on that framework in this unique way. Starting with those cutting-edge papers, this special issue extends those groundbreaking exploratory and descriptive studies, and brings much-needed theoretical rigor to the field of green advertising.

The 9 papers here represent a variety of methodological approaches, including experiments, surveys, depth interviews, and content analyses, as well as theoretical frameworks ranging from signal theory and regulatory focus to prospect theory and the theory of planned behavior. They also cast a broad geographic net, with studies drawing samples from

Taiwan, Portugal, Germany, and South Korea, in addition to the United States.

Running through all the studies, however, are three important common threads: theoretical richness, complex model building, and real-world implications. First, the papers in this collection draw on a rich tradition of psychological and sociological theories to ground their findings and generate theoretically rich insights into green advertising. In so doing, these studies help build our understanding of green advertising, the mechanisms at play, and how advertising audiences react to them. Their theoretical contributions help bring clarity to the topic of green advertising and offer road maps for future research, as well as theory building and testing.

For example, in their paper "The Role of Regulatory Focus and Self-View in 'Green' Advertising Message Framing," Kareklas, Carlson, and Muehling rely on the theory of regulatory focus to explain audience reactions to different green advertising frames. Their results replicate the theory's applicability to green advertising while shedding new light on the role of regulatory focus in the context of advertising appeals directed at the personal level compared with those at the more general, environmental level. In "Communicating Green Marketing Appeals Effectively: The Role of Consumers' Motivational Orientation to Promotion Versus Prevention," Ku et al. also studied the phenomenon of consumer regulatory focus in relationship to green motivations. Their work suggests that green appeals that are nonproduct focused can be highly motivating to many consumers. In "Green Eco-Seals and Advertising Persuasion," Bickart and Ruth rely on the Persuasion Knowledge Model (PKM) to explain the persuasiveness of eco-seals, while underscoring the importance of environmental concern as an important theoretical component. Royne et al. use Prospect Theory and Mental Accounting Theory to examine the relationship between advertising appeals and product pricing in "The Effectiveness of Benefit Type and Price Endings in Green Advertising." Their study looks at how those two elements play into perceptions of the product quality of green products relative to other types of products, given different pricing structures. The study also contributes to our understanding of consumer motivations for purchasing green products.

Second, this collection of papers brings a careful, nuanced eye to the ways in which consumers process green advertising messages and with what effects. The simple view of a reluctant green consumer has been expanded in this special issue to account for important mediating and moderating influences, such as environmental concern and advertising skepticism at the individual level, and the influence of framing and medium effects at the message level. They go beyond developing typologies of green consumers or the various kinds of green advertising to build more complex models of green consumer behaviors.

For example, two studies underscore the importance of consumer involvement in green advertising messages. In Minton et al.'s cross-cultural article, "Sustainable Marketing and Social Media: A Cross-Country Analysis of Motives for Sustainable Behaviors," involvement, which the authors operationalized as a measure of sociability and camaraderie, was an important predictor of green behaviors in the United States and Germany, but less so for consumers in South Korea. In "Victoria's *Dirty Secrets*: Effectiveness of Green Not-for-Profit Messages Targeting Brands," Cervellon takes a different view of involvement, operationalizing it in terms of environmental involvement. She shows how exposure to messages about a brand's negative environmental track record resonate more strongly with less-involved consumers than with highly involved consumers when the message is framed as a loss. Tackling involvement from a slightly different angle, Tucker et al. explore involvement in the form of past environmental behaviors and perceived consumer efficacy. In "Consumer Receptivity to Green Ads: A Test of Green Claim Types and the Role of Individual Consumer Characteristics for Green Ad Response," they show how higher levels of involvement are positive predictors of ad credibility, which leads to more positive attitudes toward the ad and the brand.

Paço and Reis, in "Factors Affecting Skepticism Toward Green Advertising," build on this attitudinal knowledge by examining the role of consumer skepticism in message processing. While consumers are indeed skeptical of green claims, Paço and Reis found that such skepticism does not negatively affect behaviors: Consumers perform and participate in green activities and buy environmentally friendly products regardless of this skepticism. Xie and Kronrod also explore the nature of skepticism in "Is the Devil in the Details? The Signaling Effect of Numerical Precision in Environmental Advertising Claims." The authors found that in certain situations, a high level of numerical precision in advertising claims can be persuasive to highly skeptical individuals. Specifically, scarcity of information enhances the importance and persuasiveness of whatever information is available.

Finally, each paper speaks to the applied and practical aspects of green advertising. Across the board, these studies raise important questions and present meaningful suggestions for industry professionals. In so doing, they shed light on one of the more frustrating and limiting aspects of green advertising: how to bridge the attitude–behavior gap among would-be green consumers. This green gap is particularly problematic for practitioners, who are left with little guidance on how to motivate consumers to purchase green products and exhibit green behaviors.

Xie and Kronrod provide information on providing explicit numeric claims to increase persuasiveness in specific situations. Ku et al. recommend that marketers prime a target audience for either a promotion-focused or a prevention-focused strategy to influence the persuasiveness of communications.

Taken together, this collection of papers offers detailed insight into the current field of green advertising while raising important questions and avenues for future research. It is our hope that the work represented in this volume energizes future studies of green advertising and lays the groundwork for another decade or so of scholarship, just as the first special issue did in 1995.

REFERENCES

FoodDrinkEurope (2011), "Environmental Sustainability Vision Toward 2030," available at http://sustainability.fooddrink europe.eu (accessed February 28, 2013).

GfK Roper Public Affairs & Media and the Yale School of Forestry & Environmental Studies (2008), "The GfK Roper Yale Survey on Environmental Issues: Consumer Attitudes Toward Environmentally Friendly Products and Eco-Labeling," available at http://environment.yale.edu (accessed February 28, 2013).

Grail Research (2009), "The Green Revolution," available at http://grailresearch.com/about_us/featuredresearch .aspx?aid=90/ (accessed February 28, 2013).

Integer Group and M/A/R/C Research (2011), "Green Report," available at www.marcresearch.com/archives.php#The% 20Checkout/ (accessed February 28, 2013).

Kilbourne, William E. (1995), "Green Advertising: Salvation or Oxymoron?" *Journal of Advertising,* 24 (Summer), 7–20.

Lindqvist, Nea (2011), "Green Segmentation," available at http:// behavioraltargeting.biz/tag/nea-lindqvist/ (accessed February 28, 2013).

McKinsey (2011), "Finding the Green in Green," available at http://csi.mckinsey.com/knowledge_by_region/asia/japan/finding_the_green_in_green/ (accessed February 28, 2013).

Mintel Oxygen Reports (2010), "Green Living," available at www .mintel.com/press-centre/press-releases/514/are-americans-willing-to-pay-more-green-to-get-more-green/ (accessed February 28, 2013).

Nielsen (2011), "Sustainable Efforts and Environmental Concerns," available at www.nielsen.com/us/en/insights/ reports-downloads/2011/sustainable-efforts-environmental-concerns.html (accessed February 28, 2013).

Ogilvy Mather (2011), "Corporations Not Cashing In on Chinese Consumers' Desire for Sustainability," available at www .ogilvy.com/News/Press-Releases/April-2011-Corporations-Not-Cashing-In-On-Chinese-Consumers-Desire-For-Sustainability.aspx (accessed February 28, 2013).

Schuhwerk, Melody E., and Roxanne Lefkoff-Hagius (1995), "Green or Non-Green? Does Type of Appeal Matter When Advertising a Green Product?" *Journal of Advertising,* 24, (Summer), 45–54.

Zinkhan, George M., and Les Carlson (1995), "Green Advertising and the Reluctant Consumer," *Journal of Advertising,* 24 (Summer), 1–6.

CONSUMER RECEPTIVITY TO GREEN ADS

A Test of Green Claim Types and the Role of Individual
Consumer Characteristics for Green Ad Response

Elizabeth M. Tucker, Nora J. Rifon, Eun Mi Lee, and Bonnie B. Reece

ABSTRACT: The overarching goal of this study is to clarify how individual characteristics may influence consumers to be more or less receptive to ecologically themed ad claims. An experiment compares the effectiveness of strong and weak green product claims with a cause-related marketing strategy to advertise a "green" product. The results suggest that consumers with positive attitudes toward environmental protection are equally receptive to all conditions tested. An analysis using a theoretically based structural equation model points to the important role played by perceived consumer effectiveness in creating positive responses.

Environmental protection has resurfaced as an important issue with consumers, policymakers, and corporations. Recent environmental disasters such as the BP oil rig explosion (Brown and Fountain 2010) and evidence of global warming (Gillis 2012) remind consumers of the importance of environmental protection, rekindle consumer awareness and interest in environmental issues (Chitra 2007), and have reinvigorated green marketing strategies (Cronin et al. 2011; Haytko and Matulich 2008). The use of green marketing emerged in the 1980s and early 1990s (Davis 1993; Ottman 1998) and has grown exponentially in the past two decades (Futerra 2008). As noted in the call for papers for this issue, a majority of practitioners surveyed report the intention to increase spending on green marketing. However, academic research has not kept pace with industry interest (Chamorro, Rubio, and Miranda 2009), and there is a gap in our knowledge regarding consumer response to ecologically themed ad appeals.

An ongoing conundrum is the gap between consumer concern for environmental issues and their purchase behaviors (Cone 2012). In other words, if consumers have positive attitudes toward environmental protection, why doesn't that translate into positive ad response and consumption behaviors? Consumer response to ecologically themed ads is a complex puzzle that involves the interplay of ad elements and consumer characteristics, and understanding ecologically themed advertising tactics and their effects is central to solving this enigma. Early research examined consumer receptivity to green ad claims (see, e.g., Ellen, Wiener, and Cobb-Walgren 1991) and the effects of claim presence and claim type on credibility (Carlson, Grove, and Kangun 1993). A large portion of research focused on the potentially deceptive and confusing nature of eco-ad claims, often through content analysis (Carlson, Grove, and Kangun 1993). Few studies examined consumer response to reasonable claims (Manrai et al. 1997; Thorson, Page, and Moore 1995), leaving a significant gap in this research stream.

Furthermore, studies examining the influence of consumer ecological attitudes and behaviors on receptivity to environmental claims provide conflicting results. Moreover, consumers report the desire to punish marketers who deceive them with false ecological claims (Cone 2012). Thus, the exact nature of consumer response to green ads still has not been well established, and it appears that the use of some ecological ad tactics can run the risk of serious backlash.

To date, the paucity of research on reasonable eco-ad claims and the inconsistent findings regarding the influence of consumer characteristics on consumer response to eco-ads have hindered the development of a generalizable model. The study presented in this paper seeks to integrate these two streams of research and develop a generalizable model of the role of consumer characteristics and eco-ad types on

This article is dedicated to the memory of the first author, Elizabeth M. Tucker. The authors thank Paula Storrer and Mark Stuenkel for creating the ads used in the study. They also thank the three anonymous reviewers and the special issue editors for their constructive comments.

consumer response to eco-ad appeals that use reasonable claims. To do this, we first present the results of an experiment that examines the effects of product claim specificity on consumer response to eco-ad appeals. Three forms of eco-ad appeals are compared for their relative effects on consumer response, using a nonecological appeal as a control. The three types of appeals that are compared are the use of (1) a strong product claim, (2) a weak product claim, and (3) a cause-related marketing appeal that makes no product claims, but offers to support environmental protection with a donation to a not-for-profit environmental advocacy group. Thus, we update the research stream by examining a popular tactic that has emerged during the past 20 years within the context of ecological appeals. Green marketing strategies have grown to encompass tactics such as cause-related marketing for product sales and corporate image enhancement (Connolly and Prothero 2003), but it is not clear which of these tactics might yield more positive consumer response than product claim strategies.

In addition, based on past findings and theories of persuasion, the research presented here develops and tests a theoretical model of consumer response to ecologically themed ads based on individual traits. The overarching goal is to clarify how consumer characteristics may influence consumers to be more or less receptive to eco-ad claims. The model outlines the roles of perceived consumer effectiveness and ecological attitudes and behaviors in determining consumer perceptions of ecologically themed advertising credibility and subsequent attitude toward the ad, brand attitude, and purchase intention. The study expands the current domain of academic knowledge, and its results suggest recommendations for advertisers. The findings offer direction for identifying consumers who may be more receptive to ecological ad appeals as well as guidance on the value of the use of ecological product claims, their relative effectiveness based on strength, and the value of creating an eco-ad appeal through the use of cause-related marketing and the avoidance of specific product claims.

LITERATURE REVIEW

Ecologically Themed Advertising Claim Types

During the late 1980s and early 1990s, marketers inundated consumers with green products and environmental claims. Because environmental benefits often occur in the future or cannot be seen at all, there is a credence quality to these claims. Thus, environmental marketing has been considered a tempting arena for exploitation by unscrupulous advertisers (Mayer, Scammon, and Gray-Lee 1993). A number of marketers employed eco-ads to inform consumers about the environmental benefits of their brands, even when claims were untrue, unknown, or unrelated to the product (Coddington 1993). Due to unfavorable publicity generated by several such cases,

consumers became skeptical of green product performance and cynical toward advertised claims (Carlson, Grove, and Kangun 1993; Moore 1993; Thorson, Page, and Moore 1995). Thus "green backlash," the negative response to products based on skepticism of ad claims, was cited as the main reason the green market failed to live up to industry expectations (Davis 1993; Moore 1993; Ottman 1998).

A number of researchers proposed classification systems for green advertising and ad claims. Carlson, Grove, and Kangun (1993) classified environmental claims as product-oriented, process-oriented, image-oriented, and environmental fact. In addition, environmental claims can be considered either substantive or associative. Substantive claims present tangible benefits, whereas associative claims present general environmental facts considered to be intangible and unrelated to the product. Davis (1993) referred to the tangibility versus intangibility of claims as claim specificity and considered the emphasis of the claim based on its position in the ad as primary or secondary. Leonidou et al. (2011) documented types of green claims that appeared in ads in the international edition of *The Economist* between 1988 and 2007. They found an increase in the percentage of ads targeted to consumers and a decrease in the percentage targeted to businesses over the period studied. Using Carlson, Grove, and Kangung's (1993) typology, product-oriented claims were most common, appearing in more than half (52.2%) the ads; process-oriented claims were seen in only 26.6% of the ads. Using Manrai et al.'s (1997) typology, over 50% of observed claims were strong and all others were weak.

Effects of Claim Types on Consumer Response: Ad Credibility and Brand Attitudes

Empirical findings of the few studies on claim type effects are mixed, perhaps due to the use of these noncommensurate typologies. Carlson, Grove, and Kangun (1993) posited that eco-ad claims themselves are potentially deceptive and may confuse consumers, and some typologies suggest a rank ordering of ad types in terms of their potential to be believed by consumers. In general, ad claims that focus on environmental facts or actions that consumers can take are viewed as having the greatest potential to be believed; these are not product claims, as they are not directly linked to product production, performance or disposal, and consumers cannot test the claims through product experience. Thorson, Page, and Moore (1995) tested for consumer attitudes toward different claims and found that "look what we are doing corporate image ads" and "instructional, let's teach our children about the environment ads" created more positive consumer attitudes than commercials with packaging and product claims. Clearly, those claims do not directly connect to product performance, disposal, or production.

Using automobiles as the product category, Manrai et al. (1997) found that moderate claim strength created more positive evaluations of the product and the company as being environmentally conscious and were more believable. They examined a product-specific claim that was manipulated by changing the percentage pollution reduction effected by a car in the stimulus ad. Using Sherif and Hovland's (1961) assimilation contrast model, they predicted that an extreme claim would be outside the latitude of acceptance of the consumer and thus rejected. A weak claim would have no meaning, and so would not engender positive consumer response. Thus, moderate claims would be expected to receive more positive response than either extreme.

The findings from studies specific to ecologically themed advertising suggest that nonproduct claims that focus on corporate image or "feel good" tactics have the potential to be more effective than product claims, and when product claims are made, moderate attribute performance may be more persuasive. Manrai et al.'s (1997) findings should be qualified, however. They claimed to manipulate claim strength by manipulating claim extremity, but claim extremity is not equivalent to claim strength. An extreme claim, such as the one in Manrai's study, presents a very high level of performance on a product attribute, and it can be argued that this was not, in fact, a strong argument but merely an extreme claim. A strong claim may be considered to be one with evidence to support a claim made in a persuasive message. Using the Elaboration Likelihood Model (ELM), studies examining argument strength effects indicate that regardless of level of involvement with an ad, strong arguments are more persuasive than weak arguments (Petty, Cacioppo, and Schumann 1983). Involvement with environmental issues will moderate these effects.

The few studies that examine claim type effects have used a variety of outcome measures, most of which would be a result of the consumer viewing the claim as credible. Yet none have directly measured the credibility of the ad and its claims. Ad credibility has emerged as an essential precursor to the development of positive attitude toward the ad and the brand (MacKenzie and Lutz 1989). To extend the research in this area, we will test the effects of ad claim type on a sequence of ad response variables that have been widely accepted as mediators of the development of brand perceptions. They include ad credibility, attitude toward the ad, and brand attitude.

Credibility has been defined as trustworthiness, believability, fairness, accuracy, completeness, and other concepts that reflect the believability of a statement (Self 1996). Empirical findings show that credibility is one of the most important factors determining the effects of a persuasive message (Petty and Cacioppo 1981). Ad credibility has been shown to influence ad effectiveness (MacKenzie and Lutz 1989) in terms of message evaluation, attitudes, and behavioral intentions

(Choi and Rifon 2002; Freiden 1982; Ohanian 1991; Petty, Cacioppo, and Schumann 1983).

Ad credibility is defined as "the extent to which the consumer perceives claims made about the brand in the ad to be truthful and believable" (MacKenzie and Lutz 1989). MacKenzie and Lutz (1989) found that ad credibility had a direct influence on both attitude toward the ad and the brand. Credibility was expected to have only an indirect effect on attitude toward the brand, so the latter finding was somewhat surprising. MacKenzie and Lutz's rationale for this result is that audience members see the ad itself as a source of information, and once the source is deemed believable, the ad can operate as a peripheral cue (Petty and Cacioppo 1981). Hence, attitude toward the brand is directly influenced by ad credibility even in low-involvement situations, without the processing of message arguments.

The credibility of an advertisement or advertiser determines the extent to which the consumer perceives the claims to be truthful and believable (Goldsmith, Lafferty, and Newell 2000; Kim and Damhorst 1998; MacKenzie and Lutz 1989). Some research findings suggest a positive relationship between environmental message credibility and ad attitude and purchase intention (Chan 2004; Kim and Damhorst 1998; Phau and Ong 2007).

Thus, we expect that strong eco-ad claims will create more positive consumer response to eco-ads than weak claims or a cause-related marketing claim.

Hypothesis 1a: Strong ad claims will create greater ad credibility than weak green ad claims.

Hypothesis 1b: Strong ad claims will create greater ad credibility than a cause-related marketing claim.

Several studies have found that ad credibility positively influences brand attitudes (MacKenzie and Lutz 1989; Rifon et al. 2004); consequently, we propose:

Hypothesis 2a: Strong ad claims will create more positive attitudes toward the ad than weak green ad claims.

Hypothesis 2b: Strong ad claims will create more positive attitude toward the ad than cause-related marketing ad claims.

Muehling and McCann's (1993) analysis of studies that examined effects of attitude toward the ad, and Brown and Stayman's (1992) meta-analysis, support the influence of attitude toward ad on brand attitudes; thus, we logically deduce:

Hypothesis 3a: Strong ad claims will create more positive attitudes toward the brand than weak green ad claims.

Hypothesis 3b: Strong ad claims will create more positive attitudes toward the brand than cause-related marketing claims.

Hypothesis 4a: Strong ad claims will create stronger purchase intentions than weak green ad claims.

Hypothesis 4b: Strong ad claims will create stronger purchase intentions than cause-related marketing claims.

Claim type effects may be moderated by several factors. Chan (2000) and Chan and Lau (2004) found that Chinese consumers' image of the environmental friendliness of the product's country of origin will influence their response; the more positive the country image, the more receptive the consumers were to product versus image claims. Manrai et al. (1997) found similar effects of consumers' positive perceptions of a country's environmental friendliness: More positive ad perceptions were associated with more positive response to moderate ad claim strength. Studies of the influence of individual consumer characteristics on response to green ad claims have mixed findings, and a central question is whether the ecologically concerned consumer would be more receptive to or more skeptical of green ad claims. Due to the mixed findings, no moderating effects are hypothesized, but we pose the following research questions:

Research Question 1: Does gender moderate ad claim effects?

Research Question 2: Does attitude toward environmental protection moderate ad claim effects?

Individual Characteristics and Response to Green Claims: A Generalizable Model

McGuire (1976) suggested that the believability, now referred to as credibility, of a communication is dependent on many aspects of the message, including message content and receiver characteristics. While it is difficult to identify situation-specific consumer characteristics that may affect advertising response on a universal basis, studies of ecological marketing identify two factors. There is evidence that ecological consumption-related behaviors and receptivity to ecological ad themes stem from an individual's perceived consumer effectiveness in dealing with the environment and from his or her ecological concern (Kassarjian 1971; Kinnear, Taylor, and Ahmed 1974; Ellen, Wiener, and Cobb-Walgren 1991).

Perceived consumer effectiveness (PCE) is a trait-like personality characteristic. It has been defined as the consumer's belief that individual conservation efforts can be effective in solving a problem such as pollution abatement (Ellen, Wiener, and Cobb-Walgren 1991; Kinnear, Taylor, and Ahmed 1974). PCE has occasionally been linked to the generalized concept of locus of control, a personality trait that influences the likelihood of a person's taking action (Schwepker and Cornwell 1991), but it is considered domain specific (Ellen, Wiener, and Cobb-Walgren 1991). Most research examined the relationship between the PCE construct and attitudinal and behavior measures (e.g., ecological concern, need for regulation, socially conscious consumption, socially responsible consumption behavior, actual energy usage) (e.g., Ellen, Wiener, and Cobb-

Walgren 1991). A number of studies suggest that PCE is significantly related to ecologically oriented consumption (Berger and Corbin 1992; Henion 1976; Roberts 1996; Schwepker and Cornwell 1991; Webster 1975; Wiener and Doescher 1991). For example, some research indicates that consumers' levels of PCE plays an important role in explaining the likelihood of performing ecologically conscious consumer behaviors (Berger and Corbin 1992; Lee and Holden 1999; Roberts 1996; Wiener and Doescher 1991), and PCE is a critical predictor of buying behavior, including green products (Vermeir and Verbeke 2006) and organic food (Verhoef 2005). In addition, there is empirical evidence that PCE is separate from and antecedent to environmental concern (Ellen, Wiener, and Cobb-Walgren 1991; Kinnear, Taylor, and Ahmed 1974).

Consumers with high levels of PCE are more likely to engage in eco-consumption than consumers without that belief. However, the relationship appears to be behavior specific; that is, consumers perceive some behaviors as effective and others as not effective (Ellen, Wiener, and Cobb-Walgren 1991). Thus, PCE is one of the most important constructs in a model of ecological consumption behavior and in explaining the relationship between individual consumer behaviors and environmental attitudes (Berger and Corbin 1992).

Environmental Concern (Attitude and Behavior)

Environmental concern as a critical topic began to receive attention in the 1970s and has recently become even more important with today's concerns related to sustainability (Royne, Levy, and Martinez 2011). Crosby, Gill, and Taylor (1981) described environmental concern as the respondent's concern about protecting the environment. Schwepker and Cornwell's (1991) review of measures of ecological concern noted a focus on favorable inclination toward the environment and awareness of environmental problems. Kassarjian (1971) reasoned that a general attitude of concern toward ecology would be the best predictor of ecologically oriented consumption. He found that ecological concern made consumers more receptive to ecological appeals, whereas Moore (1993) concluded that consumers were suspicious of ecological appeals and unwilling to act on them. Newell, Goldsmith, and Banzhaf (1998) found that consumer perceptions of deception negatively influenced ad and brand perceptions regardless of green claim veracity, yet concern for the environment had no effects. Chang (2011) found that ambivalent consumers discounted strong claims. Minton and Rose (1997) suggested the main effects of environmentally concerned attitudes and norms on choice of product, search for information, recycling, and behavioral intentions.

The results of several studies suggest that individuals with higher levels of environmental concern are more likely to engage in ecologically conscious consumer behavior (Antil 1984;

Hines, Hungerford, and Tomera 1987; Shetzer, Stackman, and Moore 1991). Gill, Crosby, and Taylor (1986) found that the effects of environmental concern on behavior are mediated by more specific attitudinal, normative, and behavioral intention variables. Zimmer, Stafford, and Stafford (1994) identified over 50 different "green" issues that could generate consumer concern, and they emphasized the need to discriminate between a generalized concern for the environment and issue-specific concerns that are more likely to drive behavior. Research profiling environmentally concerned consumers often incorporates a behavioral component intended to discriminate the merely concerned from action-oriented eco-consumers (Henion 1976; Henion, Gregory, and Clee 1981). Kinnear and Taylor (1973) and Kinnear, Taylor, and Ahmed (1974) suggested two dimensions of ecological concern: attitudinal and behavioral.

Hypothesis 5: Perceived consumer effectiveness is directly and positively related to

a: general environmental attitude.

b: general environmental behavior.

c: environmental activism behavior.

As previously discussed, the research findings are equivocal regarding how ecological concern influences response to green claims. Some found that consumers are skeptical about green claims (Chan 1999; Karna et al. 2001; Laroche, Bergeron, and Barbaro-Forleo 2001; Manrai et al. 1997; Mohr, Eroglu, and Ellen 1998; Zinkhan and Carlson 1995). Others found that consumers respond favorably to green claims (e.g., Kim, Forney, and Arnold 1997) and perceive them to be credible (Mathur and Mathur 2000), resulting in a positive attitude toward the ad and brand (Chan 2004; Kim and Damhorst 1998; Phau and Ong 2007).

In addition, studies of general advertising response indicate that advertiser credibility and ad credibility directly influence brand attitudes, which then influence purchase intentions (Choi and Rifon 2002; Goldsmith, Lafferty, and Newell 2000; MacKenzie and Lutz 1989; MacKenzie, Lutz, and Belch 1986). Using the same ad response logic posed for H1–H4, we propose:

Hypothesis 6: General environmental attitude will directly and positively influence green ad involvement.

Hypothesis 7: Past general environmental behavior will directly and positively influence green ad involvement.

Hypothesis 8: Environmental activism behavior will directly and positively influence green ad involvement.

Hypothesis 9: Green ad involvement will directly and positively influence green ad credibility.

Hypothesis 10: Green ad credibility will lead to positive attitude toward a green ad.

Hypothesis 11: Green ad credibility will lead to more positive brand attitudes.

Hypothesis 12: Attitude toward the ad will directly and positively influence brand attitude.

METHOD

Sample

Participants were recruited from several sources in a Midwestern state in the United States. Adult participants were recruited from a population of church members, an informal recreational group, a population of clerical/technical university staff who were members of a worker's union, and through snowballing procedures. Recruitment letters were distributed by the heads of the social groups to their respective group members through listservs. Students were recruited from large undergraduate courses at a major Midwestern university. The response rate for adults was 13.7% and 41.8% for students.

The sample consisted of 420 participants. The majority of participants were women (309); 83.1% of the adults and 65.8% of the students were women. Only one undergraduate and 133 of the adults (62.7%) reported being married. The majority of adults were the primary grocery shoppers (81.5%), but a minority of students (45.5%) reported being primary grocery shoppers. Participant ages ranged from 18 to 77, and the average age was 48.4 years in the adult sample and 19.9 in the student sample. Table 1 displays the sample's demographic profile.

Design and Data Collection Procedures

A one-way, posttest between-subjects experimental design was used to test the hypotheses, with three treatment groups and one control group. Participants were blocked based on their student or adult status, and were randomly assigned within each block to one of the four test conditions. The independent variable was ad claim type; one condition offered strong product-related claims, one ad offered weak product-related claims, one ad made a cause-related marketing claim, and one ad was a control. The post-stimulus questionnaire included ad perceptions (ad involvement, ad credibility, attitude toward the ad), brand perceptions (brand attitude, purchase intention), individual characteristics (environmental protection attitudes, environmental behaviors, environmental activism behaviors, perceived consumer effectiveness), and demographics. Participants were contacted via e-mail. Four URLs, one for each treatment and control group, were posted through surveygizmo. Each group responded to the same questionnaire items in the same order, but viewed a different stimulus ad. The university's Institutional Review Board approved the study protocol.

TABLE I
Demographic Profile of the Sample

	Frequency	Percentage
Gender		
Male	104	25.1%
Female	309	74.6%
Transgendered	1	.2%
Age group		
17–25	209	50.1%
26–35	36	8.6%
36–45	33	7.9%
46–55	71	17.0%
Over 55	68	16.3%
Education		
High school or less	35	8.4%
Some college, no degree	205	49.5%
Associate degree	37	8.9%
Bachelor's degree	90	21.7%
Postgraduate degree	47	11.3%
Occupation		
Student	201	48.2%
Clerical/technical	124	29.7%
Professional	51	12.2%
Homemakers	9	2.2%
Service	7	1.7%
Managerial	5	1.2%
Others	18	4.3%
Income		
$0–$14,999	111	27.5%
$15,000–$24,999	21	5.2%
$25,000–$34,999	34	8.4%
$35,000–$49,999	54	13.4%
$50,000–$69,999	68	16.9%
$70,000 +	115	28.5%
Marital status		
Married	134	32.5%
Single	242	58.7%
Divorced	31	7.5%
Widowed	5	1.2%
Grocery shoppers		
Yes	267	64.2%
No	149	35.8%

The intention was *not* to create potentially deceptive claims, but rather to create reasonable claims, and to have a strong claim that would be credible. The three treatment condition ads were created to be exactly the same; the headline and body copy appeared in the same spaces, but the content of the copy was different for each treatment. The ads displayed the same picture of a roll of toilet paper, with the same brand name, "Greenleaf," and displayed the same background scene of greenery and trees. In each ad, the claim was made in the headline, with supporting details in the body copy. The brand name appeared in the lower right hand corner. The bottom edge of the ad displayed the product details: 80 sheets per roll, two-ply, 4.5×4.4 inches, and unscented. The price was $2.99 for a four-roll package. The control ad used a layout identical to that in the treatments, but with a different brand name, "Soft 'n' Gentle," with a blue sky with clouds as the background to remove any reference to ecological themes. The headlines and body copy appear in the Appendix.

Measures

Most of the scales and items were based on existing sources, and some were created for the study. All scales, items, and internal consistency statistics appear in Table 2. Product category involvement was based on Ohanian and Tashchian's (1992) instrument. Environmental protection attitudes and behaviors were based on Kinnear and Taylor (1973), Ellen, Wiener, and Cobb-Walgren (1991), and Schwepker and Cornwell (1991); perceived consumer effectiveness was based on Ellen, Wiener, and Cobb-Walgren (1991). Ad involvement was measured using Celsi and Olson's (1988) felt involvement scale; ad credibility was based on Newell and Goldsmith (2001) and Beltramini (1988); ad attitude, brand attitude, and purchase intention were based on MacKenzie and Lutz's (1989) items.

Statistical Analyses

To test for the effects of ad claim type on consumer response, we ran a series of analyses of variance (ANOVAs). To test for the effects of personal characteristics on ad response, we used AMOS to perform a structural equation analysis.

Stimulus Materials

The four stimulus ads were professionally created. Toilet paper was selected as the product category to be advertised, as it met several criteria. A relatively low involvement product category was considered desirable to minimize the cognitive effort necessary to process the product attributes. In addition, it is common to see environmental claims associated with relatively low-involvement products. Also, it was imperative to use a product category that had clear environmental relevance.

RESULTS

To test the hypotheses, several univariate ANOVAs were performed with ad type as the main independent variable. Environmental protection attitude had been planned to be the variable used to test for the moderating influence of concern for the environment; however, that variable, as well as the environmental protection behavior variable, was severely skewed. The only variable with a reasonable range and distribution was environmental activism, and this variable was used to test

TABLE 2
Measures and Scale Reliabilities

Name of scale	Items	Cronbach's α
Environmental attitude	It is important to purchase recycled paper products to help preserve our forests. I believe the industry could reduce packaging for some consumer items. The U.S. is facing a serious solid waste disposal problem.	.82
Environmental behavior	When I buy products, I try to consider how my use will affect the environment and other consumers. Whenever possible, I buy products I consider environmentally safe.	.73
Environmental activism behavior	I have worked for environmental groups or causes. I have donated money to an environmental protection group. I have signed a petition in favor of protection of some part of the environment.	.75
Perceived consumer effectiveness	There is not much that any one individual can do to protect the environment. An individual can protect the environment by buying products that are kind to the environment.	.54
Ad involvement	The message in the ad was important to me. The ad did not do anything to meet my needs.	.68
Ad credibility	Believable/unbelievable Trustworthy/untrustworthy Convincing/not convincing Credible/not credible Reasonable/unreasonable Honest/dishonest Unquestionable/questionable Conclusive/inconclusive Authentic/not authentic	.93
Attitude toward the ad	Good/bad Pleasant/unpleasant Favorable/unfavorable	.90
Brand attitude	Buying this brand of toilet paper is a good decision. I think this is a satisfactory brand of toilet paper. I have a favorable opinion of this brand of toilet paper. I like this brand of toilet paper. I think the brand of toilet paper depicted in the ad has a lot of beneficial characteristics.	.87
Purchase intention	I would consider buying this toilet paper. My willingness to buy this brand of toilet paper is high.	.90

for the moderating effects of ecological concern. Behavioral activism was clearly the stricter standard of ecological concern. Kinnear and Taylor (1973) make the valid point that concern cannot merely be a function of expression of attitude, but must be measured by behavior as well. Measured on a seven-point scale, activism scores ranged from 1 (low) to 7 (high), with a mean of 3.35, median of 3.33, a mode of 1, and a standard deviation of 1.69. The distribution of scores was fairly symmetrical except for the high number of ones. Based on scale midpoints and the distribution of participants on the scale, participants were categorized as high or low, with those scoring 3.67 and below as low and all others as high. Though not perfect, the categorization balanced cell size concerns with categorizing participants accurately for their activism based on the absolute value of their score.

The positively skewed ecological attitude scores suggested that ad appeal effects sizes could be diminished. Thus, to test

for possible gender and student status differences, as well as their moderating effects, for each dependent variable, three 4×2 factorial univariate ANOVAs were performed, one for each potential moderator.

Effects of Ad Claims on Consumer Response

Significant effects of ad claim type were seen for ad credibility, $F(3, 414) = 2.8$, $p = .04$. There were no significant main or moderating effects of ecological activism, gender, or occupation. The strong claim condition created the highest levels of ad credibility ($M = 4.73$), followed by the weak claim condition ($M = 4.7$), then the cause-related marketing (CRM) condition ($M = 4.5$), with the control ad showing the lowest credibility ($M = 4.34$). Specific contrasts show that the control ad was significantly lower in credibility than the strong claim ad ($p = .022$), and that there were no significant differences among the other conditions. Thus, H1b was supported, but H1a was not.

There were significant main effects of ad claim, $F(3, 410) = 3.5$, $p = .036$, and activism, $F(1, 410) = 3.76$, $p = .053$, on attitude toward the ad, and no significant interaction effect. The strong ($M = 4.95$) and weak ($M = 4.98$) claim conditions were comparable, followed by the CRM condition ($M = 4.77$) and the control condition ($M = 4.59$). Specific comparisons show that the control condition was significantly different than the weak claim condition ($p = .010$). H2a and H2b were not supported. Participants with lower activism scores ($M = 4.93$) exhibited significantly more positive attitudes toward the ad than those with higher activism scores ($M = 4.72$), but the means were very high on the scale, and the meaningfulness of this difference is questionable. There were no significant main or moderating effects of gender or occupation.

Ad claim type had a significant main effect on brand attitude, $F(3, 410) = 4.16$, $p = .006$, and no moderating or main effects of activism, gender, or occupation emerged. The weak claim generated the most positive brand attitude ($M = 4.65$), followed by the strong claim ($M = 4.54$), then the CRM ad ($M = 4.48$), with the control ad generating the weakest brand attitude ($M = 4.19$). Specific comparisons indicate that the control ad was significantly different than the weak claim ad, but no other differences were significant, and H3a and H3b were not supported. Purchase intention was not significantly influenced by ad claim type, but it was significantly greater for those higher in activism ($M = 4.70$) than for those lower in activism behaviors ($M = 4.22$), $F(2, 410) = 11.63$, $p = .001$, disconfirming H4a and H4b. There were no significant main or moderating effects of gender or occupation. Overall, the findings suggest that green ad claims, in all of the forms presented here, generated similar consumer ad response outcomes.

A Test of the Model of Consumer Response

Measurement Validity

We used AMOS to perform a structural equation analysis and test the hypotheses in the proposed model of the effects of individual characteristics on response to green ads. The data used were from the participants who viewed the three green claim ads as treatment conditions. Data from participants who saw the control ad were not included in this analysis. Following the two-step approach (Anderson and Gerbing 1988), the measurement model was examined. Confirmatory factor analysis (CFA) was conducted to test the convergent validity of each construct prior to estimating the structural relationships. Convergent validity is obtained when the path coefficients from the latent constructs to their corresponding manifest indicators are statistically significant (Bagozzi and Yi

1988). As indicated by the results of CFA, all factor loadings for each latent construct are statistically significant; convergent validity was achieved. To obtain discriminant validity, the average variance extracted (AVE) for each factor should be higher than the squared pairwise correlations between factors (Fornell and Larcker 1981). All of the average variances extracted were larger than the squared pairwise correlations, suggesting discriminant validity of the factors.

Table 3 reports the results of confirmatory factor analysis; Table 4 reports the correlations of the latent constructs. The χ^2/df ratio was below 2.0, and the comparative fit index (CFI) and Tucker-Lewis Index (TLI) values were .959 and .949, respectively, which exceeded the .90 standard for model fit (McDonald and Marsh 1990). Other goodness of fit indices (GFI = .897, NFI [normed fit index] = .905) were sufficient, and the root mean square error of approximation (RMSEA) was .046, which was less than .08, showing a good fit (Browne and Cudeck 1993).

Analyzing the Structural Relationships

Seven of the 10 proposed relationships in the model were statistically significant ($p < .01$). Structural relationships in the proposed model (Figure 1) were examined, and results of the hypothesized relationships among the constructs are reported in Table 5. The first three model hypotheses (H5a, H5b, and H5c) were supported. The results indicate that an individual's level of perceived consumer effectiveness (PCE) has positive effects on his or her environmental attitude ($\beta = .64$, $t = 5.26$, $p < .01$), environmental behavior ($\beta = .81$, $t = 5.21$, $p < .01$), and environmental activism behavior ($\beta = .43$, $t = 4.28$, $p < .01$). Consumers with higher levels of PCE have more positive environment attitudes and engage in more behaviors.

It was hypothesized that ad involvement would be positively affected by environmental attitude (H6), environmental behavior (H7), and environmental activism behavior (H8). The results show that environmental attitude ($\beta = .05$, $t = .64$, $p > .1$) and environmental activism behavior ($\beta = -.03$, $t = -.53$, $p > .1$) are not a significant influence on ad involvement, while environmental behavior has a positive effect on ad involvement ($\beta = .45$, $t = 6.1$, $p < .01$). H9 proposes a positive influence of ad involvement on ad credibility, and the results support the proposed relationships ($\beta = .47$, $t = 6.45$, $p < .01$). H10 and H11 propose the effect of ad credibility on attitude toward the ad and brand attitude, and H12 posits the effect of ad attitude on brand attitude. The results of the AMOS analysis indicate that ad credibility has a positive influence on attitude toward the ad ($\beta = .78$, $t = 11.35$, $p < .01$), while it has no significant effect on brand attitude ($\beta = .15$, $t = 1.55$, $p > .1$). The impact of ad attitude on brand attitude was supported ($\beta = .54$, $t = 5.48$, $p < .01$). Thus, ad attitude mediates the effect of ad credibility on brand attitude. The

TABLE 3
Results of Confirmatory Factor Analysis

Measures	Estimate	t-value	SMC	AVE
Environmental attitude 1	.78		.61	.60
Environmental attitude 2	.74	12.46	.55	
Environmental attitude 3	.81	13.19	.66	
Environmental behavior 1	.82		.66	.76
Environmental behavior 2	.92	14.56	.84	
Environmental activism behavior 1	.75		.57	.52
Environmental activism behavior 2	.58	9.05	.34	
Environmental activism behavior 3	.82	10.23	.67	
Perceived consumer effectiveness 1	.55		.30	.44
Perceived consumer effectiveness 2	.76	6.31	.58	
Ad involvement 1	.87		.75	.62
Ad involvement 2	.60	10.30	.35	
Ad credibility 1	.72		.51	.55
Ad credibility 2	.81	17.72	.66	
Ad credibility 3	.75	12.55	.56	
Ad credibility 4	.77	13.06	.59	
Ad credibility 5	.75	12.83	.57	
Ad credibility 6	.81	13.73	.65	
Ad credibility 7	.66	11.31	.44	
Ad credibility 8	.63	10.72	.40	
Ad credibility 9	.78	13.35	.61	
Attitude toward the ad 1	.82		.67	.75
Attitude toward the ad 2	.87	18.63	.76	
Attitude toward the ad 3	.91	19.49	.82	
Brand attitude 1	.81		.66	.60
Brand attitude 2	.74	14.21	.55	
Brand attitude 3	.80	15.46	.63	
Brand attitude 4	.77	14.68	.59	
Brand attitude 5	.76	14.60	.57	

Notes: SMC = squared multiple correlations; AVE = average variance extracted.

All *t*-values are significant ($p < .01$).

$\chi^2(df)$ = 545.92 (326, $p < .05$), GFI (goodness-of-fit index) = .897, CFI (comparative fit index) = .959, TLI (Tucker-Lewis index) = .949, RMSEA (root mean square error of approximation) = .046.

One indicator of all constructs is set to 1 to standardize the measurement scale.

goodness of fit for the overall model is highly acceptable, $\chi^2(df)$ = 676.42 (342), GFI = .877, CFI = .938, TLI = .926, and RMSEA = .056.

DISCUSSION

As environmental protection increases in its salience to marketers and consumers, understanding how consumers will respond to a range of environmental advertising tactics becomes salient as well. The study presented here examined responses to three green ad tactics and tested a model of consumer response to green ads focusing on the role of individual characteristics. Thus, we offer implications for the use of these green ad tactics and the identification of consumers who are more likely to positively respond to them and why.

The main findings suggest that consumers who care about the environment, especially as displayed through past actions, will be receptive to ecologically themed ads, regardless of claim type as tested here. The results of the experiment show that all three forms of green ads were effective in creating positive credibility and attitudes. Ad hoc comparisons show no differences in the control from the CRM ad, but the analysis of variance results show that the control and weak claims generate different levels of credibility and positive ad and brand response. In addition, we found that gender and occupation, that is, student or adult status, did not moderate these effects. The

TABLE 4
Correlations of Latent Constructs

Constructs	PCE	ECOA	ECOB	ECOACT	ADINV	ADCRED	ATTAD	ATTBR
PCE	1.00							
ECOA	.38**	1.00						
ECOB	.39**	.43**	1.00					
ECOACT	.14*	.16**	.37**	1.00				
ADINV	.24**	.21**	.42**	.17**	1.00			
ADCRED	.09	.09	.09	−.01	.41**	1.00		
ATTAD	.11	.16**	.15**	−.01	.46**	.71**	1.00	
ATTBR	.20**	.19**	.36**	.11	.69**	.48**	.58**	1.00

Notes: PCE = perceived consumer effectiveness; ECOA = environmental attitude; ECOB = environmental behavior; ECOACT = environmental activism behavior; ADINV = ad involvement; ADCRED = ad credibility; ATTAD = attitude toward the ad; ATTBR = brand attitude.

** $p < .01$.

* $p < .05$.

FIGURE 1
Proposed Model

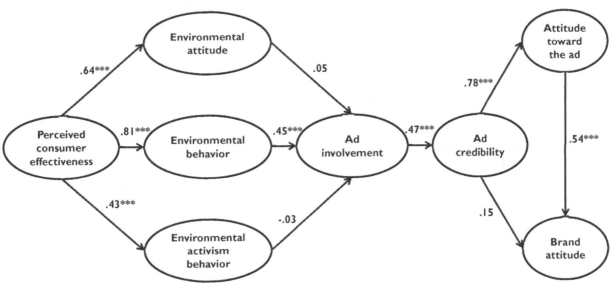

*** $p < .001$.

lack of differences in response based on ad tactic can be good news for marketers who wish to use a green message without presenting green product benefits. Of course, it is not clear whether this can be accomplished with products that lack any environmental connection, and future studies should examine whether a green CRM appeal can be effective for products with limited or no environmental relevance.

The findings of the experiment run counter to what some theories of persuasion would predict, and what some studies have found empirically. Traditional thinking is that individuals with higher levels of involvement with the advertised product or issue are more likely to be involved with a persuasive message for that issue, and will be resistant to attitude change.

Recent approaches predict that high-involvement consumers are more likely to exert greater cognitive effort and elaborate the claims in the message (Celsi and Olson 1988; Petty, Cacioppo, and Schumann 1983). This greater elaboration activates beliefs in memory that may be strongly held given the involvement with the issue, and results in resistance to attitude change. In this study, however, we see a direct and positive relationship between involvement and credibility, and the ANOVA results did not show any moderating influence of activism on ad response.

It is not clear why we observed this phenomenon, but one possibility is that the environmental attitude and behavior measures were positively skewed. With over 400 participants

TABLE 5
Results of the Model

Relationship	Proposed model	
From → to	Estimate	t-value
Perceived consumer effectiveness → environmental attitude	.64	5.26***
Perceived consumer effectiveness → environmental behavior	.81	5.21***
Perceived consumer effectiveness → environmental activism behavior	.43	4.28***
Environmental attitude → ad involvement	.05	.64
Environmental behavior → ad involvement	.45	6.12***
Environmental activism behavior → ad involvement	−.03	−.53
Ad involvement → ad credibility	.47	6.45***
Ad credibility → attitude toward the ad	.78	11.35***
Ad credibility → brand attitude	.15	1.55
Attitude toward the ad → brand attitude	.54	5.48***
Goodness of fit indices		
χ^2 (df)	676.42 (342)	
GFI	.877	
CFI	.938	
TLI	.926	
RMSEA	.056	

Notes: GFI = goodness-of-fit index; CFI = comparative fit index; TLI = Tucker-Lewis index; RMSEA = root mean square error of approximation.

*** $p < .001$.

in our study, the majority expressed positive attitudes toward environmental protection and toward behaving in ways that protect the environment. This was true for students as well as the adult participants. We had thought that students might be less concerned about environmental issues than the adults, and more focused on economic worries (getting jobs). It may be, however, that they have grown up thinking that certain environmentally beneficial behaviors are normal (e.g., separate recycling containers at home or at school). However, the implications of our findings should be qualified by the leaning of the sample toward positive environmental protection.

The lack of differences in effects of strong, weak, and CRM claims may be an artifact of the observed high levels of ecological attitudes in the sample. It is possible that our statistical tests were limited in their ability to detect the phenomenon by the restricted range of those variables. That said, the high levels of consumer interest in environmental protection is a positive sign for environmentalists who wish to raise funds for their causes, and for marketers who wish to use green claims to sell their products. These positive findings should be confirmed by further study using a probability sample that can offer generalizability to a greater population with different characteristics. However, the data support the use of a variety of tactics for those consumers who are positively inclined to protect the environment.

The AMOS results show that a consumer's perceived effectiveness for making environmental change is an important

variable for understanding consumer green attitudes, behaviors, and response to green ads. In our sample, perceived effectiveness led to more positive attitudes toward environmental protection, environmental protection behaviors in general, and degree of activist behaviors. In terms of consumer response to green ads, environmental behaviors in general predicted interest in ads with green claims (ad involvement), subsequently enhancing ad credibility. That is, consumers who have a high level of involvement perceive the green ad to be more truthful and believable. As expected, greater ad credibility generated more positive ad attitudes toward the ad, leading to more positive brand attitudes. Hence, the model suggests that individual consumers who believe that one person's actions can make a difference in environmental protection will engage in more environmental protection behaviors, and will be more receptive to ecologically themed ads with strong or weak claims, and even cause-related marketing efforts.

The key variable for creating the observed positive response is perceived consumer effectiveness. Perhaps this should not be a surprise, as studies that have tried to predict a variety of behaviors using social cognitive approaches have shown that response efficacy—the belief that a behavior can successfully create an outcome—is a key predictor of behavior enactment (in addition to self-efficacy, the belief that one can successfully accomplish the behavior; cf. LaRose, Rifon, and Enbody 2008). This finding is critical for those interested in promoting environmental protection. Based on our study, it is recommended that advocates of environmental protection try to influence an individual's belief that he or she can make a difference with his or her individual behaviors.

Some qualifications of our findings should be noted. We did not set out to identify the possibly deceptive nature of claims; rather, we explored reasonable claims and tested them in different forms, and identified consumer characteristics that would influence ad response. Thus, our findings should not be interpreted as an indication that consumers can easily be duped by green claims. The findings suggest that reasonable claims may not be rejected by those who are concerned about the environment and who want to act on that concern. In addition, we used a low involvement product category (toilet paper), and while toilet paper has relevance to environmental protection, it is quite different from a product such as a hybrid car, which carries greater involvement, risk, and potential for environmental protection. Future studies should examine how consumers respond to claims for high-involvement, high-priced products. The patterns may be different.

REFERENCES

Anderson, James C., and David W. Gerbing (1988), "Structural Equation Modeling in Practice: A Review and Recommended Two-Step Approach," *Psychological Bulletin,* 103 (3), 411–423.

Antil, John H. (1984), "Socially Responsible Consumers: Profile and Implications for Public Policy," *Journal of Macromarketing,* 4 (2), 18–39.

Bagozzi, Richard P., and Youjae Yi (1988), "On the Evaluation of Structural Equation Models," *Journal of the Academy of Marketing Science,* 16 (1), 74–97.

Beltramini, Richard F. (1988), "Perceived Believability of Warning Information Presented in Cigarette Advertising," *Journal of Advertising,* 17 (2), 26–32.

Berger, Ida E., and Ruth M. Corbin (1992), "Perceived Consumer Effectiveness and Faith in Others as Moderators of Environmentally Responsible Behaviors," *Journal of Public Policy and Marketing,* 11 (2), 79–89.

Brown, Robbie, and Henry Fountain (2010), "In Oil Inquiry, Panel Sees No Single Smoking Gun," *New York Times,* August 27, available at www.nytimes.com/2010/08/28/us/28hearings.html (accessed March 28, 2012).

Brown, Steven P., and Douglas M. Stayman (1992), "Antecedents and Consequences of Attitude Toward the Ad: A Meta-Analysis," *Journal of Consumer Research,* 19 (1), 34–51.

Browne, Michael W., and Robert Cudeck (1993), "Alternative Ways of Assessing Model Fit," in *Testing Structural Equation Models,* Kenneth A. Bollen and J. Scott Long, eds., Newbury Park, CA: Sage, 136–162.

Carlson, Les, Stephen J. Grove, and Norman Kangun (1993), "A Content Analysis of Environmental Advertising Claims: A Matrix Approach Method," *Journal of Advertising,* 22 (3), 27–39.

Celsi, Richard L., and Jerry C. Olson (1988), "The Role of Involvement in Attention and Comprehension Processes," *Journal of Consumer Research,* 15 (2), 210–224.

Chamorro, Antonio, Sergio Rubio, and Francisco J. Miranda (2009), "Characteristics of Research on Green Marketing," *Business Strategy and the Environment,* 18 (4), 223–239.

Chan, Ricky Y. K. (1999), "Environmental Attitudes and Behaviour of Consumers in China: Survey Findings and Implications," *Journal of International Consumer Marketing,* 11 (4), 25–53.

——— (2000), "The Effectiveness of Environmental Advertising: The Role of Claim Type and the Source Country Green Image," *International Journal of Advertising,* 19 (3), 349–375.

——— (2004), "Consumer Responses to Environmental Advertising in China," *Marketing Intelligence and Planning,* 22 (4), 427–437.

———, and Lorett B. Y. Lau (2004), "The Effectiveness of Environmental Claims Among Chinese Consumers: Influences of Claim Type, Country Disposition and Ecocentric Orientation," *Journal of Marketing Management,* 20 (3), 273–319.

Chang, Chingching (2011), "Feeling Ambivalent About Going Green: Implications for Green Advertising Processing," *Journal of Advertising,* 40 (4), 19–31.

Chitra, K. (2007), "In Search of the Green Consumers: A Perceptual Study," *Journal of Services Research,* 7 (1), 173–191.

Choi, Sejung Marina, and Nora J. Rifon (2002), "Antecedents and Consequences of Web Advertising Credibility: A Study of Consumer Response to Banner Ads," *Journal of Interactive Advertising,* 3 (1), 12–24.

Coddington, Walter (1993), *Environmental Marketing: Positive Strategies for Reaching the Green Consumer,* New York: McGraw-Hill.

Cone (2012), "Americans Value Honesty over Perfection in Environmental Marketing," Cone Trend Tracker, available at www.coneinc.com/research/index.php (accessed March 23, 2012).

Connolly, John, and Andrea Prothero (2003), "Sustainable Consumption: Consumption, Consumers and the Commodity Discourse," *Consumption Markets and Cultures,* 6 (4), 275–291.

Cronin, J. Joseph, Jeffery S. Smith, Mark R. Gleim, Edward Ramirez, and Jennifer Dawn Martinez (2011), "Green Marketing Strategies: An Examination of Stakeholders and the Opportunities They Present," *Journal of the Academy of Marketing Science,* 39 (1), 158–174.

Crosby, Lawrence A., James D. Gill, and James R. Taylor (1981), "Consumer/Voter Behavior in the Passage of the Michigan Container Law," *Journal of Marketing,* 45 (2), 19–32.

Davis, Joel J. (1993), "Strategies for Environmental Advertising," *Journal of Consumer Marketing,* 10 (2), 19–36.

Ellen, Pam Scholder, Joshua Lyle Wiener, and Cathy Cobb-Walgren (1991), "The Role of Perceived Consumer Effectiveness in Motivating Environmentally Conscious Behaviors," *Journal of Public Policy and Marketing,* 10 (2), 102–117.

Fornell, Claes, and David F. Larcker (1981), "Evaluating Structural Equation Models with Unobservable Variables and

Measurement Error," *Journal of Marketing Research,* 18 (1), 39–50.

Freiden, Jon B. (1982), "An Evaluation of Spokesperson and Vehicle Source Effects in Advertising," in *Current Issues and Research in Advertising,* James H. Leigh and Claude R. Martin, eds., Ann Arbor: University of Michigan Press, 77–87.

Futerra (2008), "The Greenwash Guide," available at www .futerra.co.uk/story/the-greenwash-guide-3/ (accessed March 23, 2012).

Gill, James D., Lawrence A. Crosby, and James R. Taylor (1986), "Ecological Concern, Attitudes, and Social Norms in Voting Behavior," *Public Opinion Quarterly,* 50 (4), 537–554.

Gillis, Justin (2012), "Rising Sea Levels Seen as Threat to Coastal U.S.," *New York Times,* March 13, available at www.nytimes .com/2012/03/14/science/earth/study-rising-sea-levels-a-risk-to-coastal-states.html (accessed March 28, 2012).

Goldsmith, Ronald E., Barbara A. Lafferty, and Stephen J. Newell (2000), "The Impact of Corporate Credibility and Celebrity Credibility on Consumer Reaction to Advertisements and Brands," *Journal of Advertising,* 29 (3), 43–54.

Haytko, Diana L., and Erika Matulich (2008), "Green Advertising and Environmentally Responsible Consumer Behaviors: Linkages Examined," *Journal of Management and Marketing Research,* 1, 2–11.

Henion, Karl E. (1976), *Environmental Marketing,* Columbus, OH: Grid.

———, Russell Gregory, and Mona A. Clee (1981), "Trade-Offs in Attribute Levels Made by Ecologically Concerned Unconcerned Consumers When Buying Detergents," in *Advances in Consumer Research,* vol. 8, Kent B. Monroe, ed., Ann Arbor, MI: Association for Consumer Research, 624–629.

Hines, Jody M., Harold R. Hungerford, and Audrey N. Tomera (1987), "Analysis and Synthesis of Research on Responsible Environmental Behavior: A Meta-Analysis," *The Journal of Environmental Education,* 18 (2), 1–8.

Karna, Jari, Heikki Juslin, Virpi Ahonen, and Eric Hansen (2001), "Green Advertising: Greenwash or a True Reflection of Marketing Strategies?" *Greener Management International,* 33 (Spring), 59–70.

Kassarjian, Harold H. (1971), "Incorporating Ecology into Marketing Strategy: The Case of Air Pollution," *Journal of Marketing,* 35 (3), 61–65.

Kim, Hye-Shin, and Mary Lynn Damhorst (1998), "Environmental Concern and Apparel Consumption," *Clothing and Textiles Research Journal,* 16 (3), 126–133.

Kim, Youn-Kyung, Judith Forney, and Elizabeth Arnold (1997), "Environmental Messages in Fashion Advertisements: Impact on Consumer Responses," *Clothing and Textiles Research Journal,* 15 (3), 147–154.

Kinnear, Thomas C., and James R. Taylor (1973), "The Effect of Ecological Concern on Brand Perceptions," *Journal of Marketing Research,* 10 (May), 191–197.

———, James R. Taylor, and Sadrudin A. Ahmed (1974), "Ecologically Concerned Consumers: Who Are They?" *Journal of Marketing,* 38 (2), 20–24.

Laroche, Michel, Jasmin Bergeron, and Guido Barbaro-Forleo (2001), "Targeting Consumers Who Are Willing to Pay More for Environmentally Friendly Products," *Journal of Consumer Marketing,* 18 (6), 503–521.

LaRose, Robert, Nora J. Rifon, and Richard Enbody (2008), "Promoting Personal Responsibility for Internet Safety," *Communications of the ACM,* 51 (3), 71–76.

Lee, Julie Anne, and Stephen J. S. Holden (1999), "Understanding the Determinants of Environmentally Conscious Behavior," *Psychology and Marketing,* 16 (5), 373–392.

Leonidou, Leonidas C., Constantinos N. Leonidou, Dayananda Palihawadana, and Magnus Hultman (2011), "Evaluating the Green Advertising Practices of International Firms: A Trend Analysis," *International Marketing Review,* 28 (1), 6–33.

MacKenzie, Scott B., and Richard J. Lutz (1989), "An Empirical Examination of the Structural Antecedents of Attitude Toward the Ad in an Advertising Pretesting Context," *Journal of Marketing,* 53 (2), 48–65.

———, Richard J. Lutz, and George E. Belch (1986), "The Role of Attitude Toward the Ad as a Mediator of Advertising Effectiveness: A Test of Competing Explanations," *Journal of Marketing Research,* 23 (2), 130–143.

Manrai, Lalita A., Ajay K. Manrai, Dana-Nicoleta Lascu, and John K. Ryarrs (1997), "How Green Claim Strength and Country Disposition Affect Product Evaluation and Company Image," *Psychology and Marketing,* 14 (5), 511–537.

Mathur, Lynette K., and Ike Mathur (2000), "An Analysis of the Wealth Effects of Green Marketing Strategies," *Journal of Business Research,* 50 (2), 193–200.

Mayer, Robert N., Debra L. Scammon, and Jason W. Gray-Lee (1993), "Will the FTC Guidelines on Environmental Marketing Affect the Hue of Green Marketing? An Audit of Claims on Product Labels," in *Proceedings of the 1993 Marketing and Public Policy Conference,* Mary Jane Sheffet, ed., East Lansing: Michigan State University Press, 19–30.

McDonald, Roderick P., and Herbert W. Marsh (1990), "Choosing a Multivariate Model: Noncentrality and Goodness of Fit," *Psychological Bulletin,* 107 (2), 247–255.

McGuire, William J. (1976), "Some Internal Psychological Factors Influencing Consumer Choice," *Journal of Consumer Research,* 2 (4), 302–319.

Minton, Ann P., and Randall L. Rose (1997), "The Effects of Environmental Concern on Environmentally Friendly Consumer Behavior: An Exploratory Study," *Journal of Business Research,* 40 (1), 38–48.

Mohr, Lois A., Dogan Eroglu, and Pam S. Ellen (1998), "The Development and Testing of a Measure of Skepticism Toward Environmental Claims in Marketers' Communications," *Journal of Consumer Affairs,* 32 (1), 30–55.

Moore, Karl James (1993), "Emerging Themes in Environmental Consumer Behavior," in *Proceedings of the 1993 Marketing and Public Policy Conference,* Mary Jane Sheffet, ed., East Lansing: Michigan State University Press, 109–122.

Muehling, Darrel D., and Michelle McCann (1993), "Attitude Toward the Ad: A Review," *Journal of Current Issues and Research in Advertising,* 15 (1), 25–58.

Newell, Stephen J., and Ronald E. Goldsmith (2001), "The Development of a Scale to Measure Perceived Corporate Credibility," *Journal of Business Research,* 52 (3), 235–247.

————, Ronald E. Goldsmith, and Edgar J. Banzhaf (1998), "The Effect of Misleading Environmental Claims on Consumer Perceptions of Advertisements," *Journal of Marketing Theory and Practice,* 6 (2), 48–60.

Ohanian, Roobina (1991), "The Impact of Celebrity Spokespersons' Perceived Image on Consumers' Intention to Purchase," *Journal of Advertising Research,* 31 (1), 46–54.

————, and Armen Tashchian (1992), "Consumers' Shopping Effort and Evaluation of Store Image Attributes: The Roles of Purchasing Involvement and Recreational Shopping Interest," *Journal of Applied Business Research,* 8 (6), 40–49.

Ottman, Jacquelyn A. (1998), *Green Marketing: Opportunity for Innovation,* 2nd ed., Lincolnwood, IL: NTC Business Books.

Petty, Richard E., and John T. Cacioppo (1981), *Attitudes and Persuasion: Classic and Contemporary Approaches,* Dubuque, IA: Wm. C. Brown.

————, John T. Cacioppo, and David Schumann (1983), "Central and Peripheral Routes to Advertising Effectiveness: The Moderating Role of Involvement," *Journal of Consumer Research,* 10 (2), 135–146.

Phau, Ian, and Denise Ong (2007), "An Investigation of the Effects of Environmental Claims in Promotional Messages for Clothing Brands," *Marketing Intelligence and Planning,* 25 (7), 772–788.

Rifon, Nora J., Sejung Marina Choi, Carrie S. Trimble, and Hairong Li (2004), "Congruence Effects in Sponsorship: The Mediating Roles of Sponsor Motive and Credibility," *Journal of Advertising,* 33 (1), 29–42.

Roberts, James A. (1996), "Green Consumers in the 1990s: Profile and Implications for Advertising," *Journal of Business Research,* 36 (3), 217–231.

Royne, Marla B., Marian Levy, and Jennifer Martinez (2011), "The Public Health Implications of Consumers' Environmental Concern and Their Willingness to Pay for an Eco-Friendly Product," *The Journal of Consumer Affairs,* 45 (2), 329–343.

Schwepker, Charles H., Jr., and T. Bettina Cornwell (1991), "An Examination of Ecologically Concerned Consumers and Their Intention to Purchase Ecologically Packaged Products," *Journal of Public Policy and Marketing,* 10 (2), 77–101.

Self, Charles C. (1996), "Credibility," in *An Integrated Approach to Communication Theory and Research,* Michael B. Salwen and Don W. Stacks, eds., Mahwah, NJ: Lawrence Erlbaum, 421–441.

Sherif, Muzafer, and Carl Iver Hovland (1961), *Social Judgment: Assimilation and Contrast Effects in Communication and Attitude Change,* New Haven: Yale University Press.

Shetzer, Larry, Richard W. Stackman, and Larry F. Moore (1991), "Business Environment Attitudes and the New Environmental Paradigm," *Journal of Environmental Education,* 22 (4), 14–21.

Thorson, Esther, Thomas Page, and Jeri Moore (1995), "Consumer Response to Four Categories of 'Green' Television Commercials," in *Advances in Consumer Research,* vol. 22, Frank R. Kardes and Mita Sujan, eds., Provo, UT: Association for Consumer Research, 243–250.

Verhoef, Peter C. (2005), "Explaining Purchases of Organic Meat by Dutch Consumers," *European Review of Agricultural Economics,* 32 (2), 245–267.

Vermeir, Iris, and Wim Verbeke (2006), "Sustainable Food Consumption: Exploring the Consumer 'Attitude-Behavioral Intention' Gap," *Journal of Agricultural and Environmental Ethics,* 19 (2), 169–194.

Webster, Frederick E., Jr. (1975), "Determining the Characteristics of the Socially Conscious Consumer," *Journal of Consumer Research,* 2 (3), 188–196.

Wiener, Joshua, and Tabitha Doescher (1991), "A Framework for Promoting Cooperation," *Journal of Marketing,* 55 (2), 38–47.

Zimmer, Mary R., Thomas F. Stafford, and Marla Royne Stafford (1994), "Green Issues: Dimensions of Environmental Concern," *Journal of Business Research,* 30 (1), 63–74.

Zinkhan, George M., and Les Carlson (1995), "Green Advertising and the Reluctant Consumer," *Journal of Advertising,* 24 (2), 1–6.

APPENDIX

Stimulus Ad Copy

Strong Claim

Greenleaf: Made from 100% recycled paper without toxic bleaching. Greenleaf brand toilet tissue is made from 100% post-consumer recycled paper. And, because no bleach is used during production, Greenleaf generates significantly fewer toxic pollutants.

Weak Claim

Greenleaf: Protecting our planet and our future. Every Greenleaf product is made considering the balance between the needs of people and the needs of nature. Greenleaf brand toilet tissue—seriously committed to a greener future.

Cause-Related Marketing Claim

Greenleaf: 5¢ of every sale is donated to the Nature Conservancy. The Nature Conservancy is a worldwide, nonprofit organization devoted to preserving biodiversity wherever it is found. Greenleaf supports these efforts by donating 5¢ from every sale to the Nature Conservancy.

Control Ad

Soft 'n' Gentle: There are a few things softer but not many. Soft 'n' Gentle is a soft bathroom tissue with two absorbent layers. It's perfect for the whole family. Available in white and your favorite pastel colors.

THE ROLE OF REGULATORY FOCUS AND SELF-VIEW IN "GREEN" ADVERTISING MESSAGE FRAMING

Ioannis Kareklas, Jeffrey R. Carlson, and Darrel D. Muehling

ABSTRACT: This research draws on theoretical perspectives related to regulatory focus and self-view in the context of "green" advertising appeals. A pattern of results similar to that typically reported in the literature is replicated (i.e., promotion-framed messages are more persuasive for individuals with an active independent self-view, whereas prevention-framed messages are more persuasive for individuals with an active interdependent self-view)—but only when persuasive messages focus on personal health appeals. A considerably different set of relationships is observed when messages focus on environmental appeals. Consistent with our theoretical expectations regarding goal compatibility effects, prevention- (as opposed to promotion-) focused environmental appeals generated more favorable attitudes for individuals who are situationally primed to have an independent self-view. In the interdependent self-view condition, the promotion-focused appeals performed as well as or better than the prevention-focused appeals. The theoretical and managerial implications of these findings are discussed, and future research directions are offered.

For decades, consumers have expressed concerns about environmental issues and their impact on the future of our planet (Zinkhan and Carlson 1995). These concerns have led many to seek out "green" products—resulting in a sizable, attractive, and potentially profitable market segment for companies to pursue (MDG Advertising 2012; Zinkhan and Carlson 1995). Concurrent with this marketplace growth, a mounting body of literature examining theoretical and empirical issues related to green topics has emerged. As such, several journals have devoted special issues exploring the relationship between ecological concerns and green marketing/advertising practices (e.g., *Journal of Public Policy & Marketing* in 1991; *Journal of Business Research* in 1994; *Journal of Advertising* in 1995 and this current issue).

While extant research has provided the marketing discipline with critical insights into the sociodemographic and psychographic makeup of green consumers (Laroche, Bergeron, and Barbaro-Forleo 2001; Roberts 1996; Shrum, McCarty, and Lowrey 1995; Webster 1975), few studies to date have examined the impact of message framing (specifically, regulatory focus) as it relates to consumers' responses to green advertising. According to regulatory focus theory (Higgins 1997), individuals have two distinct types of orientations in their goal pursuits, each of which has a unique impact on message persuasiveness: the pursuit of positive outcomes (i.e., a promotion focus), or the avoidance of negative consequences (i.e., a prevention focus). A quick perusal of green advertising campaigns suggests that marketers often utilize one of two message strategies consistent with these goal orientations. They either stress that which is to be gained by consumers who "buy green" (e.g., safer water and cleaner air), or they emphasize what consumers stand to lose if they do not adopt a green philosophy (e.g., the loss of our country's forest lands). But are each of these strategies equally effective? Might their relative influence be subject to certain boundary conditions?

In this paper, we address these questions by examining the effectiveness of message frames in the context of an environmentally focused advertising campaign. However, we also recognize that one's self-view (i.e., whether the consumer responds to the advertised message from a "me" perspective, as opposed to an "us" or "others" perspective) may moderate these relationships. In fact, a growing body of research has suggested that one's "self-construal" may be an antecedent of regulatory focus effects, such that individuals with an *independent* self-construal (i.e., a focus on one's self) are more likely to be persuaded by messages that emphasize the attainment of positive outcomes (i.e., consistent with promotion), whereas individuals with an *interdependent* self-construal (i.e., a focus on others) are more likely to be persuaded by messages that emphasize the avoidance of negative consequences (i.e., consistent with prevention) (Aaker and Lee 2001; Lee, Aaker, and Gardner 2000).

Studies that have investigated this interactive effect (often referenced in terms of "goal compatibility"), however, have not tended to focus on the effects of green advertising messages. Moreover, these studies have been largely conducted using ad treatments featuring personal benefits as reasons for product adoption, as opposed to environmental benefits—an issue we consider to be especially relevant for the advancement of advertising theory and practice in the present context. Given that environmental appeals often focus on how green products are produced, distributed, and disposed of in an environmentally sustainable manner, one might expect them to be more compatible with societal goals (e.g., protecting the environment for everyone's benefit), as opposed to being closely aligned with personal goals. However, it is not clear how and to what extent the prompting of a more global perspective affects judgments, when one is already in a self-focused frame of mind. Therefore, a different interpretation of the effects of goal compatibility on consumers' judgments may be needed to more fully understand the impact of green advertising appeals.

To address this outstanding issue, we explore goal compatibility in the context of two separate appeals (environmental appeals versus personal health appeals) used to promote an organic brand of milk. Our expectation is that appeal type will differentially influence the interplay of regulatory focus and self-view on participants' ad processing, and subsequently, their attitudes toward the advertised brand. In the sections that follow, we briefly review the concepts of regulatory focus and self-construal, and then present the details of two empirical studies. In Study 1, we examine whether and to what extent the manipulation of regulatory focus and self-view affects consumers' attitudes toward a brand of organic food for which an environmental appeal is utilized. In Study 2, we extend our investigation to include both personally focused as well as environmentally focused ad appeals, using goal compatibility as a means of predicting differing persuasive effects. The theoretical and practical implications of our findings are subsequently presented and discussed.

THEORETICAL DEVELOPMENT

Regulatory Focus

Regulatory focus, initially conceptualized as a relatively stable individual difference variable, suggests that individuals tend to have a natural tendency to be either promotion-oriented or prevention-oriented (Higgins 1997, 1998). Individuals who exercise a promotion focus in their goal pursuits tend to concentrate on hopes and advancement needs—needs that relate to accomplishment and progress. In contrast, individuals who exercise a prevention focus tend to be concerned about safety, responsibility, and security needs—needs that focus on protection. Furthermore, Higgins et al. (2001) found that a promotion orientation is often associated with eagerness (a desire to get things done), whereas prevention is associated with vigilance (making sure the task is accomplished correctly). These tendencies have been measured using the Regulatory

Focus Questionnaire (Higgins et al. 2001), and have also been situationally manipulated for certain tasks/goals (Higgins et al. 1994; Kees, Burton, and Tangari 2010). As such, regulatory focus has been viewed from the standpoint of differences across individuals (i.e., chronic regulatory focus), as well as variability across situations (i.e., situational regulatory focus).

As it relates to advertising processing, regulatory focus predicts that advertising that stresses the pursuit of gains is expected to be more persuasive for individuals exhibiting a promotion focus. In contrast, ads stressing the avoidance of losses are expected to be more persuasive for prevention-focused individuals. Such "regulatory fit" (Avnet and Higgins 2006) has been shown to intensify ad- and brand-related responses (Kees, Burton, and Tangari 2010; Kim 2006). As an example, Kim (2006) examined how framing affected the effectiveness of health-based antismoking advertising messages. Results showed that when regulatory goals were congruent with the antismoking message frame, participants perceived lower pharmacological and psychological benefits related to smoking, and indicated that they were less likely to smoke cigarettes in the future.

Common operationalizations of regulatory focus tend to view promotion and prevention goal orientations from a personal perspective, that is, what a *person* stands to gain or lose (Pham and Higgins 2005). This characterization would appear to be most appropriate for the vast majority of consumer decisions where one is concerned with her or his personal welfare. However, in the case of green advertising focusing on environmental appeals, consumer decisions are likely to also involve the consideration of global issues that transcend the personal domain (Arnocky, Stroink, and DeCicco 2007). In this case, environmentally related goals with a promotion- and prevention-orientation may involve benefits or losses to others well beyond the individual consumer and his or her egoistic desires. For green advertising efforts involving environmental appeals, this would suggest that a promotion focus might entail taking actions that contribute positively to the state of the environment for everyone's sake. In contrast, a prevention orientation would be consistent with vigilant actions that reduce the deterioration of the environment and its harmful effects on all of us. Therefore, whether one's goal orientation is focused on promotion or prevention, the emphasis would appear to be more outwardly directed, that is, with respect to others. In either case, regulatory fit is expected to result in satisfaction and a feeling of rightness toward messages that are framed in a manner consistent with consumers' regulatory orientations (Cesario, Higgins, and Scholer 2008; Higgins 2002). We believe this alternative perspective of promotion and prevention is especially relevant when one considers how the effects of regulatory focus interact with one's self-construal in the context of environmentally focused advertisements.

Self-Construal

Self-construal is often characterized as a constellation of thoughts, feelings, and actions concerning the relation of the self to others, and the self as distinct from others (Singelis 1994). From an information-processing perspective, Baumeister (1998) suggests that self-construal may also be considered a process, explaining how individuals develop and define information about the relationship between one's self and others (see also DeCicco and Stroink 2007). Self-construal was initially considered in a cultural context (for a review, see Fiske et al. 1998). Specifically, Western cultures tend to construe the self as distinct from the social context and foster autonomy and independence, whereas Eastern cultures tend to construe the self as part of a larger social context and encourage interdependence (Markus and Kitayama 1991). Such cultural influences are believed to contribute to the chronic accessibility of individuals' self-construals.

However, extant research has demonstrated that distinct self-views can also be activated by using situational manipulations (Aaker and Williams 1998). Therefore, researchers have both measured individuals' self-view using the Self-Construal scale (Singelis 1994) and have used priming techniques to situationally activate either an independent or an interdependent self-view (Aaker and Lee 2001). Of particular note, Lee, Aaker, and Gardner (2000) and Aaker and Lee (2001) found convergent results in their studies, regardless of whether self-construal was measured (using participants from a Western versus an Eastern culture), or was situationally activated. Furthermore, extant research suggests that the different ways of construing the self are not necessarily mutually exclusive, but in fact may coexist within individuals (DeCicco and Stroink 2007). Hence, consumers may act in ways that reflect a mutual coexistence of independent and interdependent self-views. For example, Griskevicius, Tybur, and Van den Bergh (2010) recently demonstrated that consumers are motivated to purchase green products for altruistic reasons related to their environmental benefits (i.e., in line with interdependent goals) but also to satisfy their status motives (i.e., congruent with independent goals).

Of particular relevance to the current investigation, a recent addition to the literature on self-construal has been the recognition of a third model, known as the "metapersonal" view of the self (Arnocky, Stroink, and DeCicco 2007; DeCicco and Stroink 2007). Specifically, the metapersonal self-construal is defined as a sense of one's self that is characterized by deep interconnections with all life forms (Arnocky, Stroink, and DeCicco 2007). Unlike the independent view of the self that is described by individual attributes, or the interdependent view of the self that is construed by connections to close others (such as one's family), the metapersonal view of the self is described by a "universal focus" that is concerned with how

one is connected to all forms of life (DeCicco and Stroink 2007). It is our contention that when exposed to an environmentally themed ad, some contextually driven thoughts may be evoked—thoughts that would appear to be in line with the metapersonal view of self.

The addition of the metapersonal self-view is beneficial when attempting to understand and interpret individuals' responses to environmental appeals—appeals that are likely to evoke thoughts of a more global nature that extend beyond one's self and family. Indeed, Arnocky, Stroink, and DeCicco (2007) examined independent, interdependent, and metapersonal self-construal types in the context of environmental concern, cooperation, and conservation. Their findings demonstrate that the metapersonal self-view is most concerned about the environment for its own sake (as opposed to egoistic or self-directed environmental concerns), though it does bear some resemblance to the interdependent self in terms of its consideration for the well-being of others (see also Schultz 2001). Moreover, consistent with the findings of Utz (2004), the interdependent and metapersonal self-construals were predictive of cooperative attitudes in a "commons dilemma" dealing with sharing limited environmental resources, whereas the independent self-construal was negatively correlated with cooperation (Arnocky, Stroink, and DeCicco 2007).

Self-Construal and Its Relation to Regulatory Focus

Regarding the relationship of self-view and regulatory focus, research suggests that individuals' accessible self-construal is an antecedent to the effects described by regulatory focus theory. Specifically, Aaker and Lee (2001) demonstrated that promotion-focused messages were more persuasive when individuals had an active, independent self-view, whereas prevention-focused messages were more persuasive when individuals had an active, interdependent self-view. The theoretical rationale for these findings is goal compatibility; extant research suggests that independent goals are more compatible with a promotion focus, since they relate to autonomy and achieving success by showing how one is different from others (Aaker and Lee 2001; Cesario, Higgins, and Scholer 2008). In contrast, interdependent goals are most often related to a desire to belong to a collective group, and fulfilling one's obligations and responsibilities to others so as to maintain harmony in social settings (Heine et al. 1999). Hence, the interdependent self is often concerned with avoiding mistakes that may impede one from belonging with others, which tends to be more compatible with a prevention focus (Lee, Aaker, and Gardner 2000).

With regard to the metapersonal self-construal, extant research has not examined how the goals characteristic of this view of the self may be compatible with a promotion versus a prevention focus. However, given the work of Arnocky, Stroink, and DeCicco (2007) and DeCicco and Stroink (2007), we expect that the metapersonal self-view will be more in line with the others-focused interdependent self, as opposed to the self-interested independent self. If such is the case, an environmentally focused ad is more likely to evoke contrasting (even conflicting) perspectives for an individual who is situationally primed to have an independent self-view. This is because the contextually induced metapersonal self is expected to encourage others-focused thinking, while the independent-self encourages self-centered thinking. However, for individuals situationally primed with an interdependent self-view, compatible self-view perspectives are expected, as the metapersonal self is consistent with an others-focused manner of thinking.

In our first study, we examine the role of regulatory focus and self-view in the context of organic food advertisements. Our expectation is that a pattern of relationships will emerge that differs from what has been previously established in the literature. We expect this difference in findings to be attributed to environmental appeals being contextually associated with universal goals, commensurate with the interdependent or metapersonal views of the self, but in contrast to the independent self-view. Contrary to most findings reported in the literature (e.g., Aaker and Lee 2001; Chen, Ng, and Rao 2005; Hamilton and Biehal 2005), we believe that when environmental appeals are used, the interplay of the situationally induced self-view and contextually driven (metapersonal) thoughts will result in a different pattern of relationships as they relate to goal compatibility. Due to the contrasting self-view perspectives in the independent-primed condition, greater care, time, and vigilance (consistent with a prevention-focused regulatory orientation) are expected. But the assimilation of congruent self-views in the interdependent condition should prompt little hesitancy and instead encourage eagerness and a motivation to take action (consistent with a promotion-based focus).

However, green ads may also focus on personal benefits and concerns. Therefore, in our second study, we explore the notion of goal compatibility further by examining both environmental appeals and personal health appeals. In doing so, we hope to replicate the findings of our first study (for participants exposed to environmental appeals), while finding a contrasting effect for participants exposed to personal health appeals (one that is consistent with the findings of previous research on the topic).

STUDY 1

In Study 1, we investigate how different message frames (i.e., promotion- versus prevention-focused) interact with consumers' situationally manipulated self-view (i.e., independent versus interdependent) to predict brand attitudes. We focus on environmental appeals, which are commonly used in green advertising, and examine the interactive effects of regulatory focus and self-view on consumers' attitudes toward an organic brand of milk. It is our contention that advertising appeals used in organic food promotions provide a useful consumption context for studying consumers' responses to green marketing efforts, as these messages typically use environmental and/or personal health appeals. In keeping with this notion, Banerjee, Gulas, and Iyer (1995) considered "organic" appeals (e.g., health aspects of environmentalism, the goodness of natural products/ingredients) as one of seven appeals relevant to their content analysis of green advertising. Moreover, some empirical evidence suggests that consumers' concerns for the environment, coupled with their concerns for their overall personal health and nutrition, are dominant factors driving organic food–related attitudes and purchase intent.[1]

Participants, Measures, and Procedures

We recruited 306 undergraduate business students (46.3% female) from a major Western university to participate in this study. We examined participants' evaluations of an organic brand of milk called "The Farmer's Cow." While this is an existing brand sold in the Eastern United States, it was presented to participants in our study as "a new brand of organic milk," produced by a group of six local dairy farms and now available in their local grocery stores. A 2 (regulatory focus: promotion versus prevention) × 2 (self-view prime: independent versus interdependent) between-subjects design was used. Participants were randomly assigned to one of the four experimental conditions, all of which used environmental appeals (it should be noted that the scripts used for these appeals were adapted from ad copy actually used by The Farmer's Cow organic milk company in their promotions). Each participant read a short narrative and was shown an advertisement for The Farmer's Cow organic milk, followed by a questionnaire assessing their brand attitudes. We also collected demographic information from the participants and checks of our manipulations.

Extant research has shown that self-view (Aaker and Williams 1998) and regulatory focus (Lee, Aaker, and Gardner 2000) can be manipulated using situational primes. The situational prime used to activate the desired self-view in our study was manipulated by using a picture focusing on a single individual (independent prime condition) or a group of people (interdependent prime condition), accompanied by text focusing on potential benefits of product adoption to the reader or his or her family. Regulatory focus was manipulated through differences in the text that accompanied the advertisement. For example, participants exposed to promotion-focused environmental appeals read how organic farming helps maintain the state's natural landscape and improves air, water, and soil quality. In contrast, participants exposed to prevention-focused environmental appeals read how organic farming helps to prevent the deterioration of the state's natural landscape and keeps harmful chemicals out of the air, water, and soil.

Attitude toward the brand was measured using three, seven-point items (α = .93), adapted from Shamdasani, Stanaland, and Tan (2001). Participants were asked to respond to items pertaining to The Farmer's Cow brand, including: "I feel negative toward this brand"/"I feel positive toward this brand"; "This brand is awful"/"This brand is great"; and "I disapprove of this brand"/"I approve of this brand."

To assess our manipulation of regulatory focus, we asked participants two questions anchored with nine-point bipolar scale items. Specifically, participants were asked the extent to which their thoughts at the time of ad exposure were about "Maintaining the beauty of [state's] natural landscape" versus "Preventing the decline of [state's] natural landscape," and "Enhancing the state's scenic views" versus "Reducing the deterioration of the state's scenic views."

Two separate indices of self-construal were used to assess the effectiveness of the self-view manipulations. Participants were asked to respond to six items, identical to those used by Aaker and Lee (2001). Specifically, the first three items asked participants the extent to which they thought just about themselves while reading about The Farmer's Cow (averaged to provide a self-thoughts index; α = .96), while the remaining three items asked participants the extent to which they thought about themselves and their family (averaged to provide an others-thoughts index; α = .96).

Given our underlying assumption that participants' self-views may also be influenced by the contextual nature of the green ad appeal (i.e., a focus on environmental benefits, as opposed to personal benefits), an additional measure was employed in an attempt to assess participants' contextually-influenced self-views and to provide some indication of a metapersonal view of self being evoked. This measure included a forced-choice and a nine-point bipolar scale item. Participants were first asked to choose between "Your own personal benefits" and "Society's benefits" when asked the question, "When you were reading about The Farmer's Cow milk brand, describe the extent to which your thoughts were about . . ." A follow-up measure (using the same question stem as above) asked participants to then respond to an item, with endpoints "Your own personal benefits" (1) and "Society's benefits" (9).

Results

To assess the viability of our manipulation of regulatory focus, a 2 (regulatory focus: promotion versus prevention) × 2 (self-view: independent versus interdependent) ANOVA (analysis of variance) was conducted using the two regulatory focus items (maintaining beauty/preventing decline, enhancing views/

reducing deterioration) noted previously as the dependent variable. The main effect for self-view, as well as the interaction of self-view and regulatory focus, were not significant ($p > .05$), as expected. However, the analysis produced a significant main effect for both the first ($F(1, 302) = 19.14$, $p < .001$) and second ($F(1, 302) = 17.75$, $p < .001$) regulatory focus manipulation-check items. In both cases, participants who were exposed to the promotion condition more closely identified with promotion-related thoughts (item one: M = 4.08; item two: M = 4.82) compared with participants exposed to the prevention condition (item one: M = 5.14; item two: M = 5.90).

We also tested our manipulation of self-construal using a 2 (regulatory focus: promotion versus prevention) × 2 (self-view: independent versus interdependent) ANOVA including the self-thoughts index and others-thoughts index as the dependent variables, respectively, and again observed no significant main effect for regulatory focus or for the interaction of regulatory focus and the measures of self-construal. However, as anticipated, we did obtain a significant main effect for both self-construal indices (independent self-view, $F(1, 302) = 4.86$, $p < .05$; interdependent self-view, $F(1, 302) = 44.88$, $p < .001$). Participants who were exposed to the independent-primed condition reported having higher levels of self-related thoughts (M = 3.94) compared with participants who were exposed to the interdependent-primed condition (M = 3.49), while participants who were exposed to the interdependent-primed condition reported having higher levels of others-related thoughts (M = 4.30) compared with participants who were exposed to the independent-primed condition (M = 3.08). In summary, all the manipulations worked as intended (see the top portion of Table 1).

To address our primary research question (i.e., the impact of the ad treatments on participants' brand attitudes), a 2 (regulatory focus: promotion versus prevention) × 2 (self-view: independent versus interdependent) ANOVA was conducted using attitude toward the brand as the dependent variable (see the top portions of Tables 2 and 3 for a summary of the results and descriptive statistics, respectively). Results showed a significant two-way interaction between regulatory focus and self-view, $F(1, 302) = 6.72$, $p < .01$. Consistent with our expectations for ads featuring environmental claims, simple effects follow-up tests showed that for participants with a primed independent self-view, a prevention-framed message, M = 5.19; $F(1, 302) = 6.91$, $p < .01$, yielded more favorable brand attitudes than did a promotion-framed message (M = 4.65). However, for individuals with a primed interdependent self-view, a promotion-framed message (M = 5.55) generated attitudes that were more favorable than a prevention-framed message; however, these differences were not statistically significant, M = 5.34; $F(1, 302) = .61$, $p > .44$. Figure 1 illustrates the findings from this study.

TABLE 1
Manipulation Checks

Study 1

Manipulation-check question	Treatment condition			
	Regulatory focus		Self-view	
	Prevention	Promotion	Interdependent	Independent
Maintaining beauty (1) versus preventing decline (7)	**5.14 (2.12)**	**4.08 (2.07)**	4.52 (2.33)	4.70 (1.96)
Enhancing landscape (1) versus reducing deterioration (7)	**5.90 (2.15)**	**4.82 (2.28)**	5.27 (2.43)	5.45 (2.11)
Self-related thoughts	3.89 (1.67)	3.83 (1.64)	**3.49 (1.52)**	**3.94 (1.77)**
Others-related thoughts	3.76 (1.72)	3.63 (1.75)	**4.30 (1.65)**	**3.08 (1.60)**

Study 2

Manipulation-check question	Treatment condition			
	Regulatory focus		Self-view	
	Prevention	Promotion	Interdependent	Independent
Promotion (1) versus prevention (7)	**4.34 (1.25)**	**3.98 (1.60)**	4.13 (1.39)	4.16 (1.51)
Self-related thoughts	3.72 (1.31)	3.81 (1.30)	**3.49 (1.25)**	**4.00 (1.30)**
Others-related thoughts	3.84 (1.37)	3.80 (1.20)	**4.13 (1.25)**	**3.55 (1.25)**

Notes: Standard deviations are in parentheses. Row cells in boldface are statistically different from one another.

As a follow-up to these findings, we first conducted an ANOVA using the contextually influenced self-view measures referenced above as the dependent variable. Results of these analyses yielded nonsignificant findings for both main effects (regulatory focus and self-construal) and their interaction term (all ps > .05), as expected. Our underlying assumption was that the environmentally based messages would generate thoughts consistent with a global focus, irrespective of the primed self-view and regulatory focus conditions. Consistent with these expectations, further analyses indicated that responses to the contextual thoughts scale were not significantly different for participants in the primed independent self-view condition ($M = 4.73$) compared with those who were in the primed interdependent self-view condition, $M = 5.14$; $F(1, 303) = 1.53$, $p = .22$. Moreover, for those individuals in the primed independent self-view condition ($n = 149$) who selected the "society's benefits" choice option (43% of respondents), their mean responses to the nine-point "personal versus societal" scale item were significantly greater ($M = 6.94$) than the scale midpoint of 5.00 ($t = 11.35$, $p < .01$)—suggesting they were indeed focusing on societal thoughts. Furthermore, those individuals who reported having more societal benefits thoughts were also more inclined to believe that consuming organic food had a positive effect on the environment ($M = 5.29$), compared with participants whose thoughts were focused on personal benefits, $M = 4.95$;

$F(1, 300) = 6.29$, $p < .05$[2]—offering further evidence of the persuasive impact of the ad's message on participants' brand attitudes in this treatment condition.

Discussion

The results of our first study produced a pattern of relationships different from those reported in the literature dealing with the interactive effects of regulatory focus and self-view (e.g., Aaker and Lee 2001; Lee, Aaker, and Gardner 2000). Specifically, we found that when using environmental appeals, prevention-focused messages were more persuasive (i.e., led to more favorable brand attitudes) when participants were situationally primed to have an independent self-view. The findings with regard to the interdependent condition were in the expected direction, but did not reach statistical significance. Furthermore, some empirical evidence was provided in support of our supposition that environmental appeals may evoke contextually related thoughts consistent with a metapersonal view of the self, which may have affected the relative influence of the situationally primed self-view thoughts.

To further explore the pattern of relationships we observed in Study 1, we conducted a second study, pitting ads featuring environmental appeals for an organic food product against ones featuring personal health appeals for the same product. Our expectation was that we would replicate the expected findings

TABLE 2
The Impact of Self-View and Regulatory Focus on Attitude Toward the Advertised Brand

Study 1: Two-way ANOVA results			
Source	df	Mean square	F
Self-view (SV)	1, 302	20.89	13.73***
Regulatory focus (RF)	1, 302	2.07	1.36
SV × RF	1, 302	10.23	6.72**

Study 2: Three-way ANOVA results			
Source	df	Mean square	F
Self-view (SV)	1, 177	.80	.88
Regulatory focus (RF)	1, 177	.03	.04
Appeal type (AT)	1, 177	.41	.45
SV × RF	1, 177	.00	.00
SV × AT	1, 177	2.44	2.68
RF × AT	1, 177	.07	.08
SV × RF × AT	1, 177	7.76	8.53**

Study 2: Two-way ANOVA results (environmental appeal)			
Source	df	Mean square	F
Self-view (SV)	1, 79	2.53	2.54
Regulatory focus (RF)	1, 79	.00	.00
SV × RF	1, 79	3.99	4.01*

Study 2: Two-way ANOVA results (personal health appeal)			
Source	df	Mean square	F
Self-view (SV)	1, 95	.13	.16
Regulatory focus (RF)	1, 95	.02	.02
SV × RF	1, 95	4.63	5.70*

Note: ANOVA = analysis of variance.

* $p < .05$.

** $p < .01$.

*** $p < .001$.

from Study 1, but only for the environmental appeal ad; for the personal health appeal ad, a pattern of findings consistent with those reported in the literature was expected.

STUDY 2

The purpose of this study was to examine the interactive effects of regulatory focus and self-construal on consumers' attitudes toward an organic brand of milk, across two different types of message appeals (i.e., personal health appeals versus environmental benefits).

Participants, Measures, and Procedures

Two hundred and sixty undergraduate business students (48.1% female) from a large western university participated in this experiment. We used a 2 (regulatory focus: promotion versus prevention) × 2 (self-view: independent versus interdependent) × 2 (appeal type: personal health benefits versus environmental benefits) between-subjects design. Participants were randomly assigned to one of eight experimental conditions. We used the same procedures as in the first study to situationally activate the desired self-view and regulatory focus

TABLE 3
Attitude Toward the Advertised Brand by Treatment Condition

	Study 1 results			
	Interdependent		**Independent**	
Prevention	5.34 (1.21)		5.19 (1.25)[a]	
Promotion	5.55 (1.05)[b]		4.65 (1.43)[ab]	

	Study 2 results			
	Personal health appeal		**Environmental appeal**	
	Interdependent	**Independent**	**Interdependent**	**Independent**
Prevention	5.57 (.90)[a]	5.20 (.92)[c]	5.39 (1.01)[e]	5.48 (1.01)
Promotion	5.10 (.92)[ab]	5.62 (.91)[bc]	5.85 (1.01)[de]	5.05 (1.00)[d]

Notes: Standard deviations are in parentheses. Contrasts for means with the same superscripts are statistically significant.

FIGURE 1
Study 1 Results: Brand Attitudes as a Function of Self-View and Regulatory Focus

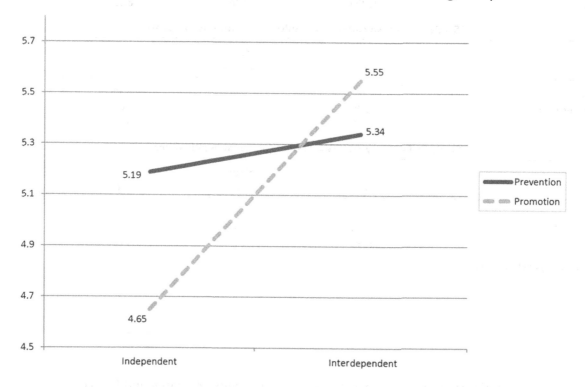

orientation, with the only exception that we now used personal health appeals rather than environmental appeals in four of the eight ad treatment conditions. For example, participants assigned to the promotion-focused personal health appeal condition read that drinking organic milk helps promote a healthy lifestyle and that studies show that organic milk increases energy levels by providing essential nutrients. In contrast, participants assigned to the prevention-focused per-

sonal health appeal condition read that drinking organic milk helps prevent an unhealthy lifestyle, and that studies show that organic milk reduces the risk of disease. The scripts used for the environmentally focused ads were similar in content to those used in Study 1 and featured the same brand (The Farmer's Cow). (See the Appendix for details of the ad scripts corresponding to the experimental conditions employed in the second study.)

Results

To assess our manipulation of regulatory focus, a 2 (regulatory focus: promotion versus prevention) × 2 (self-view: independent versus interdependent) × 2 (appeal type: personal health benefits versus environmental benefits) ANOVA was conducted, using a regulatory focus measure similar to that used in Study 1 as the dependent variable (but modified to reflect the difference in ad appeal types). Results showed a significant main effect for regulatory focus, $F(1, 255) = 3.84$, $p < .05$, but no significant effect for self-construal or its interaction with regulatory focus ($ps > .05$), as anticipated. Consistent with our expectations, compared with participants in the promotion-focused condition ($M = 3.98$), participants who were exposed to the prevention condition reported having higher levels of prevention-related thoughts, such as disease prevention (in the personal health benefit appeal condition) and reducing toxins (in the environmental benefits appeal condition) ($M = 4.34$).

We also tested our manipulation of self-construal using a 2 (regulatory focus: promotion versus prevention) × 2 (self-view: independent versus interdependent) × 2 (appeal type: personal health benefits versus environmental benefits) ANOVA, including the self- and others-thoughts indices as the dependent variables, respectively. Results showed a significant main effect for having an independent self-view, $F(1, 256) = 10.21$, $p < .01$, and for having an interdependent self-view, $F(1, 256) = 13.99$, $p < .001$. Participants exposed to the independent self-construal condition reported having higher levels of self-related thoughts ($M = 4.00$) compared with participants exposed to the interdependent self-construal condition ($M = 3.49$), while participants exposed to the interdependent condition reported having higher levels of others-related thoughts ($M = 4.13$) compared with participants exposed to the independent condition ($M = 3.55$). As expected, the main effects for regulatory focus and its interaction with self-construal were not significant for either self-view index (all $ps > .05$). In summary, all of the manipulations worked as intended. (See the bottom portion of Table 1.)

To assess the impact of the ad treatments on participants' brand attitudes, a 2 (regulatory focus: promotion versus prevention) × 2 (self-view: independent versus interdependent) × 2 (appeal type: personal health benefits versus environmental benefits) ANCOVA (analysis of covariance) was conducted, using attitude toward the brand as the dependent variable (refer to the bottom portions of Tables 2 and 3). Results showed a significant three-way interaction, $F(1, 177) = 8.53$, $p < .001$.[3] To examine the differential effects due to appeal type, we conducted a 2 (regulatory focus: promotion versus prevention) × 2 (self-view: independent versus interdependent) ANCOVA within each appeal type condition. Similar to the findings obtained in Study 1, the results showed a significant

two-way interaction between regulatory focus and self-view when the focus of the advertising claims was on environmental appeals, $F(1, 79) = 4.01$, $p < .05$.

Simple effects follow-up tests showed that for those individuals who had been situationally primed to have an independent self-view, a prevention-framed message was generally more persuasive, that is, it yielded more favorable brand attitudes, $M = 5.48$; $F(1, 79) = 1.84$, $p = .09$, than a promotion-framed message ($M = 5.05$). In addition, simple effects follow-up tests showed that a promotion-framed message, $M = 5.85$; $F(1, 79) = 2.13$, $p = .07$, was generally more persuasive than a prevention-framed message ($M = 5.39$) when participants were situationally primed to have an interdependent self-view.

Within the personal health benefits appeal condition, the results showed a significant two-way interaction between regulatory focus and self-view, $F(1, 95) = 5.70$, $p < .05$. When the focus of the advertising message was on personal health benefits, simple effects follow-up tests revealed that a promotion-framed message was more persuasive, $M = 5.62$; $F(1, 95) = 3.086$, $p < .05$, than a prevention-framed message ($M = 5.20$) with an independent self-view, whereas a prevention-framed message was more persuasive, $M = 5.57$; $F(1, 95) = 2.63$, $p < .05$, than a promotion-framed message ($M = 5.10$) with an interdependent self-view. Figure 2 illustrates the findings from Study 2.

Discussion

The results of this study extend previous work on self-construal and regulatory focus by examining two different message appeals for an organic food product. Specifically, when using environmentally focused appeals, we found that prevention-framed messages (as compared with promotion-framed messages) were more persuasive (i.e., yielded more favorable brand attitudes) for participants who were situationally primed to be independent. In addition, we found that the promotion-focused messages were more persuasive than the prevention-focused messages in the situationally primed interdependent condition. Consistent with Study 1, we surmise that this pattern of relationships stems from the interplay between the contextually based environmental (metapersonal) thoughts and the situationally primed self-view thoughts.[4] In addition, it is our expectation that environmental appeals generally prompt a different type of promotion or prevention goal-orientation—one that focuses on benefits to others more so than to one's self.

When using personal health appeals, we did not expect messages to induce thoughts related to the metapersonal view of the self, as the arguments advocated were expected to benefit the individual consumer as opposed to others. Consistent with this expectation, we found that promotion-framed messages were more persuasive for individuals with a situationally

FIGURE 2
Study 2 Results: Brand Attitudes as a Function of Self-View, Regulatory Focus, and Message Appeal

Environmental Appeals

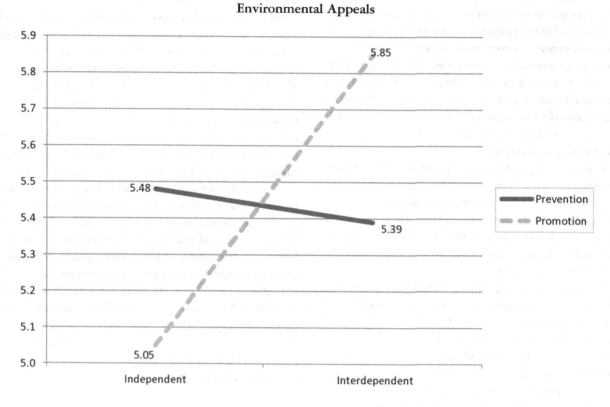

Personal Health Appeals

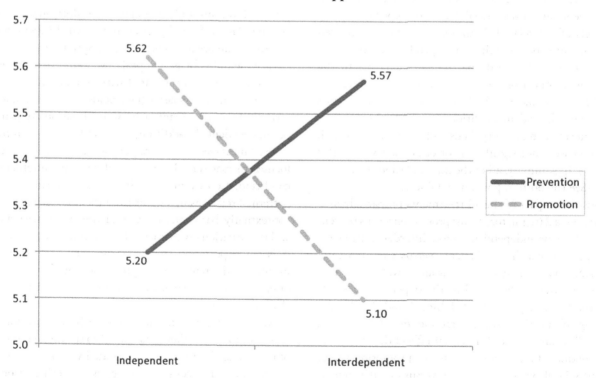

manipulated independent self-view, whereas prevention-framed messages were more persuasive for individuals with a situationally manipulated interdependent self-view. Thus, the findings previously reported in the literature were replicated.

GENERAL DISCUSSION

We believe the current investigation makes several theoretical and practical contributions to the green advertising literature. While extant research has examined the influence of self-construal on regulatory focus, to the best of our knowledge, our work is the first to extend this domain into the context of green advertising strategies. In addition, given the noted synergies between green marketing and organic food products, we investigate regulatory focus and self-view effects as they relate specifically to attitudes toward organic brands. These insights are intended to provide guidance to advertisers who wish to create more effective advertising campaigns to promote organic food, as well as to extend our theoretical understanding of how consumers process alternate types of green advertising messages differently. In general, our findings suggest that focusing on either environmental benefits or personal health benefits can change consumers' attitudes favorably toward organic brands, provided that messages are framed appropriately. To do so, however, one must take into consideration the contrasting results we observed with regard to the interactive effects of regulatory focus and self-view for the two types of ad appeals investigated.

Marketing and social-psychology researchers have begun to recognize that the different ways of construing the self may coexist within individuals, regardless of one's cultural background, and can be situationally activated or suppressed (Aaker and Lee 2001; Aaker and Williams 1998). Our findings suggest that green advertising messages using environmental appeals present such a consumption context. In our studies, one view of the self was made contextually salient, while another view was situationally primed by the use of ad executional features. Results indicated that after being exposed to an ad focusing on environmental benefits, participants in Study 1 who were primed to focus on themselves had contextually driven thoughts about societal benefits as well nonetheless. We argue that evidence of the evocation of these thoughts supports recent theorizing involving the metapersonal self (DeCicco and Stroink 2007) and provides a new perspective on how views of one's self may differentially affect consumers' responses to advertising in an environmental context. It is our contention that the use of environmental appeals is likely to be associated with universal goals in line with the metapersonal view of the self, when the improvement or deterioration of the environment is made salient during the decision process. In fact, recent work by Arnocky, Stroink, and DeCicco (2007) has demonstrated that the metapersonal self-construal is pre-

dictive of environmental conservation behavior, biospheric environmental concern (i.e., attitudes that are related to the intrinsic value of the environment), and ecological cooperation. Moreover, in his study of over 4,000 "green" consumers, Thøgersen (2011) found that buying organic food was, indeed, positively related to unselfish values (universalism). In interpreting these findings, Thøgersen (2011) postulated that they are indicative of the fact that green consumers are not only driven by selfishness (as is often presumed), but are motivated to help solve environmental problems as well.

Due to the likely conflict between these contextual thoughts and the primed egoistic, independent goals, vigilance (a prevention-focused response) was expected to occur. As posited by Cesario, Higgins, and Scholer, "vigilant means are concerned with ensuring against mismatches to the desired end state" (2008, p. 446). Therefore, in the independent-prime condition, a prevention-focused environmental message (offering ways to prevent further environmental deterioration) was more goal-compatible and was found to be more persuasive than a promotion-focused message. Using a set of ad stimuli and procedures closely aligned with the first study, we obtained a similar pattern of effects in Study 2.

However, when participants were exposed to environmental appeals and were situationally primed to have interdependent thoughts, they were more persuaded by promotion- (as compared to prevention-) framed messages. This was especially the case for participants in Study 2. In this situation, we reason that the assimilation of similar self-views (both of which are outwardly focused) would facilitate less scrutiny and greater ease to pursue the desired goal—which is compatible with eagerness, a promotion-oriented goal orientation (Novak and Hoffman 2009). Once again, as discussed by Cesario, Higgins, and Scholer, "eager means are concerned with ensuring matches to the desired end state" (2008, p. 446).

Relatedly, we posit that when exposed to environmental appeals, participants' thoughts may have been focused on the attainment of universal goals, specifically, the potential benefits that could be achieved for the welfare of all humans alike. This may have placed them in a cooperative frame of mind, which is more compatible with a promotion as opposed to a prevention focus. In other words, by focusing on the common good that could be achieved for everyone's sake, promotion-framed messages offered a more compatible means to seek goals related to the coexistence of participants' metapersonal and interdependent self-views. Our conjecture is further supported by an examination of the recommendations to consumers recently provided by the Environmental Protection Agency (EPA) for addressing the issue of climate change. Specifically, the EPA's recommendations (EPA 2012) tend to emphasize a "promotion-focused" attainment of group (i.e., interdependent or metapersonal) goals (e.g., "Change a light, and you help change the world," "Tell family and friends that energy efficiency is good for their homes and good for the environment").

Goal Compatibility Findings and Extensions

Extant literature has documented that in some domains (e.g., in the case of financial decisions), alternate findings such as ours (i.e., when using environmental appeals) have been observed with regard to goal compatibility. Specifically, Hsee and Weber (1999) observed that participants with a chronically accessible interdependent self-construal were more risk seeking in the financial domain, which is compatible with a promotion as opposed to a prevention orientation. Similarly, Mandel (2003) found that those primed with an interdependent self-construal were more likely to make risky financial choices. Our findings suggest that goal compatibility in the context of green advertising messages employing environmental appeals seems to operate in the same manner. In our studies, when participants were exposed to environmental appeals and primed to be interdependent, they may have focused more on global collaboration as a way to address environmental concerns, consistent with a focus on promotion. Conversely, when they were primed to be independent, but had societal thoughts contextually activated (in line with metapersonal goals), they may have adopted a more vigilant decision process that is more consistent with risk aversion and a focus on prevention.

Furthermore, research has documented that the alternatives under consideration can themselves activate states of prevention and promotion (Pham and Higgins 2005). For example, Zhou and Pham (2004) found that when evaluating individual stocks, consumers were more sensitive to gains than losses (consistent with a focus on promotion), whereas when evaluating mutual funds in a retirement account, they paid more attention to losses as opposed to gains (compatible with prevention). Zhou and Pham (2004) posited that their findings are indicative of the fact that states of promotion and prevention can be contextually activated by the targets of judgment under consideration.

Therefore, it should be readily apparent that advertising practitioners wishing to generalize our findings to their own green campaign plans must account for the fact that appeal type is likely to differentially influence the impact of regulatory focus and self-view on participants' attitudes toward green brands. Furthermore, it should be noted that while both constructs are often conceptualized in terms of consumer information-processing tendencies, regulatory focus and self-view are variables that can also be directly implemented in advertising campaigns by strategic use of ad copy and visual placements. For example, ads featuring a single individual (and corresponding text) are capable of evoking an independent self-view, whereas ads featuring a group of individuals

can successfully facilitate the activation of an interdependent self-view. Similarly, ad copy focusing on the advantages of adopting a green philosophy for personal (or societal) gain might effectively encourage a promotion-focused processing orientation, whereas ad copy focusing on the disadvantages of not adopting such a philosophy may be capable of prompting a prevention-focused processing orientation.

Future Research Directions

Additional work is needed to investigate the conditions under which a contextually based self-view may prevail over a situationally activated self-view. Agrawal and Maheswaran (2005) found that brand commitment moderated the effects of chronic versus primed self-view on persuasion, such that participants with high (low) commitment provided more favorable evaluations when appeals were consistent with the chronic (primed) view of the self. Therefore, in a green advertising context, future research may wish to explore how commitment to the green movement interacts with one's view of self in driving consumers' responses.

In the current research setting, we may have had as many as three self-views contributing to participants' responses to the environmentally based advertisement: a chronically accessible self-view (one that is shaped by the culture in which one is raised), a situationally primed self-view (that may be manipulated by ad features), and a contextually based self-view (that is influenced by the subject matter or general theme of the advertisement). Although our findings are promising in this regard, further work is clearly needed to more fully understand how the interplay of these various self-views may differentially affect consumers' responses. For example, what mechanisms are at play when an advertisement evokes competing or compatible self-views? What may cause one view of self to dominate over another in these conditions?

Relatedly, future research should attempt to extend our findings in other consumption contexts that involve purchase decisions related to the satisfaction of both individual and group goals. For example, researchers should further investigate whether framing the outcomes of environmental appeals as benefiting the individual (consistent with an independent self-view), or benefiting the individual's family (consistent with an interdependent self-view), or benefiting all humans (consistent with the metapersonal view of the self) has a differential impact on the effectiveness of messages framed in terms of promotion versus prevention.

It is our hope that the insights gained from our two empirical studies will not only assist advertising managers in their pursuit of effective green advertising strategies, but will serve as a catalyst for additional research and theoretical development regarding the effects of green advertising on consumers' brand attitudes.

NOTES

1. In a separate study (not reported here), the authors tested an SEM (structural equation model) and found that measures of "concern for personal health" (e.g., perceptions that organic food is nutritious and natural) and "concern for the environment" (e.g., organic food production reduces soil pollution and the use of harmful chemicals) successfully predicted consumers' attitudes and intentions to purchase organic food. In addition, proenvironmental lifestyle and "deal proneness" (negative relationship) were predictors of organic food purchase intentions. Details of this study are available from the authors, upon request.

2. The belief scale (α = .93) included the statement "Consuming organic food . . ." followed by five, seven-point items, anchored on strongly disagree (1)/strongly agree (7) ("Improves the state of the environment," "Reduces the use of artificial fertilizers in agriculture," "Reduces the amount of chemicals that run off into lakes and watercourses," "Reduces soil pollution," and "Reduces the use of herbicides and pesticides in agriculture").

3. In this analysis, we excluded lactose intolerant participants and those who reported having an aversion to drinking milk. Measures of participants' perceptions of organic food (as they relate to naturalness, social responsibility, and proenvironmental behavior) were included as covariates. The ANCOVA results revealed no significant differences for either of the two-way interactions or for the main effects.

4. It should be noted that unlike Study 1, no direct assessment was made of participants' contextually driven (metapersonal) thoughts in Study 2. Instead, we pitted an ad that focused on environmental benefits against one that focused on personal benefits, and observed a pattern of results similar to what was hypothesized and observed in Study 1.

REFERENCES

Aaker, Jennifer L., and Angela Y. Lee (2001), "'I' Seek Pleasures and 'We' Avoid Pains: The Role of Self-Regulatory Goals in Information Processing and Persuasion," *Journal of Consumer Research,* 28 (June), 33–49.

———, and Patti Williams (1998), "Empathy Versus Pride: The Influence of Emotional Appeals Across Cultures," *Journal of Consumer Research,* 25 (December), 241–261.

Agrawal, Nidhi, and Durairaj Maheswaran (2005), "The Effects of Self-Construal and Commitment on Persuasion," *Journal of Consumer Research,* 31 (4), 841–849.

Arnocky, Steven, Mirella Stroink, and Teresa DeCicco (2007), "Self-Construal Predicts Environmental Concern, Cooperation, and Conservation," *Journal of Environmental Psychology,* 27 (4), 255–264.

Avnet, Tamar, and E. Tory Higgins (2006), "How Regulatory Fit Affects Value in Consumer Choices and Opinions," *Journal of Marketing Research,* 43 (1), 1–10.

Banerjee, Subhabrata, Charles S. Gulas, and Easwar Iyer (1995), "Shades of Green: A Multidimensional Analysis of Environmental Advertising," *Journal of Advertising,* 24 (2), 21–31.

Baumeister, Roy F. (1998), "The Self," in *The Handbook of Social Psychology,* 4th ed., Daniel T. Gilbert, Susan T. Fiske, and Gardner Lindzey, eds., New York: McGraw-Hill, 680–740.

Cesario, Joseph, E. Tory Higgins, and Abigail A. Scholer (2008), "Regulatory Fit and Persuasion: Basic Principles and Remaining Questions," *Social and Personality Psychology Compass,* 2 (1), 444–463.

Chen, Haipeng (Allan), Sharon Ng, and Akshay R. Rao (2005), "Cultural Differences in Consumer Impatience," *Journal of Marketing Research,* 42 (3), 291–301.

DeCicco, Teresa L., and Mirella L. Stroink (2007), "A Third Model of Self-Construal: The Metapersonal Self," *International Journal of Transpersonal Studies,* 26, 82–104.

Environmental Protection Agency (2012), "Climate Change," available at www.epa.gov/climatechange/ (accessed March 1, 2012).

Fiske, Alan, Shinobu Kitayama, Hazel R. Markus, and Richard Nisbett (1998), "The Cultural Matrix of Social Psychology," in *The Handbook of Social Psychology,* vol. 2, Daniel T. Gilbert and Susan T. Fiske, eds., Boston: McGraw-Hill, 915–981.

Griskevicius, Vladas, Joshua M. Tybur, and Bram Van den Bergh (2010), "Going Green to Be Seen: Status, Reputation, and Conspicuous Conservation," *Journal of Personality and Social Psychology,* 98 (3), 392–404.

Hamilton, Rebecca W., and Gabriel J. Biehal (2005), "Achieving Your Goals or Protecting Their Future? The Effects of Self-View on Goals and Choices," *Journal of Consumer Research,* 32 (2), 277–283.

Heine, Steven J., Darrin R. Lehman, Hazel R. Markus, and Shinobu Kitayama (1999), "Is There a Universal Need for Positive Self-Regard?" *Psychological Review,* 106 (4), 766–794.

Higgins, E. Tory (1997), "Beyond Pleasure and Pain," *American Psychologist,* 52 (12), 1280–1300.

——— (1998), "Promotion and Prevention: Regulatory Focus as a Motivational Principle," in *Advances in Experimental Psychology,* vol. 30, Mark P. Zanna, ed., San Diego: Academic Press, 1–46.

——— (2002), "How Self-Regulation Creates Distinct Values: The Case of Promotion and Prevention Decision Making," *Journal of Consumer Psychology,* 12 (3), 177–191.

———, Christopher J. R. Roney, Ellen Crowe, and Charles Hymes (1994), "Ideal Versus Ought Predilections for Approach and Avoidance: Distinct Self-Regulatory Systems," *Journal of Personality and Social Psychology,* 66 (2), 276–286.

———, Ronald S. Friedman, Robert E. Harlow, Lorraine Chen Idson, Ozlem N. Ayduk, and Amy Taylor (2001), "Achievement Orientations from Subjective Histories of Success: Promotion Pride Versus Prevention Pride," *European Journal of Social Psychology,* 31 (1), 3–23.

Hsee, Christopher K., and Elke U. Weber (1999), "Cross-National Differences in Risk Preference and Lay Predictions," *Journal of Behavioral Decision Making,* 12 (2), 165–179.

Kees, Jeremy, Scot Burton, and Andrea Heintz Tangari (2010), "The Impact of Regulatory Focus, Temporal Orientation, and Fit on Consumer Responses to Health-Related Advertising," *Journal of Advertising,* 39 (1), 19–34.

Kim, Yeung-Jo (2006), "The Role of Regulatory Focus in Message Framing in Antismoking Advertisements for Adolescents," *Journal of Advertising*, 35 (1), 143–151.

Laroche, Michel, Jasmin Bergeron, and Guido Barbaro-Forleo (2001), "Targeting Consumers Who Are Willing to Pay More for Environmentally Friendly Products," *Journal of Consumer Marketing*, 18 (6), 503–520.

Lee, Angela Y., Jennifer L. Aaker, and Wendi L. Gardner (2000), "The Pleasures and Pains of Distinct Self-Construals: The Role of Interdependence in Regulatory Focus," *Journal of Personality and Social Psychology*, 78 (6), 1122–1134.

Mandel, Naomi (2003), "Shifting Selves and Decision Making: The Effects of Self-Construal Priming on Consumer Risk-Taking," *Journal of Consumer Research*, 30 (1), 30–40.

Markus, Hazel R., and Shinobu Kitayama (1991), "Culture and the Self: Implications for Cognition, Emotion, and Motivation," *Psychological Review*, 98 (2), 224–253.

MDG Advertising (2012), "Green Advertising Worldwide to Hit $3.5 Trillion in 2017," available at www.mdgadvertising.com/blog/green-advertising-worldwide-to-hit-3-5-trillion-in-2017-2/ (accessed March 1, 2012).

Novak, Thomas P., and Donna L. Hoffman (2009), "The Fit of Thinking Style and Situation: New Measures of Situation-Specific Experiential and Rational Cognition," *Journal of Consumer Research*, 36 (3), 56–72.

Pham, Michel Tuan, and E. Tory Higgins (2005), "Promotion and Prevention in Consumer Decision Making: The State of the Art and Theoretical Propositions," in *Inside Consumption: Consumer Motives, Goals, and Desires*, S. Ratneshwar and David Glen Mick, eds., London: Routledge, 8–43.

Roberts, James A. (1996), "Green Consumers in the 1990s: Profile and Implications for Advertising," *Journal of Business Research*, 36 (3), 217–231.

Schultz, Wesley (2001), "The Structure of Environmental Concern: For Self, Other People, and the Biosphere," *Journal of Environmental Psychology*, 21 (4), 327–339.

Shamdasani, Prem N., Andrea J. S. Stanaland, and Julaina Tan (2001), "Location, Location, Location: Insights for Advertising Placement on the Web," *Journal of Advertising Research*, 41 (4), 7–21.

Shrum, L.J., John A. McCarty, and Tina M. Lowrey (1995), "Buyer Characteristics of the Green Consumer and Their Implications for Advertising Strategy," *Journal of Advertising*, 24 (2), 71–82.

Singelis, Theodore M. (1994), "The Measurement of Independent and Interdependent Self-Construals," *Personality and Social Psychology Bulletin*, 20 (5), 580–591.

Thøgersen, John (2011), "Green Shopping: For Selfish Seasons or the Common Good," *American Behavioral Scientist*, 55 (8), 1052–1076.

Utz, Sonja (2004), "Self-Construal and Cooperation: Is the Interdependent Self More Cooperative Than the Independent Self?" *Self and Identity*, 3 (3), 177–190.

Webster, Frederick E., Jr. (1975), "Determining the Characteristics of the Socially Conscious Consumer," *Journal of Consumer Research*, 2 (3), 188–196.

Zhou, Rongrong, and Michel T. Pham (2004), "Promotion and Prevention Across Mental Accounts: When Financial Products Dictate Consumers' Investment Goals," *Journal of Consumer Research*, 31 (1), 125–135.

Zinkhan, George M., and Les Carlson (1995), "Green Advertising and the Reluctant Consumer," *Journal of Advertising*, 24 (2), 1–6.

APPENDIX

Messages Corresponding to Ad Treatment Conditions in Study 2

1. Promotion-Focused Ad Using Personal Health Appeals

Nothing is better than a cool glass of delicious milk. And when the milk is organic, you can enjoy it even more knowing that it is fresh, wholesome, natural milk. Plus, drinking milk helps promote a healthy lifestyle. Studies show that organic milk increases your energy level by providing you with essential nutrients such as calcium, phosphorus, and vitamin D. Furthermore, you can enjoy these benefits with a better and fresher taste. Please become part of The Farmer's Cow story by buying our organic milk at your local grocery store.

2. Prevention-Focused Ad Using Personal Health Appeals

Nothing is better than a cool glass of delicious milk. And when the milk is organic, you can enjoy it even more knowing that it is produced without pesticides, antibiotics, or artificial growth hormones. Plus, drinking milk helps prevent an unhealthy lifestyle. Studies show that organic milk reduces your risk of disease by providing you with essential nutrients such as calcium, phosphorus, and vitamin D. Furthermore, you can enjoy these benefits without the addition of artificial growth hormones (rBST). Please become part of The Farmer's Cow story by buying our organic milk at your local grocery store.

3. Promotion-Focused Ad Using Environmental Appeals

Our dairy farmers work in harmony with nature's own balance. Organic farming helps cleanse our environment by ensuring that air, water, and soil remain pure. Furthermore, our farmers seek to maintain biodiversity, which is so important to promoting a healthy ecosystem. When you buy locally produced milk, you help to make a difference by increasing the use of [state's] natural landscape. The working fields and woodlands of [state] farms help maintain our state's unique flavor, providing open space with scenic views and habitat for all kinds of wildlife. Please become part of The Farmer's Cow story by buying our organic milk at your local grocery store.

4. Prevention-Focused Ad Using Environmental Appeals

Our dairy farmers work in a way that does not harm the balance of nature. Organic farming helps to reduce the toxic load on our environment by keeping unnecessary chemicals out of the air, water, and soil. Furthermore, our farmers rely upon biodiversity, which is important in preventing the deterioration of a healthy ecosystem. When you buy locally produced milk, you help to make a difference by stopping the decline of [state's] natural landscape. The working fields and woodlands of [state] farms help maintain our state's unique flavor, providing open space with scenic views and habitat for all kinds of wildlife. Please become part of The Farmer's Cow story by buying our organic milk at your local grocery store.

COMMUNICATING GREEN MARKETING APPEALS EFFECTIVELY

The Role of Consumers' Motivational Orientation to Promotion Versus Prevention

Hsuan-Hsuan Ku, Chien-Chih Kuo, Ching-Luen Wu, and Chih-Ying Wu

ABSTRACT: This study investigates the effect of consumers' self-regulatory focus on their response to green versus nongreen advertising appeals in terms of perceived attractiveness and purchase intention. Study 1 finds that prevention-focused participants are more strongly persuaded when "product-related" appeals emphasize green rather than nongreen product attributes, whereas the converse holds true for those who are promotion-focused. Study 2 finds that with respect to "non–product-related" appeals and for both categories of self-regulatory focus, green is significantly more persuasive than nongreen. Purchasing decisions by promotion-focused individuals are found to reflect a concern for experiential advancement; prevention-focused counterparts are motivated to minimize loss.

There is clear evidence that consumers in the contemporary world marketplace generally exhibit a heightened awareness of environmental issues and consequently experience significant levels of environmental concern (Laroche, Bergeron, and Barbaro-Forleo 2001). In response, many consumer-product manufacturers have followed popular sentiment by adopting overtly "green" marketing strategies (Pickett-Baker and Ozaki 2008) with the aim of gaining an edge over their competitors. Green marketing is considered one of the major trends in modern business (Kassaye 2001). Its strategic aims have been expressed in more environmentally focused advertising campaigns (Schuhwerk and Lefkoff-Hagius 1995) and an increasing number of claims of ecological responsibility made at the point of sale (Banerjee, Gulas, and Iyer 1995; Phau and Ong 2007).

Previous research on green marketing and advertising has specifically addressed issues related to the determinants of green-influenced purchasing decisions. Drawing on communication and information-processing theories, Schuhwerk and Lefkoff-Hagius (1995) examined the relative persuasiveness of various appeals to different target audiences in advertisements for a "green product," that is, one that is less harmful to the environment than a direct alternative. Phau and Ong (2007) compared the influence of different environmental message strategies on the credibility and effectiveness of appeals. Several studies have investigated the formation of consumers' perceptions of products classified as "green" and discuss the implications for companies and marketers engaged in their promotion and commercialization (D'Souza et al. 2006; Tanner and Kast 2003).

An increasingly frequent research topic in the literature is the role of consumers' regulatory goals and foci in determining the effectiveness of advertising campaigns (Aaker and Lee 2001; Kim 2006). Relatively little is known, however, about the way in which this process of self-regulation affects their respective responses to "green advertising." The present research therefore attempts to measure the relative persuasiveness of green versus nongreen message appeals, moderated by the personal regulatory foci of consumers in a target audience. It furthermore distinguishes between the applications of each type of appeal to both "product-related" and "non–product-related" attributes, a distinction attributable to Keller (1993), which reflects how directly the product attributes on which the appeals focus relate to the performance of the product. *Product-related attributes* are "the ingredients necessary for performing the product function sought by consumers," whereas *non–product-related attributes* are the "external aspects of the product that relate to its purchase or consumption." Keller cites packaging as a case in point, insofar as it is an integral element of the purchase and consumption process, but does not generally relate directly to the necessary ingredients for product performance. Drawing on this definition of the difference, according to Montoro Rios et al. (2006), a green appeal that emphasizes the environmental attributes of the product can be considered as product-related (environmental-friendly composition) or non–product-related (beliefs in the possibility of packaging recycling). The literature clearly distinguishes between a self-regulatory focus that is primarily either on "promotion" or "prevention." The former relates to one's ideals, hopes, and aspirations; the latter to responsibilities, duties, and security. A basic tenet of regulatory focus theory (Higgins 1997) is that individuals attend especially closely to information relevant to the dominant focus and allocate greater weight to product attributes compatible with that focus (Chernev 2004; Florack and Scarabis 2006). In other words, their attitude toward a product is more favorable when its deliverable benefits match their self-regulatory orientation (Aaker and Lee 2001; Cesario, Grant, and Higgins 2004).

Building on prior research, our paper extends the notion of compatibility to the relationship between a consumer's focus on promotion or prevention and the type of advertising appeals to which he or she is exposed (in this case, green versus nongreen). Specifically, in Study 1, we propose that marketers can benefit from making product-related green appeals in communications targeted at prevention-focused consumers, whereas such appeals can have a negative influence on the product preferences of others whose focus is on promotion. Study 2 tests whether, in the case of both promotion-focused and prevention-focused individuals, framing non–product-related attributes in green terms enhances the product's appeal. The results of these two studies thereby highlight the importance of understanding how personal self-regulatory focus affects the persuasiveness of green appeals.

The next section reviews relevant prior research studies and findings, which provides the basis for two research hypotheses. Two experiments are then described. We conclude by discussing the findings of the study, identifying its managerial implications, and suggesting fruitful directions for further research.

THEORETICAL BACKGROUND AND HYPOTHESES

Consumer's Self-Regulatory Focus

Individuals differ in their approach to the pursuit of positive goals and avoidance of negative goals. Regulatory focus theory (Higgins 1997) offers one key to the understanding of these differences, its main thesis being that people in general, and by extension consumers in particular, are guided in their purchasing behavior by either *promotion* or *prevention.* The former concerns the attainment of such positive personal outcomes as advancement and achievement, the latter the avoidance of negative outcomes relating to protection and security (Micu and Chowdhury 2010; Mourali, Böckenholt, and Laroche 2007; Rossiter, Percy, and Donovan 1991). Both self-regulatory behavioral systems can take the form of a persisting individual predisposition in one direction or the other, or can be activated ad hoc by situational circumstances (Higgins 2002; Higgins et al. 2001). For example, Aaker and

Lee (2001) have shown that advertising messages can evoke either a promotion or prevention response by varying the emphasis on such promotion-related benefits as the enhancement of energy levels versus such prevention-related alternatives as reduced risk of heart disease.

Recent research has provided considerable evidence that these two modes of self-regulation are associated with distinct variations of personal decision-making strategy. The promotion focus reflects an orientation characterized by "eagerness" and the prevention focus to one placing the emphasis on "vigilance" (Higgins 2002; Lee and Aaker 2004). Eager strategists are concerned with achieving "hits" and ensuring against "misses," whereas vigilant counterparts aim to "correct rejections" and ensure against "false hits" (Crowe and Higgins 1997). In a study by Roney, Higgins, and Shah (1995), for example, promotion-focused individuals undertaking the task of searching for anagrams exhibited a high degree of persistence and determination to keep searching for an elusive solution. In contrast, prevention-focused individuals experiencing difficulty were motivated to abandon the search, to avoid committing an explicit error. The findings of Crowe and Higgins (1997) also support the impact of these different strategic inclinations on behavior. Thus, when individuals undertake a task that, for example, requires them to decide whether they did or did not detect a signal, those with a promotion focus would be expected to exhibit a "risky" responses bias, whereas those whose focus is on prevention would adopt a "conservative" response bias and take longer to respond.

With the increasing recognition in recent years of the significance of goals and motives in the shaping of consumer behavior, consumer researchers have found that the concept of self-regulatory focus furnishes a powerful and parsimonious framework for the investigation of such phenomena as persuasion and choice decisions (Chernev 2004; Pham and Avnet 2004; Zhou and Pham 2004). Specifically, researchers building on regulatory focus theory have proposed that advertising persuasion may depend on whether an audience member's personal goals relate mainly to prevention or promotion. When the persuasive appeal is compatible with an individual's own self-regulatory focus, he or she will be more persuaded and will have better recall of the claims made in the advertisements (Aaker and Lee 2001).

Influence of Regulatory Focus and Green Appeals on Persuasion

Contemporary marketplaces are characterized by an increasing level of concern for the environment. Such sensitivity to environmental issues leads to an increased availability of green, proenvironment products, yet consumers' purchasing behavior is not necessarily more green than before (Pickett-Baker and Ozaki 2008). Often, strongly expressed concerns for the environment are not reflected in consumption practices (Chang 2011; Essoussi and Linton 2010). Studies on the consumption of environmentally sustainable products have demonstrated that perceived product performance is a significant barrier to purchase (Ottman 1998), and it is known that some consumers associate green products with inferior performance in use. The key thus lies in understanding the variable that is differentially affecting the influence of green appeals on preference.

Product-Related Appeals

In general, it is argued that promotion goals regulate behavior with respect to positive outcomes, either by maximizing their presence or minimizing their absence. In contrast, prevention goals act either by minimizing the presence of negative outcomes or maximizing their absence (Freitas and Higgins 2002; Idson, Liberman, and Higgins 2000). In the context of a promotion focus, the desired endpoint is the presence of positive outcomes; in the case of a prevention focus, it is the absence of negative outcomes. Of particular relevance to persuasive effect is the concept of regulatory fit, which suggests that consumers tend to give particular weight to goal-consistent information. Outcomes that match an individual's self-regulatory orientation are likely to be viewed as relatively more important than those that are inconsistent with the goal (Chernev 2004). It is further conceptualized that attributes compatible with personal goal orientation tend to be weighted more strongly in choice making, permitting direct prediction of the choice outcome.

With regard to product-related attributes, directly related to product performance, the fact that individuals with a self-regulatory focus on promotion are motivated to pursue such positive outcomes as "advancement" and "eagerness" means that they will be more concerned with "getting the job done," will place particular emphasis on "strength" in their choices, and will respond positively to claims that the product is, for example, "powerful" or "effective." Those whose focus is on prevention, who are motivated to pursue "safety" and "vigilance" are more likely to respond favorably to appeals emphasizing the "healthiness" or "gentleness" of the product, even if there may be a cost in terms of reduced effectiveness.

A very recent study by Luchs et al. (2010) presents evidence that products perceived to be "ethical" are associated in consumers' minds with gentleness-related attributes; those seen as less ethical are associated with strength-related attributes. These categorizations can be linked to consumers' self-regulatory foci on prevention and promotion. Since those whose focus is on prevention are likely to allocate greater weight to safety or vigilance than to power or effectiveness, advertising messages emphasizing green features compatible with their personal consumption goals can be expected to exert an enhanced persuasive effect. In the case of promotion-focused

consumers, however—those who tend to place most weight on power and effectiveness—it could be a strategic liability to base a marketing campaign on the claim of greenness, with its appeal to security and vigilance. Thus, green product-related appeals that emphasize a product's superior performance in terms of gentleness-related criteria (such as safety or health) enhance the preferences of prevention-focused consumers, whereas that positive effect is reduced if the self-regulatory focus is on promotion. This prediction can be expressed more formally as follows:

> *Hypothesis 1a: For individuals with a self-regulatory focus on promotion, framing the product-related appeal in nongreen terms will be more persuasive than framing it in green terms.*

> *Hypothesis 1b: For individuals with a self-regulatory focus on prevention, framing the product-related appeal in green terms will be more persuasive than framing it in nongreen terms.*

Non–Product-Related Appeals

Non–product-related attributes, defined as external aspects of the product that relate to its purchase or consumption, typically do not relate directly to the product performance. However, there has been a continued increase in the use of non–product-related attributes as an instrument for product and brand differentiation.

The inclusion of a green, non–product-related appeal in an advertising message can be expected to be interpreted as a signal of added value, compared with a nongreen alternative, in relation to the social benefits offered. These associations with environmental concerns can deliver expected satisfaction by promoting a feeling of accomplishment or satisfying a motivation of safety, depending on the consumers' purchasing motivations, and are more effective in persuasion.

Non–product-related environmental claims might influence the consumer's response to the product in use, in the form of a perceived experiential benefit: that the decision to choose it rather than another has made a contribution to social welfare (Montoro Rios et al. 2006). Positive environmental associations signal to the consumer that using the product will deliver such consumer benefits by virtue of, for instance, its recyclable packaging. In the case of individuals with a self-regulatory focus dominantly on promotion—those who are shown to be strategically inclined to seek "advancement"—the payoff comes in the shape of the satisfaction and fulfillment of knowing that they are contributing to the environmental cause. The green appeal thus reinforces the brand image by delivering a feeling of accomplishment as an outcome of purchase (Hoeffler and Keller 2002).

In the case of individuals with a prevention focus—those who are negatively oriented and motivated to remove or avoid any problem—green purchases may not reflect a concern with enhancement of experience, but rather with safety and the minimizing of losses. The perception of environmental benefits could be related to the product's credentials with respect to care of the environment, which appeals to safety motivations and the avoidance or elimination of negative outcomes. A green non–product-related attribute may thus help to attain prevention goals, and produce more positive reactions to an advertising message. The following hypothesis thus posits that:

Hypothesis 2: In the case of both promotion-focused and prevention-focused consumers, framing the non–product-related appeal in green terms will be more persuasive than framing it in nongreen terms.

STUDY 1

Design and Sample

This study tested H1a and H1b, which postulated that consumers whose self-regulatory focus is on promotion would be more persuaded by product-related nongreen appeals than by product-related green appeals, whereas the reverse would hold true for those with a self-regulatory focus on prevention. A between-participants 2 × 2 design manipulated two product-related advertising appeals, nongreen versus green, and two self-regulation foci, prevention versus promotion. The experimental participants were 125 undergraduate students enrolled in management or business courses at a large university in Taiwan.

Stimuli and Procedure

Magazine Articles

Magazine articles served as the stimulus to evoke either the promotion or prevention focus. Each participant read two articles, both based on real-life stories. Of the two designed to reveal a focus on promotion, one told how efficient high-technology products could help individuals to be more professional and success oriented, and the other featured people being energized by bodybuilding activities. Of the two evoking a prevention focus, one focused on individuals pursuing security by means of medical insurance schemes and the other on reducing the risk of osteoporosis by the use of bone-care products. The rationale for the two contrasting stories for each condition was to increase the generalizability of the findings and to reduce the idiosyncratic effects of any individual story. The pretest had shown that the subsample of the same student population thought the articles related to a self-regulatory focus on promotion evoked the notion of self-enhancement, while those related to a prevention focus conveyed a sense of self-protection. On a seven-point scale anchored at 1 = "protection" and 7 = "enhancement," the mean scores were M = 5.73 and 4.13, respectively; t = 4.27, p < .001.

Product-Related Appeals

To manipulate these stimuli, participants were exposed to a print advertisement in which the headline appeal related to either the green or nongreen credentials of the product. The ads featured a fictitious household cleaning product, "Clean Angel," chosen to avoid the confounding effects of preexistent knowledge of a real brand. The nongreen appeal communicated by one headline was "Exclusive high-tech formula removes stubborn stains and grime!"; in the other, the appeal was that a "natural plant formula" removed them. The noncopy elements of the advertisements did not vary. To enhance external validity, participants were simultaneously exposed to a filler advertisement, in both the green and nongreen manipulations.

Procedure

Participants were given a mock magazine, *Modern Life,* containing the two focus-evoking articles, one of the purpose-designed advertisements, and the filler advertisement. They were instructed to look at all three stimuli, just as they might at home. To avoid interference with the manipulation of the two articles, they were instructed to put aside thoughts about themselves coming into their minds as they read the stories, and then to rate how easy it had been to understand what the articles were saying. After those preliminary responses, they completed measures of perceived product attractiveness and intention to purchase, followed by ratings testing the experimental manipulations of the magazine articles and the self-regulatory focus. Lastly, they provided standard demographic data.

Independent Variables

To check whether the articles in the mock magazine evoked a focus on promotion or prevention, participants were directed to report how much reliance they would place on two corresponding decision-making criteria, by means of seven-point scales anchored respectively at 1 = "protection" and 7 = "enhancement," and 1 = "avoiding loss" and 7 = "pursuing effectiveness." As predicted, the promotion-focused condition achieved higher mean scores than the prevention-focused condition, M_{pro} = 4.85 versus M_{pre} = 3.94; $F(1, 123)$ = 13.54, p < .001.

Analysis further confirmed that prevention-focused consumers were more likely to give a heavier weighting to "gentle" or "safe" than to "powerful" or "effective," and that their promotion-focused counterparts would exhibit exactly the reverse tendency. All participants responded to the question "How important is each of these dimensions/characteristics to you when buying a home cleaning product?" They answered on a seven-point scale anchored at "very unimportant" and "very important." As predicted, "gentle" and "safe" were rated more important than "powerful" and "effective" for participants known to have a self-regulation focus on prevention (M = 5.62 and 4.94, respectively; t = 3.33, p < .01). For those whose focus was on promotion, the reverse held true (M = 5.48 and 5.14, respectively; t = 1.77, p < .1).

An additional test was conducted to check for variation in the comprehensibility of the two sets of magazine stories, which dealt with high-tech products and bodybuilding for promotion-focused participants and health insurance and medication for their prevention-focused counterparts. There was no significant difference in the reported ease of comprehension, M_{pro} = 5.52 versus M_{pre} = 5.27; $F(1, 123)$ = 1.51.

Dependent Variables

Product Attractiveness

This variable was measured by three, seven-point scales adapted from a study by Zhang and Buda (1999), anchored at "bad"/"good," "not nice"/"nice," and "unlikable"/"likable," as shown in the Appendix. The Cronbach's α of .90 indicates high internal reliability.

Purchase Intention

For this variable, three, seven-point scales developed by Dodds, Monroe, and Grewal (1991), anchored at 1 = "very low" and 7 = "very high," measured a participant's willingness to buy "Clean Angel," the likelihood of buying it, and the probability of considering its purchase. The scale items appear in the Appendix. The internal validity of this scale was again high, at α = .96.

Results

H1a and H1b were tested by ANOVA (analysis of variance), followed by contrast analysis. Neither green versus nongreen appeals nor prevention versus promotion self-regulatory foci had significant effects on the two dependent variables: product attractiveness, $F(1, 121)$ = .42 and $F(1, 121)$ = .42, respectively, and purchase intention, $F(1, 121)$ = .52 and $F(1, 121)$ = .27, respectively.

Figure 1A shows that as expected, the interaction effect on product attractiveness of the green and nongreen product-related appeals and the respondents' self-regulatory focus was significant, $F(1, 121)$ = 23.29, p < .001. In support of H1a, contrast analysis found that participants with a focus on prevention reported higher levels of perceived product attractiveness when the headline claim was green ("natural plant formula") (M = 4.75) than when it was nongreen ("exclusive high-tech formula"), M = 3.75; $F(1, 61)$ = 15.69, p < .001. Confirming H1b, a product-related green appeal resulted in

significantly lower product attractiveness among participants with a focus on promotion (M = 3.99) than when the appeal was nongreen, M = 4.75; $F(1, 60)$ = 8.34, p < .01.

Figure 1B shows that the interaction effect on purchase intention of the green and nongreen product-related appeals with the respondents' self-regulatory focus interaction was also significant, $F(1, 121)$ = 27.28, p < .001. As predicted, compared with the nongreen condition (M = 3.43), participants whose focus was on prevention reported stronger purchase intentions when the headline claim was green, M = 4.38; $F(1, 61)$ = 8.21, p < .01. By comparison, promotion-focused consumers' purchase intentions were higher with respect to a product-related nongreen appeal (M = 4.64) than in the case of a product-related green appeal, M = 3.39; $F(1, 60)$ = 23.33, p < .001. These findings offer further support for H1a and H1b.

For each category of appeal, a meaningful picture emerges from examination of the pattern of differences in perceived product attractiveness and purchase intention between the self-regulatory foci. When that was nongreen, promotion-focused participants exhibited a higher level of both perceived product attractiveness and intention to purchase than their prevention-focused counterparts: $F(1, 61)$ = 14.00, p < .001 versus $F(1, 61)$ = 17.46, p < .001. By contrast, when the appeal was green, participants whose focus was on prevention focus reported higher levels of perceived attractiveness and purchase intention scores than those focused on promotion: $F(1, 60)$ = 9.41, p < .01 versus $F(1, 60)$ = 10.46, p < .01.

Discussion

The findings of Study 1 support the hypothesis that the effect of green versus nongreen product-related appeals on an individual's perception of the attractiveness of a product and intention to purchase it is moderated by differences in self-regulatory focus. Participants with a focus on prevention generally favored products that emphasized their greenness in the advertising. In contrast, for those whose focus was on promotion, the nongreen headline claims were preferred. The results suggest that with regard to product-related attributes, a claim of greenness—appealing as a virtue in its own right—will be seen as an asset by prevention-focused consumers, but as a liability by promotion-focused consumers.

STUDY 2

Design and Sample

This study tested H2, which predicts that in the case of both promotion-focused and prevention-focused consumers, framing the non–product-related appeal in green terms will be more persuasive than framing it in nongreen terms. A between-participants 2 × 2 design manipulated two

FIGURE 1
Study 1 (Interaction Effects: Regulatory Focus × Product-Related Appeal)

A. Product Attractiveness

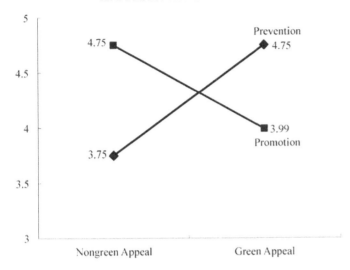

B. Purchase Intentions

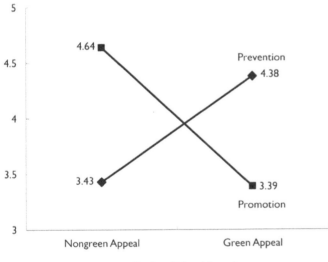

non–product-related advertisement headlines, nongreen versus green, and two self-regulation foci, prevention versus promotion. The experimental participants were 128 undergraduate students drawn from the same sampling frame that was used in Study 1. None had participated in Study 1 or the pretest.

Stimuli and Procedure

The procedure of Study 2 follows that of Study 1, with one modification. To manipulate the non–product-related appeals,

the emphasis in the advertisements was on the design of the spray nozzle that delivered the product to the surface to be cleaned, not on the product itself. The nongreen claim was: "Unique spray nozzle design. Super-fine spray! Economic usage!" The green alternative was: "Unique spray nozzle design. Eco-friendly materials! Recycled and pollution-free!" The noncopy elements of the advertisements did not vary.

Independent Variables

Self-Regulatory Focus

As in Study 1, to check whether the articles in the mocked-up magazine evoked a focus on promotion or prevention, participants were directed to report how much reliance they would place on two corresponding decision-making criteria, by means of seven-point scales anchored respectively at 1 = "protection" and 7 = "enhancement," and 1 = "avoiding loss" and 7 = "pursuing effectiveness." As expected, the mean score for promotion-focused participants was significantly higher than for their prevention-focused counterparts: M_{pro} = 5.48 versus M_{pre} = 4.25; $F(1, 126)$ = 42.85, $p < .001$. In addition, the two groups of participants did not differ significantly in their assessment of the ease of comprehension of the stories: M_{pro} = 5.17 versus M_{pre} = 4.92; $F(1, 126)$ = 1.30.

Non–Product-Related Appeals

A test was conducted to confirm that the two non–product-related appeals, green versus nongreen, offered no significant performance benefits. Participants were asked, "How relevant is the claim emphasized in the headline to the performance benefits of a home cleaning product?"; they answered on a seven-point scale anchored at 1 = "very irrelevant" and 7 = "very relevant." As expected, participants reported a low level of relevance in the case of both the green and nongreen appeals: M_{green} = 3.43 versus $M_{nongreen}$ = 3.54; $F(1, 126)$ = .09.

Dependent Variables

The same scales used in Study 1 were also used in this study to measure perceived product attractiveness and intention to purchase. Internal reliability was acceptable for both scales, at α = .79 and .94, respectively.

A basic prediction of regulatory focus theory is that individuals are more concerned with information that is relevant to the activated regulatory focus. When advertising appeals are presented in a way that is compatible with their purchasing motivations, they are more likely to be persuaded. To confirm that the green purchasing decisions of participants whose self-regulatory focus was on promotion (in this case, the acceptance of environment-friendly packaging) reflected a motive of self-enhancement, while those of their prevention-focused counterparts were related to a drive for self-protection, participants in the non–product-related green-appeal conditions were asked how attractive they personally found the non–product-related appeals for the eco-friendly packaging expressed either in terms of "avoiding harm to the environment" or "enhancing environmental benefits." They answered on a seven-point scale anchored at "very unattractive" and "very attractive."

Results

ANOVA found that the main effects of the self-regulatory focus were not significant for either product attractiveness, $F(1, 124) = .10$, or purchase intention, $F(1, 124) = .67$, but that the non–product-related appeal had significant main effects on both product attractiveness, $F(1, 124) = 7.66$, $p < .01$, and purchase intention, $F(1, 124) = 26.62, p < .001$. Figures 2A and 2B show that when cross-indexed with self-regulatory focus, non–product-related appeals had a significant effect on purchase intention, $F(1, 124) = 5.30, p < .05$, but not on product attractiveness, $F(1, 124) = .06$.

Contrast analysis found that prevention-focused participants who read the non–product-related green headline ($M = 4.73$) gave a higher rating to product attractiveness than those reacting to the nongreen scenario, $M = 4.33$; $F(1, 60) = 3.19, p < .1$. Similarly, among participants with a focus on promotion, the green headline resulted in significantly higher ratings for product attractiveness than when the appeal was nongreen, $M = 4.72$ and 4.25 respectively; $F(1, 64) = 4.54, p < .05$.

Compared with the effect of nongreen appeals on prevention-focused participants ($M = 3.19$), green appeals emphasizing the ecological credentials of the product evoked stronger purchase intention, $M = 4.69$; $F(1, 60) = 31.94, p < .001$. Similarly, promotion-focused consumers who saw the green headline reported a stronger intention ($M = 4.06$) than those reacting to the nongreen appeal, $M = 3.49$; $F(1, 64) = 3.68$, $p < .1$. These findings support H2.

As expected, the green non–product-related appeal had a significantly more persuasive effect on both promotion-focused and prevention-focused participants than the nongreen alternative. Furthermore, it was found that those two subsamples of participants were motivated by different concerns. Those in the green-appeal subsample whose self-regulatory focus was on promotion were more concerned with enhancing environmental benefits ($M = 5.84$) than with avoiding harm to the environment ($M = 4.81$; $t = 3.52, p < .01$), whereas their prevention-focused counterparts aimed for the avoidance of environmental harm ($M = 5.03$) rather than for the enhancement of environmental benefits ($M = 4.55$; $t = 2.34, p < .05$).

Further comparison shows that prevention-focused participants who were exposed to a green non–product-related

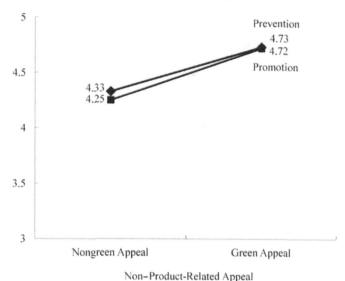

FIGURE 2
Study 2 (Interaction Effects: Regulatory Focus × Non–Product-Related Appeal)

A. Product Attractiveness

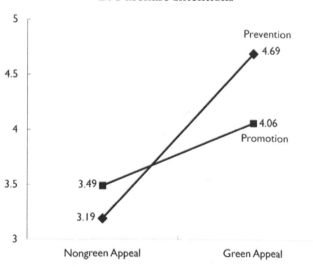

B. Purchase Intentions

headline exhibited stronger intention to purchase than those whose focus was on promotion, $F(1, 61) = 4.94, p < .05$. No difference was found, however, with respect to perceived product attractiveness for either of the self-regulatory foci, $F(1, 61) = .00$. In the case of nongreen appeals, there was no significant difference between participants' product attractiveness and purchase intention ratings, whether in the prevention or promotion conditions: $F(1, 63) = .19$ versus $F(1, 63) = 1.08$.

Discussion

The results of Study 2 show that participants with a self-regulatory focus on prevention reported higher levels of perceived product attractiveness and intention to purchase when exposed to the green non–product-related appeal than in response to the nongreen alternative. The same pattern was found for the promotion-focused participants. Although both subsamples were more likely to be persuaded by green-related appeals, they were motivated by different concerns. Prevention-focused participants prioritized the avoidance of environmental harm rather than the achievement of environmental benefits, while their promotion-focused counterparts rated such potential gains more important than potential losses.

CONCLUSIONS

The appeals encoded in advertising messages, as a key element of advertising strategy, have to be carefully developed to speak to a target audience's personal motivations in the context of purchasing behavior. Previous research on consumers' self-regulatory focus has shown that compatibility between advertising messages and consumers' purchasing motivation has an impact on persuasion (Aaker and Lee 2001; Micu and Chowdhury 2010). Our study adopted the perspective of regulatory focus theory (Higgins 1997), which organizes the basis of the motives determining consumers' goals and actions in terms of a focus on either "promotion" or "prevention," as a framework for analyzing consumers' responses to green versus nongreen advertising appeals.

Study 1 found that for consumers with a self-regulatory focus on prevention, the effectiveness of a message linking product-related attributes to a green appeal was greater than linking them to a nongreen appeal. Those whose focus was on promotion exhibited exactly the opposite tendency. The findings thus support the proposition in the literature that promotion-focused consumers are generally motivated by gain-related situations, whereas the behavior of prevention-focused consumers tends to reflect their security needs. Intention to purchase is thus enhanced by messages that either signal a product's strength or promise "gentle" benefits, according to which is compatible with the prospective purchaser's promotion or prevention focus.

The use of non–product-related attributes as an instrument for product and brand differentiation has been steadily gaining importance in marketing and advertising strategy. Study 2, which compared a green versus a nongreen appeal with respect to non–product-related attributes, found that in the case of consumers with both types of self-regulatory focus, product preference was enhanced by green rather than nongreen appeals. The results furthermore show that in the case of those with a dominant focus on promotion, increased product pref-

erence reflects the expectation of the environmental benefits achievable by green purchasing. Prevention-focused consumers, who are more concerned with security than achievement, are ready to consider green purchase as a means to avoid harm to the environment.

Though a number of consumer behavior studies have applied regulatory focus theory in a variety of contexts, little is known about the relative persuasiveness of green or nongreen appeals for individuals whose regulatory foci differ. This paper adds to the extant literature in two ways. First, it demonstrates that green appeals have to be carefully devised and developed, not only to match the consumers' purchasing motivations, but also to be appropriate to the product-related or non–product-related attributes to which they refer. Second, it advances the notion that product evaluations are a function of the compatibility of consumers' goals with the attributes describing choice alternatives. The findings of Chernev (2004) support the proposition that those that are compatible with individuals' self-regulatory foci tend to be given greater weight in choice making. Specifically, prevention-focused individuals are more likely to favor reliability-related attributes than promotion-focused consumers, who are more likely to place relatively more weight on attributes relating to performance. The research reported here has taken a step further forward, in finding that even with regard to an attribute that is associated with the product's performance, prevention-focused consumers whose concern is with safety and vigilance are especially likely to value gentleness, and thereby favor products that emphasize their greenness in their advertising. By contrast, promotion-focused consumers, concerned with advancement and eagerness, judge greenness to be more of a liability since it is not especially associated with "strength" and "getting the job done." Furthermore, for those attributes not associated with how well a product will perform a given task, green is more persuasive than nongreen among promotion-focused individuals, reflecting their concern for experiential advancement. Among prevention-focused individuals, it can be seen as an aspect of care for the environment, evoking safety motivations.

Managerial Implications

The findings of this paper have significant practical implications for marketing and advertising planners. First, the studies reported here offer evidence that participants whose regulatory focus had been experimentally manipulated do respond differently to green and nongreen product-related and non–product-related appeals. The inference for advertising strategy is that although marketers may not know with any certainty whether or not their target consumers' purchase choices will be dictated by their promotion-focused or prevention-focused self-regulatory orientations, they can aim to "prime" the target audience's goal orientation to influence the persuasiveness of their advertising in broadly predictable directions.

Second, these findings offer practical insights into the tailoring of advertising appeals and claims to consumers' purchasing motivations. Marketers should encode green appeals in terms of product-related attributes in their advertising messages, to convince potentially prevention-focused consumers that the product has benefits related to "gentleness." However, nongreen appeals should be chosen if consumers are likely to be promotion focused and will therefore tend to respond to positive outcomes and to value "strength" as a product attribute.

Third, given the finding that the green non–product-related appeal was more persuasive than the nongreen counterpart for both types of self-regulatory focus, its deployment in advertising messages can convey the distinctiveness of the product, even if its non–product-related attributes do not seem to offer any provable functional utility.

Limitations and Suggestions for Future Research

Our study has investigated the influence of consumers' self-regulatory foci on their responses to green versus nongreen appeals in advertising. Future research can explore their preferences for a green product explicitly portrayed as being "strong" or a less green alternative described in explicitly "gentle" terms.

The green messages designed for this research study were framed in a way that emphasized the product's environmentally friendly features. However, the strategy in the framing of green advertising messages could be to explicitly negate potentially undesirable features that consumers might attribute to the product in the absence of evidence to the contrary—for example, by asserting that it is free from harmful ingredients. Future research might therefore examine the effect of message framing on persuasion by green appeals.

With regard to the experimental manipulation of the green appeal, the emphasis in the advertisements was on the product-related ingredients (Study 1) or non–product-related materials (Study 2) that the product contained. To provide additional evidence for compatibility effects, the emphasis of the message could be varied between the gaining of benefit, for promotion-oriented consumers, versus the avoidance of loss, for a prevention-oriented target audience. It is predicted that green appeals emphasizing prevention or promotion benefits compatible with a consumer's self-regulatory focus will enhance the persuasion effect. For individuals with a focus on promotion, the persuasiveness of the advertising and product preference will both be higher when the emphasis in a green message is on benefit gained rather than loss avoided, and vice versa for those whose focus is on prevention.

REFERENCES

Aaker, Jennifer L., and Angela Y. Lee (2001), "'I' Seek Pleasures and 'We' Avoid Pains: The Role of Self-Regulatory Goals in Information Processing and Persuasion," *Journal of Consumer Research,* 28 (June), 33–49.

Banerjee, Subhabrata, Charles S. Gulas, and Easwar Iyer (1995), "Shades of Green: A Multidimensional Analysis of Environmental Advertising," *Journal of Advertising,* 24 (Summer), 21–31.

Cesario, Joseph, Heidi Grant, and E. Tory Higgins (2004), "Regulatory Fit and Persuasion: Transfer from 'Feeling Right,'" *Journal of Personality and Social Psychology,* 86 (March), 388–404.

Chang, Chingching (2011), "Feeling Ambivalent About Going Green: Implications for Green Advertising Processing," *Journal of Advertising,* 40 (Winter), 19–31.

Chernev, Alexander (2004), "Goal-Attribute Compatibility in Consumer Choice," *Journal of Consumer Psychology,* 14 (1/2), 141–150.

Crowe, Ellen, and E. Tory Higgins (1997), "Regulatory Focus and Strategic Inclinations: Promotion and Prevention in Decision-Making," *Organizational Behavior and Human Decision Processes,* 69 (February), 117–132.

Dodds, William B., Kent B. Monroe, and Dhruv Grewal (1991), "Effects of Price, Brand, and Store Information on Buyers' Product Evaluations," *Journal of Marketing Research,* 28 (August), 307–319.

D'Souza, Clare, Mehdi Taghian, Peter Lamb, and Roman Peretiatkos (2006), "Green Products and Corporate Strategy: An Empirical Investigation," *Society and Business Review,* 1 (2), 144–157.

Essoussi, Leila Hamzaoui, and Jonathan D. Linton (2010), "New or Recycled Products: How Much Are Consumers Willing to Pay?" *Journal of Consumer Marketing,* 27 (5), 458–468.

Florack, Arnd, and Martin Scarabis (2006), "How Advertising Claims Affect Brand Preferences and Category-Brand Associations: The Role of Regulatory Fit," *Psychology and Marketing,* 23 (September), 741–755.

Freitas, Antonio L., and E. Tory Higgins (2002), "Enjoying Goal-Directed Action: The Role of Regulatory Fit," *Psychological Science,* 13 (1), 1–6.

Higgins, E. Tory (1997), "Beyond Pleasure and Pain," *American Psychologist,* 52 (December), 1280–1300.

——— (2002), "How Self-Regulation Creates Distinct Values: The Case of Promotion and Prevention Decision Making," *Journal of Consumer Psychology,* 12 (3), 177–191.

———, Ronald S. Friedman, Robert E. Harlow, Lorraine Chen Idson, Ozlem N. Ayduk, and Amy Taylor (2001), "Achievement Orientations from Subjective Histories of Success: Promotion Pride Versus Prevention Pride," *European Journal of Social Psychology,* 31 (January/February), 3–23.

Hoeffler, Steve, and Kevin Lane Keller (2002), "Building Brand Equity Through Corporate Societal Marketing," *Journal of Public Policy and Marketing,* 21 (Spring), 78–89.

Idson, Lorraine Chen, Nira Liberman, and E. Tory Higgins (2000), "Distinguishing Gains from Nonlosses and Losses from Nongains: A Regulatory Focus Perspective on Hedonic Intensity," *Journal of Experimental Social Psychology,* 36 (3), 252–274.

Kassaye, W. Wossen (2001), "Green Dilemma," *Marketing Intelligence and Planning,* 19 (6), 444–455.

Keller, Kevin Lane (1993), "Conceptualizing, Measuring, and Managing Customer-Based Brand Equity," *Journal of Marketing,* 57 (1), 1–22.

Kim, Yeung-Jo (2006), "The Role of Regulatory Focus in Message Framing in Antismoking Advertisements for Adolescents," *Journal of Advertising,* 35 (Spring), 143–151.

Laroche, Michel, Jasmin Bergeron, and Guido Barbaro-Forleo (2001), "Targeting Consumers Who Are Willing to Pay More for Environmentally Friendly Products," *Journal of Consumer Marketing,* 18 (6), 503–520.

Lee, Angela Y., and Jennifer L. Aaker (2004), "Bringing the Frame into Focus: The Influence of Regulatory Fit on Processing Fluency and Persuasion," *Journal of Personality and Social Psychology,* 86 (February), 205–218.

Luchs, Michael G., Rebecca Walker Naylor, Julie R. Irwin, and Rajagopal Raghunathan (2010), "The Sustainability Liability: Potential Negative Effects of Ethicality on Product Preference," *Journal of Marketing,* 74 (September), 18–31.

Micu, Camelia C., and Tilottama G. Chowdhury (2010), "The Effect of Message's Regulatory Focus and Product Type on Persuasion," *Journal of Marketing Theory and Practice,* 18 (Spring), 181–190.

Montoro Rios, Francisco J., Teodoro Luque Martinez, Francisca Fuentes Moreno, and Paloma Cañadas Soriano (2006), "Improving Attitudes Toward Brands with Environmental Associations: An Experimental Approach," *Journal of Consumer Marketing,* 23 (1), 26–33.

Mourali, Mehdi, Ulf Böckenholt, and Michel Laroche (2007), "Compromise and Attraction Effects Under Prevention and Promotion Motivations," *Journal of Consumer Research,* 34 (August), 234–247.

Ottman, Jacquelyn A. (1998), *Green Marketing: Opportunity for Innovation,* New York: McGraw-Hill.

Pickett-Baker, Josephine, and Ritsuko Ozaki (2008), "Pro-Environmental Products: Marketing Influence on Consumer Purchase Decision," *Journal of Consumer Marketing,* 25 (5), 281–293.

Pham, Michel Tuan, and Tamar Avnet (2004), "Ideals and Oughts and the Reliance on Affect Versus Substance in Persuasion," *Journal of Consumer Research,* 30 (March), 503–518.

Phau, Ian, and Denise Ong (2007), "An Investigation of the Effects of Environmental Claims in Promotional Messages for Clothing Brands," *Marketing Intelligence and Planning,* 25 (7), 772–788.

Roney, Christopher J. R., E. Tory Higgins, and James Shah (1995), "Goals and Framing: How Outcome Focus Influences Motivation and Emotion," *Personality and Social Psychology Bulletin,* 21 (11), 1151–1160.

Rossiter, John R., Larry Percy, and Robert J. Donovan (1991), "A Better Advertising Planning Grid," *Journal of Advertising Research,* 31 (October/November), 11–21.

Schuhwerk, Melody E., and Roxanne Lefkoff-Hagius (1995), "Green or Non-Green? Does Type of Appeal Matter When Advertising a Green Product?" *Journal of Advertising,* 24 (Summer), 45–54.

Tanner, Carmen, and Sybille Wölfing Kast (2003), "Promoting Sustainable Consumption: Determinants of Green Purchases by Swiss Consumers," *Psychology and Marketing,* 20 (October), 883–902.

Zhang, Yong, and Richard Buda (1999), "Moderating Effects of Need for Cognition on Responses to Positively Versus Negatively Framed Advertising Messages," *Journal of Advertising,* 28 (Summer), 1–15.

Zhou, Rongrong, and Michel Tuan Pham (2004), "Promotion and Prevention Across Mental Accounts: When Financial Products Dictate Consumers' Investment Goals," *Journal of Consumer Research,* 31 (June), 125–135.

APPENDIX

Description of Multi-Item Indicators

Product Attractiveness Indicators

How attractive do you find the product?

1. Bad/good.
2. Not nice/nice.
3. Unlikable/likable.

Purchase Intention Indicators

1. My willingness to buy the product is: (very low to very high).
2. The likelihood of purchasing this product is: (very low to very high).
3. The probability that I would consider buying the product is: (very low to very high).

GREEN ECO-SEALS AND ADVERTISING PERSUASION

Barbara A. Bickart and Julie A. Ruth

ABSTRACT: Although advertisers present assurance or certification cues to burnish their "green" credentials, the impact of such "eco-seals" on persuasion is not well understood. We examine consumer characteristics (environmental concern and brand familiarity) and advertiser-controlled characteristics (the seal and advertising appeal) to understand conditions under which eco-seals are more or less persuasive, including effects on attitudes and intentions. Based on the Persuasion Knowledge Model (PKM), we hypothesize and present experimental results showing that consumers with high versus low environmental concern perceive eco-seals differently, depending on brand familiarity, eco-seal source, and ad appeal. Our findings have theoretical and practical implications for green marketing strategy and messaging.

As firms shift business models toward sustainability concerns, consumers are increasingly presented with cues regarding the environmental and social impact of products (Mintel 2011, 2012). For example, Coca-Cola is engaged in a multiyear, multimillion-dollar campaign touting its environmental sustainability efforts (Zmuda 2010), and Clorox recently doubled its annual ad budget to promote GreenWorks™ cleaning products, which are positioned as better for the environment (Neff 2009). These types of initiatives are aimed at bolstering consumer perceptions of brands on the basis of "green" marketing. However, some of these marketing communications efforts have been criticized as "greenwashing" because they are ambiguous, confusing, or lack evidence about environmental impact (Chang 2011; Cone 2011; Mintel 2011). Even supporters of firms' environmental initiatives complain that "the resulting 'eco-babble' [is] of little practical use" to consumers (Bustillo 2009, p. B1).

Marketers are attempting to cut through the ambiguity by incorporating assurance cues regarding the environmental impact of products (Cone 2011). For example, Wal-Mart is developing a "sustainability index" that signals the environmental impact of products in their assortment (Rockwood 2010; Rosenbloom 2009). SC Johnson (2012) has developed the Greenlist™ classification program and label that is applied to their brands that qualify, such as Fantastik® cleaning products. Government seals, such as the Environmental Protection Agency's EnergyStar® program, are available to brands that apply for and meet or exceed standards for energy efficiency. Variously referred to as certification, assurance, or verification seals, these classification programs and labels are cues regarding the product's performance on an important characteristic, such as environmental attributes and impact.

The purpose of our research is to investigate conditions under which environmentally oriented assurance or certification cues, which we refer to as "eco-seals," are more or less persuasive, including effects on attitudes and purchase intentions. While eco-seals are proliferating (Bounds 2009), there are important gaps in knowledge about their persuasiveness. For example, while consumers' environmental knowledge and concern has grown in recent years (Cone 2011), we do not yet fully understand how eco-seals are processed by consumers with high compared to low concern about environmental issues—two very different target markets.

In addition to consumer characteristics, some advertiser-controlled characteristics may affect consumer processing of eco-seals. For example, advertisers may use eco-seals that are created by the firm itself or by a third party such as a government entity (Arquitt and Cornwell 2007). Research shows that the source of a third-party seal affects comprehension (Beltramini and Stafford 1993) and perceptions of product quality (Dean and Biswas 2001). Yet we do not know how persuasion is affected by the use of a third-party eco-seal versus one developed and bestowed by the firm. This gap in research is important given that third-party seals are perceived as relatively independent and unbiased compared with other endorsements (Dean and Biswas 2001), such as the firm itself. In addition, advertisers recognize that their choice of ad appeals affects persuasion (Kees, Burton, and Tangari 2010; Sung and Choi 2011). While consumers who are not highly concerned about environmental issues would appear to be an unattractive target market for green products, perhaps an ad appeal that heightens vigilance about environmental issues would affect the persuasiveness of eco-seals.

The authors contributed equally and are listed alphabetically.

To address these gaps, we draw on the Persuasion Knowledge Model (PKM) as a theoretical foundation to develop hypotheses regarding consumer response to eco-seals. Persuasion knowledge is an appropriate theoretical foundation because it is based on the notion that consumer beliefs about marketers' tactics shape consumer persuasion and because it can account for the role of consumer skepticism (here with regard to environmental claims and cues) (Chang 2011). We highlight the role of a consumer characteristic—level of environmental concern (Mohr, Eroglu, and Ellen 1998; Obermiller 1995)—because of the importance of motivation and knowledge in shaping persuasion (Petty and Cacioppo 1986). We hypothesize and show how environmental concern shapes persuasion depending on brand familiarity, the presence versus absence of an eco-seal, and whether the source of the seal is a manufacturer or government entity. We also address how ad appeals framed toward the consumer's prevention or promotion goals affect the persuasive impact of eco-seals, depending on the consumer's level of concern.

In presenting our theory and findings, we make two primary contributions. First, we show that two factors—brand familiarity and eco-seal sponsor—differentially affect the persuasive impact of eco-seals for consumers who vary in their environmental concern. With the Persuasion Knowledge Model as our theoretical foundation, we describe how these differences are attributable to varying assumptions held about eco-seal sponsors by high- versus low-concern consumers. Second, we show how choice of advertising appeal can increase or reduce the persuasiveness of eco-seals for high versus low environmental concern consumers, two segments that are readily identifiable and accessible (Cone 2011; Mintel 2011). Our findings have implications for advertising theory and practice with respect to developing eco-seals and advertising messages that will persuade consumers who vary in environmental concern.

ENVIRONMENTAL CLAIMS AND PERSUASION

Eco-seals provide some information regarding environmental attributes and impact. For example, SC Johnson's Greenlist™ products not only meet legal and regulatory requirements for the product category, but the Greenlist cue also signifies that the product has a low impact on the environment and human health. Yet consumers may lack knowledge of the organization making the certification or criteria for the certification decision (Cone 2011; Dean and Biswas 2001).

In general, advertising claims that are difficult for consumers to verify are likely to prompt skepticism, consumer distrust, or disbelief of marketer actions (Forehand and Grier 2003). Not surprisingly, environmental claims are often viewed skeptically and are miscomprehended (Beltramini and Stafford 1993; Cone 2011; Carlson, Grove, and Kangun 1993; Shrum,

McCarty, and Lowrey 1995). For example, research by Miller and Sinclair (2009) suggests that consumer response to green-oriented advocacy advertising (e.g., by a coal company) elicits questions about the advertiser's intentions, consistent with the PKM. Accordingly, we believe eco-seals such as "Green Seal √ Certified™" also may be susceptible to persuasion knowledge processing because of the ambiguity of the cue and/or the consumer's lack of knowledge or ability to verify the seal certification process.

The Persuasion Knowledge Model suggests that consumers hold intuitive theories about how marketers try to influence them (Friestad and Wright 1994). Active "in virtually all interactions with marketers," persuasion knowledge allows consumers to "recognize, analyze, interpret [and] evaluate . . . persuasion attempts" and to form attitudes on that basis (Friestad and Wright 1994, p. 3). Consistent with the Elaboration Likelihood Model (ELM) (Petty and Cacioppo 1986; see also Chaiken and Trope 1999), the PKM acknowledges that consumers bring motivation and knowledge of the topic to bear on persuasion attempts. In the context of green advertising, the consumer's level of environmental concern is an important individual difference variable that relates to knowledge and motivation with respect to environmental issues (Mohr, Eroglu, and Ellen 1998; Obermiller 1995). Thus, higher levels of environmental concern should increase consumers' ability and motivation to process an advertising message, and as a result, should moderate the impact of eco-seals on persuasion (Petty and Cacioppo 1986).

Figure 1 summarizes our conceptual model of the impact of eco-seals on persuasion. We propose that the eco-seal is interpreted in light of contextual cues, such as brand familiarity, and is moderated by the consumer's concern for the environment, which in turn affects attitudes toward the ad and brand and purchase intentions in sequence (MacKenzie and Spreng 1992). We elaborate on these relationships in the next sections.

While proliferating, eco-seals are used by some but not all brands. Thus, an important question concerns how consumers respond to the presence or absence of an eco-seal in advertising. We expect that low environmental concern (LEC) consumers will be indifferent to the presence or absence of an eco-seal because environmental issues are not important to them. Thus, unless there is a reason to question the brand's effectiveness, the presence or absence of a cue about this unimportant issue is expected to have little effect on attitude formation.

However, because high environmental concern (HEC) consumers care about environmental issues, the presence or absence of an eco-seal is expected to influence persuasion. HEC consumers are vigilant about environmental information, but eco-seals are ambiguous cues. As a result, HEC consumers are likely to assess the presence of this ambiguous cue in light of

FIGURE 1
Conceptual Model for Study 1

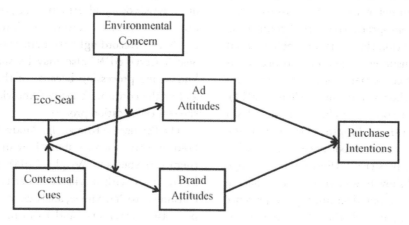

a more reliable contextual cue, such as brand familiarity (e.g., Simmons, Bickart, and Buchanan 2003). In general, familiar brands are evaluated more favorably than unfamiliar brands (e.g., Hoyer and Brown 1990). Thus, among HEC consumers, the signal value of the presence of an eco-seal will depend on brand familiarity, with that value being more favorable for familiar brands. In fact, whereas the presence of an eco-seal for an unfamiliar brand may increase skepticism among HEC consumers, the absence of an eco-seal will not tap into their concern and will not heighten an impact of brand familiarity. Thus, among HEC consumers, we expect that the presence of an eco-seal will yield the most favorable attitudes and intentions when presented by a high-familiarity brand, and the most unfavorable impact when presented by a low-familiarity brand.

In sum, we expect a three-way interaction between environmental concern, eco-seal, and brand familiarity, as follows:

Hypothesis 1: When environmental concern is low, the presence or absence of an eco-seal by a high- or low-familiarity brand will not affect (a) ad attitudes, (b) brand attitudes, or (c) purchase intentions.

In contrast:

Hypothesis 2: When environmental concern is high, (a) ad attitudes, (b) brand attitudes, and (c) purchase intentions will be more favorable for a familiar (an unfamiliar) brand when the eco-seal is present (absent).

We also expect that, consistent with MacKenzie and Spreng (1992), attitudes toward the ad and brand will mediate effects of the eco-seal on purchase intentions. Thus, we propose:

Hypothesis 3: The impact of eco-seal, brand familiarity, and environmental concern on purchase intentions will be mediated by (a) attitudes toward the ad, and (b) brand attitudes.

STUDY 1

The objective of this study was to determine whether consumer environmental concern moderates persuasion in the presence or absence of an eco-seal. In addition, we examine the role of brand familiarity. We used a 2 (eco-seal: present versus absent) × 2 (brand familiarity: known brand versus unknown brand) experimental design and environmental concern was measured. Participants were 197 students in an introductory statistics class, who completed the experiment for course credit. The majority of participants were between the ages of 19 and 21 (94%); 48% were female.

Participants were told that they were completing an advertising study. They first saw a control ad (for packaged lunch meat), followed by the target ad for an all-purpose household cleaner. A survey shows that nearly 30% of household cleaners introduced in 2011 were promoted with green claims, and that 50% of U.S. adults 18 years old or older report always or sometimes purchasing "green" household cleaners (Mintel 2012). Thus, this product is an apt stimulus for study. We created four versions of the all-purpose cleaner ad, which varied on two dimensions (see Appendix 1). First, the brand was either an actual, known brand (409) or a fictional, unknown brand (Grip). We selected 409 because it did not have a "green" product on the market at the time of the study. Second, the package shown in the ad either did or did not include an eco-seal. The eco-seal was "Green Seal √ Certified™" and was fictitious.

After viewing the filler and target ads, participants were told they would evaluate one ad selected at random. All participants then viewed the target ad for a second time and completed the dependent measures including brand attitudes, brand purchase intentions, attitude toward the ad, and environmental concern (see Appendix 2 for measures and reliability). Participants were then debriefed.

TABLE 1
Study 1: Mean Intentions and Attitudes by Condition

	No seal		Seal	
	Unfamiliar brand	Familiar brand	Unfamiliar brand	Familiar brand
Low environmental concern				
Brand intentions	2.97	4.35	3.30	4.17
	(1.22)	(1.48)	(1.38)	(1.60)
Brand attitudes	3.73	4.63	3.61	4.40
	(.96)	(.84)	(.99)	(1.05)
Ad attitudes	3.22	4.49	3.24	4.04
	(1.44)	(1.13)	(1.22)	(1.42)
High environmental concern				
Brand intentions	4.02	4.10	3.30	4.54
	(1.40)	(1.84)	(1.59)	(1.07)
Brand attitudes	4.44	4.65	3.99	4.72
	(1.14)	(1.00)	(1.27)	(.82)
Ad attitudes	4.09	4.45	3.58	4.35
	(1.63)	(1.54)	(1.46)	(1.06)

Notes: SD in parentheses; environmental concern based on median split.

Results

Manipulation Checks

Participants were asked to rate their familiarity with both 409 and Grip household cleaners on seven-point scales (1 = "not at all familiar" and 7 = "very familiar"). As expected, familiarity was higher for the 409 brand (M = 3.36) than the Grip brand, M = 1.68; $F(1\ 196)$ = 86.63, p < .01. No other effects were significant.

To test the eco-seal manipulation, participants were asked whether the product in the ad had an eco-seal on the container (yes/no). Overall, 57% of participants answered this question correctly. Consistent with the manipulation, 50% of participants in the eco-seal condition said that the package had a seal, compared with 36% in the no-seal condition, $\chi^2(1)$ = 3.50, p < .06. This effect did not vary across brands. Because the effect of this manipulation was weak, we also ran the analyses including only those participants who correctly identified their eco-seal condition (n = 112) and the results were similar to those reported below.

Findings

We expected that the effect of eco-seal and brand familiarity on the dependent variables would be moderated by environmental concern. Since environmental concern is a continuous variable that should not be dichotomized (Fitzsimons 2008), we used regression analysis. Because we expected that attitudes toward the ad and brand would mediate effects of the independent variables on purchase intentions, we examine the purchase intentions variable first. Purchase intention was regressed on dummy variables representing eco-seal (–1 = absent; 1 = present) and brand familiarity (–1 = unknown brand; 1 = known brand), environmental concern (mean centered, M = 5.03, SD = 1.29), and the interactions of these variables. Interest in household cleaners was included as a covariate and was significant (B = .14, SE [standard error] = .07, t = 2.10, p < .05).

Descriptive results for all dependent measures are shown in Table 1 and regression results are shown in Table 2. There was a significant effect of brand familiarity (B = .44, SE = .11, t = 4.17, p < .01), indicating that purchase intentions were more favorable for the familiar brand. More important, consistent with H1 and H2 (and shown in Figure 2), the three-way interaction between familiarity, eco-seal, and environmental concern on purchase intentions was significant (B = .17, SE = .08, t = 2.05, p < .05).

Because we hypothesized environmental concern as a moderator, we examined the significance of the brand familiarity × eco-seal interaction at low and high levels of environmental concern using the PROCESS macro (Hayes 2012). This macro allowed us to estimate simple slopes and regions of significance for the three-way interaction using OLS regression via the procedure described by Aiken and West (1991). Consistent with H1, for participants low in environmental concern (one SD below the mean; SD = 1.29), the brand familiarity × eco-seal interaction was not significant (p > .36). As shown in the top panel of Figure 2, LEC participants' intentions were more positive when the brand was

TABLE 2
Study 1: Regression Results (Unstandardized Coefficients)

	Dependent variable model	Mediator variable models		Dependent variable model with mediators
	Purchase intentions	Attitude toward the ad	Brand attitudes	Purchase intentions
Constant	3.47*	3.67*	3.91*	−.32
Eco-seal	−.03	−.13	−.10	.08
Brand familiarity	.44*	.39*	.31*	.11
Environmental concern	.08	.10	.08	−.01
Seal × brand familiarity	.08	.01	.07	.04
Seal × environmental concern	−.12	−.01	−.05	−.08
Brand familiarity × environmental concern	−.04	−.05	−.04	.01
Seal × brand familiarity × environmental concern	.17**	.16**	.10***	.06
Interest in category	.14**	.09	.13*	.03
Attitude toward the ad (A_{ad})				.33*
Brand attitudes (Att_{Br})				.66*
Overall model (F)	3.65*	3.23*	4.27*	26.02*

* $p < .01$.

** $p < .05$.

*** $p < .10$.

familiar, regardless of whether or not the package included a seal, which supports H1. For HEC participants (one SD above the mean), the brand familiarity × eco-seal interaction was significant ($B = .31$, $SE = .15$, $t = 2.06$, $p < .05$). As shown in the bottom panel of Figure 2, for HEC participants, when the package did not include an eco-seal, there was no effect of brand familiarity on purchase intentions ($p > .69$); in contrast, when the package included an eco-seal, intentions were more favorable for the familiar brand ($B = .70$, $SE = .20$, $t = 3.47$, $p < .01$). It is interesting to note that the eco-seal appears to hurt evaluations of an unfamiliar brand for HEC consumers. Intentions to purchase the unfamiliar brand were significantly lower when an eco-seal was present than when it was not ($B = −.49$, $SE = .21$, $t = 2.36$, $p < .05$), while the presence of the seal did not affect intentions to purchase the familiar brand ($p > .56$). These findings provide support for H2.

To test whether attitudes toward the ad (A_{ad}) and brand (Att_{Br}) are mediators, we first ran two regression models with A_{ad} and Att_{Br} as dependent variables, and the dummy variables representing eco-seal, brand familiarity, and environmental concern and their interactions as the independent variables, with interest in household cleaners as a covariate. These results are shown in Table 2. To test the significance of the omnibus indirect effects of the proposed mediators, we used the MEDIATE macro (Hayes and Preacher 2011). This macro provides bootstrap confidence interval estimates for the indirect effect of

the independent variables on the dependent variable through each mediator (for a description of this approach, see Zhao, Lynch, and Chen 2010). As shown in the middle columns of Table 2, the three-way interaction of eco-seal, brand familiarity, and environmental concern was significant or marginally significant for A_{ad} and Att_{Br}, and the patterns of means and effects were similar to those on purchase intentions. In addition, bootstrapping techniques employed to test indirect effects confirmed the mediating role of A_{ad} (95% confidence intervals excluding zero; .0075 to .0802) and Att_{Br} (95% confidence interval excluding zero; .0178 to .1562; Preacher, Rucker, and Hayes 2007; Zhao, Lynch, and Chen 2010). Thus, H3a and H3b are supported.

These results suggest that HEC consumers' inferences about the eco-seal are affected by brand familiarity. One possibility is that HEC consumers make different inferences about the eco-seal source depending on brand familiarity. We asked participants in the eco-seal condition who they thought was the "certification organization." Response options included the manufacturer, a government agency, a nongovernment third party, and "other." We compared the proportion saying that the eco-seal source was the manufacturer (coded 1) versus all other options (coded 0) using a logistic regression, with a dummy variable representing brand familiarity (coded 0 = familiar brand, 1 = unfamiliar brand), environmental concern (mean-centered), and their interaction as predictors.

FIGURE 2
Study 1: Purchase Intentions × Environmental Concern, Brand Familiarity, and Eco-Seal

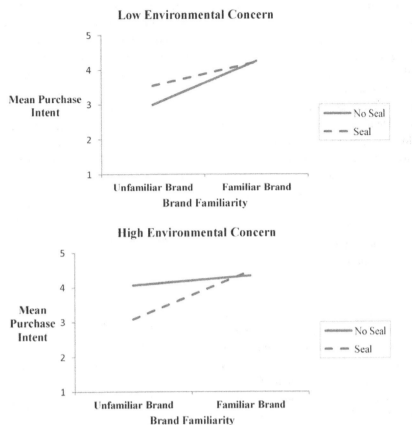

The results show a marginally significant brand familiarity × environmental concern interaction ($B = .31$, $SE = .18$, $Z = 1.63$, $p < .10$). Using the PROCESS macro (Hayes 2012), we examined the effect of brand familiarity at low and high levels of environmental concern. At low levels of concern (one SD below the mean, $SD = 1.37$), brand familiarity did not affect beliefs about the eco-seal source ($p > .53$). In contrast, at high levels of environmental concern (one SD above the mean), participants were more likely to identify the manufacturer as the source when brand familiarity was high (estimated proportion = .39) versus low (estimated proportion = .15; $B = .63$, $SE = .35$, $Z = 1.79$, $p < .07$).

Summary and Discussion

The results of this study suggest that environmental concern affects consumer response to eco-seals. Consistent with our hypotheses, when concern is low, the presence or absence of an eco-seal on a package does not affect purchase intentions generated through an ad, regardless of consumer familiarity with the brand. However, when the consumer's environmental concern is high, eco-seals generate more favorable intentions for familiar brands and less favorable intentions for unfamiliar

brands. These effects are mediated through attitudes toward the ad and brand. In addition, we provide some evidence suggesting that these differences may be due to the inferences HEC consumers make about the eco-seal source. Specifically, we find that when environmental concern is high, consumers appear to be more likely to infer that the manufacturer is the eco-seal source when brands are familiar versus unfamiliar.

These results suggest the possibility that the source may have an impact on how consumers respond to eco-seals. We examine this possibility directly in Study 2, where we provide information about the eco-seal source. The results of Study 1 suggest that when environmental concern is high, consumers will have more favorable attitudes and intentions, perhaps under an inference that the manufacturer sponsors the eco-seal. High-concern consumers may be eager to find products that have green attributes, and so seek out brands that voluntarily provide affirming information about their green credentials. In this way, high-concern consumers may make positive attributions about the behavior of firms that have developed green eco-seals, attributing the development of the eco-seal and products labeled with it to the firm's ability and effort (i.e., internal locus of causality) rather than chance or task requirements (i.e., external locus of causality). On balance, attributions are more favorable when causes for behavior are attributed to internal versus external sources (Weiner 1986). Accordingly, we expect that high environmental concern consumers will hold favorable attitudes and intentions toward firms that have developed their own eco-seals rather than "borrowing" the eco-seal from another source, such as the government.

In contrast, it is possible that low-concern consumers may react more favorably to a seal sponsored by a third party or government agency because this source is less biased than the manufacturer (Beltramini and Stafford 1993; Dean and Biswas 2001). Following the PKM, low-concern consumers may have less nuanced knowledge structures and may rely on an automatic assumption that government seals are more independent and thus may become suspicious when the manufacturer is identified as the eco-seal source.

In addition, it is possible that different ways of framing the advertising appeal might affect the persuasiveness of the eco-seal through fostering greater message vigilance. MacInnis, Moorman, and Jaworski (1991) propose that ad executions can influence consumers' motivation to process ads, in line with the impact of consumer environmental concern. In this study, we examine whether advertising appeals oriented toward the consumer's prevention or promotion goals affect the persuasiveness of eco-seals. According to regulatory focus theory (Higgins 1997), individuals can attain goals through focus on promotion (e.g., achieving positive outcomes and aspirations) or prevention (e.g., avoiding negative outcomes and ensuring security). Research shows differential impacts for prevention- versus promotion-oriented ads (Aaker and Lee 2001; Kees, Heintz, and Tangari 2010; Sung and Choi 2011) and indicates that compared with consumers holding promotion goals, those holding prevention goals are more likely to process ads in a persuasion-knowledge mind-set (Kirmani and Zhu 2007).

By application, we expect that a prevention-oriented ad appeal will heighten the salience of the ambiguous eco-seal cue because of the salience of avoiding negative outcomes. We expect that when an ad appeal is oriented toward prevention, a potentially biased eco-seal source (the manufacturer) will have a more negative influence on persuasion than a less biased source (government agency). We expect this pattern only for low-concern consumers, as these individuals are more likely to be influenced by peripheral cues in the ad (Petty and Cacioppo 1986). HEC consumers are likely to process the ad more thoroughly regardless of the ad appeal. In addition, based on the findings of Study 1, it appears that HEC consumers may make different inferences regarding the source of the eco-seal. Specifically, rather than being skeptical about marketers' tactics, HEC consumers may make positive attributions that the manufacturer is proactive in developing and communicating environmental information through an eco-seal. This reasoning is consistent with the signal value of cues, and with the notion that there are threats to the brand's reputation if the signal is false (Boulding and Kirmani 1993). In contrast, for both consumer segments, a promotion appeal is not expected to heighten skepticism about marketers' tactics and is therefore not expected to moderate the impact of other variables. In other words, when a promotion appeal is used, the source of the eco-label is either not noticed or is not given weight in the brand evaluation process, and thus will not differentially affect persuasion.

Hence, we hypothesize that participants' concern with environmental issues will moderate the effects of eco-seal source and advertising appeal (prevention versus promotion) on attitudes and purchase intentions, as follows:

Hypothesis 4: When a prevention appeal is used, a manufacturer (government) eco-seal will result in more favorable (a) ad attitudes, (b) brand attitudes, and (c) purchase intentions when environmental concern is high (low).

In contrast:

Hypothesis 5: When a promotion appeal is used, the eco-seal sponsor will not affect (a) ad attitudes, (b) brand attitudes, or (c) purchase intentions.

Similar to Study 2, we also expect that attitudes toward the ad and brand will mediate effects of eco-seal source, ad appeal, and environmental concern on purchase intentions. Thus, we propose:

Hypothesis 6: The impact of eco-seal, brand familiarity, and environmental concern on purchase intentions will be mediated by (a) attitudes toward the ad, and (b) brand attitudes.

STUDY 2

The objective of this study was to determine whether environmental concern moderates consumer response to eco-seal source and type of advertising appeal. Thus, we used a 2 (eco-seal source: product manufacturer versus government) × 2 (ad appeal: prevention versus promotion) design. Environmental concern was measured, as in Study 1.

The procedure was identical to that used for Study 1, except that a fictitious eco-seal—SmartCheck™—was used in all conditions and the target ad was for Clean Well hand sanitizer, a real brand that had limited distribution at the time of the study. Our participants were not familiar with the brand ($M = 1.37$ on a seven-point scale, where 7 = "very familiar"). Approximately 12% of personal care products introduced in 2011 were promoted with green claims, and 35% of U.S. adults 18 years old or older report always or sometimes purchasing "green" personal care products (Mintel 2012). While hand sanitizers may be lower in "green-ness" in practice, the use of different eco-seals, product categories, and brands across the two studies extends generalizability. The ad included a headline, four claims, and a description of the source of the eco-seal (see Appendix 3). We manipulated the ad appeal via the headline, which was prevention oriented ("Protecting You from Illness the Natural Way") or promotion oriented ("Keeping You Healthy the Natural Way"). The eco-seal source was identified as either "Our Company" or the "U.S. Consumer Product Safety Commission." In addition to measuring the same constructs used in Study 1 (see Appendix 2), we measured agreement with five beliefs about the hand sanitizer ("maintains good health," "effective in killing germs," "prevents illness," "is safe to use," and "is good for the environment"), each using a seven-point Likert scale.

Participants included 108 undergraduate students who participated in exchange for course credit and 36 graduate students who participated in exchange for a donation to their student organization (total = 144). The average age of participants was 23.2 years; 53% were female.

Results

Manipulation Checks

We expected that the government agency (U.S. Consumer Product Safety Commission) would be perceived as a less biased and more independent eco-seal source than a manufacturer. Participants evaluated the likelihood that certification programs developed by both the product manufacturer and the U.S. Consumer Product Safety Commission would be independent (versus not independent) and not biased (versus biased), both on seven-point semantic differential scales. The items were highly correlated ($r_{manufacturer}$ = .75; $r_{U.S. Product Safety Commission}$ = .82) and therefore were averaged. As expected, certification programs developed by government agencies were seen as more independent than those developed by manufacturers, Ms = 4.98 versus 2.57, $F(1, 140)$ = 186.05, $p < .001$. These perceptions did not vary by manipulations ($ps > .43$).

In addition, attitudes toward and trust in the Smart-Check certification were both higher when the source was the U.S. Consumer Product Safety Commission than when it was the manufacturer, attitudes: Ms = 4.86 versus 4.34, $F(1, 140)$ = 6.07, $p < .05$; trust: Ms = 4.48 versus 3.89, $F(1, 140)$ = 6.95, $p < .01$, and no other effects were significant ($ps > .10$).

We assessed the success of the ad appeal manipulation based on regulatory focus goals. Following Kirmani and Zhu (2007), participants assessed agreement with the statement "before I saw the ad, I suspected it would contain undue persuasion" on a seven-point Likert scale. As expected, agreement was higher in the prevention appeal condition (M = 4.32) than in the promotion appeal condition, M = 3.88; $F(1, 140)$ = 5.27, $p < .023$. No other effects were significant.

Findings

To test our hypotheses that environmental concern, a continuous variable, moderates the effects of eco-seal source and ad appeal on A_{ad}, Att_{Br}, and purchase intentions, we used regression analysis. Dependent variables were regressed on dummy variables indicating eco-seal source (coded 1 = company and −1 = government), ad appeal (coded 1 = promotion and −1 = prevention), environmental concern (mean centered; M = 4.96, SD = 1.27), and their interactions, as well as product category interest as a covariate. Given our predictions that effects on purchase intentions would be mediated by A_{ad} and Att_{Br}, we first present results regarding purchase intentions. The descriptive statistics for dependent measures are shown in Table 3 and the regression results are presented in Table 4.

Purchase Intentions. H4 and H5 suggest a three-way interaction effect of eco-seal, ad appeal, and environmental concern on the dependent variables. For purchase intentions, the predicted three-way interaction was not significant ($p > .89$). However, there was a significant interaction between eco-seal source and environmental concern (B = .23, SE = .09, t = 2.53, $p < .05$). Using the PROCESS macro (Hayes 2012) and the procedure suggested by Aiken and West (1991), we examined this interaction for consumers with low and high levels of environmental concern (one SD above and below the mean, SD = 1.27). For consumers with low levels of concern, there was no effect of eco-seal source on intentions ($p > .15$). In contrast, for consumers with high levels of concern, intentions were more favorable when the eco-seal source was the manufacturer than when it was a government agency (B = .34, SE = .15, t = 2.17, $p < .05$; see Figure 3).

Brand Attitudes. The predicted three-way interaction was significant (B = −.18, SE = .08, t = 2.30, $p < .05$; see Table 4). As hypothesized, the eco-seal source × environmental concern interaction effect on Att_{Br} was significant when the appeal was framed in terms of prevention (B = .40, SE = .10, t = 3.90, $p < .01$), but not when framed in terms of promotion ($p > .64$). As shown in the top panel of Figure 4, when the appeal was promotion focused, eco-seal source did not affect Att_{Br}. In contrast, as shown in the lower panel of Figure 4, when the appeal was prevention focused, the effects of eco-seal source on Att_{Br} varied with environmental concern. For LEC consumers, brand attitudes were more favorable when the eco-seal source was a government agency (B = −.50, SE = .20, t = 2.53, $p < .01$); for HEC consumers, attitudes were more favorable when the source was the manufacturer (B = .52, SE = .17, t = 3.02, $p < .01$).

Attitude Toward the Ad. There was a significant interaction between eco-seal source and environmental concern on A_{ad}

TABLE 3
Study 2: Mean Intentions and Attitudes by Condition

	Low environmental concern		High environmental concern	
	Manufacturer	Government agency	Manufacturer	Government agency
Promotion focus				
Brand intentions	2.73	3.03	3.79	2.82
	(1.39)	(1.39)	(1.38)	(1.70)
Brand attitudes	4.30	4.21	4.86	4.26
	(1.14)	(1.07)	(.90)	(1.57)
Ad attitudes	3.22	3.80	4.01	3.72
	(1.07)	(1.30)	(1.34)	(3.77)
Prevention focus				
Brand intentions	2.73	3.07	3.72	3.18
	(1.43)	(1.27)	(1.88)	(1.73)
Brand attitudes	3.68	4.44	5.03	3.95
	(1.31)	(.83)	(1.19)	(1.40)
Ad attitudes	3.18	3.83	4.07	3.87
	(1.29)	(.86)	(1.34)	(1.20)

Notes: SD in parentheses; environmental concern based on median split.

TABLE 4
Study 2: Regression Results (Unstandardized Coefficients)

	Dependent variable model	Mediator variable models		Dependent variable model with mediators
	Purchase intentions	Attitude toward the ad	Brand attitudes	Purchase intentions
Constant	1.83*	3.20*	3.75*	−1.24*
Eco-seal source	.06	−.16	.05	.09
Ad appeal	−.01	.03	.09	−.07
Environmental concern	.15***	.28*	.18**	−.05
Source × appeal	.04	−.01	.05	.02
Source × concern	.23*	.16**	.22*	.05
Appeal × concern	.005	.06	.08	−.06
Source × appeal × concern	−.01	−.07	−.18*	.10
Interest in category	.43*	.17*	.20*	.27*
Attitude toward the ad (A_{ad})				.40*
Brand attitudes (Att_{Br})				.47*
Overall model (F)	8.49*	4.14*	5.58*	26.47*

* $p < .01$.

** $p < .05$.

*** $p < .10$.

($B = .16$, $SE = .08$, $t = 2.02$, $p < .05$; see Table 2). At low levels of concern (one *SD* below the mean), A_{ad} was more favorable when the government agency was the eco-seal source ($B = −.36$, $SE = .15$, $t = 2.49$, $p < .01$), while at high levels of concern (one *SD* above the mean), the source did not affect A_{ad} ($p > .69$).

FIGURE 3
Study 2: Purchase Intentions × Environmental Concern and Eco-Seal Source

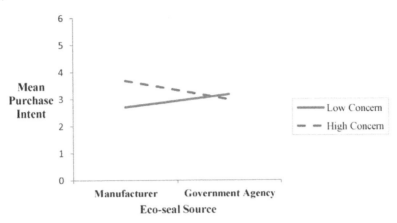

Mediation Model. The regression models used to test the mediation effects of A_{ad} and Att_{Br} on purchase intentions are shown in Table 4. As shown in the middle columns, the two-way interaction between eco-seal source and environmental concern was significant for both attitudes toward the ad and brand. We used the MEDIATE macro to test the significance of the omnibus indirect effects of the proposed mediators (Hayes and Preacher 2011). This macro conducts mediation analyses with multiple mediators and calculates confidence intervals for indirect effects of mediators using the bootstrapping techniques recommended by Zhao, Lynch, and Chen 2010. The bootstrapping techniques employed to test indirect effects confirmed the mediating role of A_{ad} (95% confidence intervals excluding zero; .0050 to .1134) and Att_{Br} (95% confidence interval excluding zero; .0122 to .1491; Preacher, Rucker, and Hayes 2007; Zhao, Lynch, and Chen 2010).

Summary

Consistent with the results of Study 1, environmental concern affects how consumers interpret eco-seal source cues presented in advertising. The results support H4b and H5b on brand attitudes and partially support H4a and H5a on attitudes toward the ad and H4c and H5c on purchase intentions. In general, HEC consumers have more favorable A_{ad}, Att_{Br}, and purchase intentions when the eco-seal source is the brand's manufacturer, whereas these measures are more favorable for LEC consumers when the eco-seal source is a government agency. These results point to differences in underlying perceptions held by high and low environmental concern consumers, consistent with persuasion knowledge theorizing. As expected, these effects are mediated by A_{ad} and Att_{Br}, consistent with H6a and H6b.

We also found that ad appeal influences the impact of eco-seal source on brand attitudes. For both LEC and HEC

consumers, a prevention appeal appears to increase vigilance, in that the effect of the eco-seal source cue was greater under these conditions. The nature of these effects varied, however, with the level of concern. When a prevention appeal is used, HEC consumers had more favorable brand attitudes when the manufacturer was the source, while the opposite pattern occurs for LEC consumers. We also measured beliefs that the brand prevents illness, as well as four related beliefs. An analysis using the MEDIATE macro (Hayes and Preacher 2011) showed that this brand belief mediates the effect of the three-way interaction on brand attitude (95% confidence intervals excluding zero: −.2091 to −.0221). Results were not significant for the other brand beliefs. Our results suggest that ad appeal can affect how consumers use green cues, such as an eco-seal, in processing an ad for an environmentally friendly product.

DISCUSSION

Our theory and findings have important implications for advertisers who promote on the basis of green marketing, including the use of eco-seals. Given the history of U.S. certification and the labeling of "organic" products, including a 20-year gap between recognizing a need for agreed-upon government standards for organic certification and the establishment of such a program (Bounds 2009), it may be many years until government eco-certification programs are designed, agreed upon, and implemented in the United States. Until that time, firms may want or need to advertise their products and brands on the basis of the environmental and sustainability qualifications, and manufacturer-designed eco-seals are an option to be considered.

Our research provides a theoretical foundation for understanding how consumers process eco-seals and conditions under which certification cues will yield more or less favorable

FIGURE 4
Study 2: Brand Attitudes × Eco-Seal Source, Environmental Concern, and Message Appeal

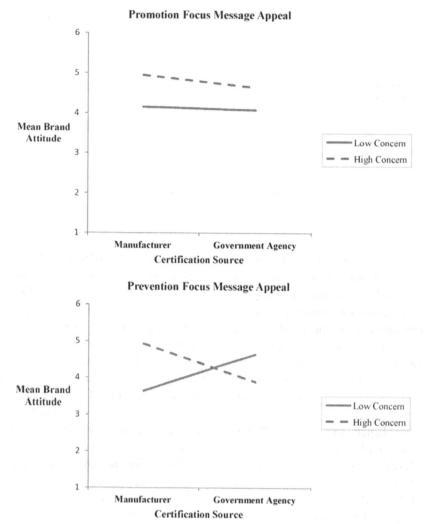

attitudes and purchase intentions. Moreover, because green marketing is viewed somewhat skeptically by consumers, our theory building provides insights that will be of use to researchers who seek to understand how green marketing messages affect persuasion, especially in light of advertisers' strategic choice of message appeal. Our research also will be of interest to public policymakers who seek to understand how green advertising and eco-seals may affect consumer well-being.

Impact of Eco-Seals Varies by High- Versus Low-Concern Consumers

One important implication of our findings is that the impact of eco-seals depends on the target market's level of environmental concern. It appears that the types of inferences consumers make about the eco-seal source vary with environmental concern,

which in turn differentially influences persuasion. Our results suggest that HEC consumers respond more favorably to eco-seals that are sponsored by the manufacturer, whereas LEC consumers respond more favorably to eco-seals sponsored by an independent third party. This asymmetry in persuasion for high- versus low-concern consumers is interesting in light of perceptions associated with manufacturer and government eco-seal sources. High-concern and low-concern consumers appear to make different inferences about the source's possible bias; unlike low-concern consumers, who perceive the manufacturer as a biased certification source, high-concern consumers appear to reward the manufacturer for efforts on an issue of concern. In this way, the Persuasion Knowledge Model can perhaps be extended to also accommodate consumers' positive attributions about marketer intentions and behaviors. That is, high-concern consumers may infer increased levels of commitment and better performance on environmental attributes by highly familiar manufacturers that develop their own eco-seals. This interpretation is also consistent with the finding that HEC consumers penalize low-familiarity brands that present manufacturer eco-seals.

We also found that the persuasive impact of an eco-seal whose source is unidentified differs for high- versus low-concern consumers. When consumer concern is high, an on-package eco-seal shown in an ad helps familiar brands but hurts unfamiliar brands. In contrast, when consumer concern is low, the presence of an ambiguous eco-seal seems to have little persuasive impact. Still, post hoc analysis suggests that the presence of the seal reduces the difference in evaluations between familiar and unfamiliar brands. Specifically, when there is no seal, LEC consumers evaluate the familiar brand more favorably than the unfamiliar brand (see top panel of Figure 2, $B = .63$, $SE = .23$, $t = 2.72$, $p < .01$). In contrast, when an eco-seal is presented, the difference in persuasion for familiar and unfamiliar brands is no longer significant ($B = .34$, $SE = .21$, $t = 1.66$, $p < .10$). Thus, the results across the two studies suggest that while low-concern consumers appear to use the eco-seal as a cue to interpret the (unfamiliar) brand, high-concern consumers seem to use the brand as a cue to interpret the eco-seal. Taken together, the findings provide insights into differential processing and persuasion for two important and accessible consumer segments: high versus low environmental concern consumers.

Implications for Green Advertising

Our findings have implications for advertising theory and practice with respect to the persuasive impact of green advertising and eco-seals. First, advertisers and marketers should be very clear about their target, as the persuasive impact of advertiser-controlled content depends on consumer characteristics, including level of environmental concern and familiarity with the brand. Second, advertisers may want to play up or play down the eco-seal sponsor, depending on the target audience. Third, the advertiser's message appeal should be developed with care, since it appears that a message appeal framed around the consumer's promotion goals has little differential impact on persuasion. At the same time, our results show that prevention-oriented appeals can be persuasive under certain conditions. A prevention message appeal will be most persuasive when the brand presents a manufacturer eco-seal and is targeting high-concern consumers, or if the brand presents a government eco-seal and is targeting low-concern consumers. It also appears that prevention appeals may prompt greater vigilance with respect to the eco-seal and its implications for beliefs about the brand. As such, message appeals and eco-seals may hold promise not just for changing attitudes and intentions, but also for specific aspects of brand beliefs and brand meaning.

Public Policy Issues

Concerns have been raised about the potential for consumer confusion from the use of eco-seals, particularly given that the source of the seals varies and is often not readily evident to consumers (Bustillo 2009). From a public policy perspective, results from our Study 1 suggest that different consumers may interpret an ambiguous eco-seal in different ways. Given the differential persuasive impact of government versus manufacturer eco-seals revealed in Study 2, policymakers may want to advocate for the eco-seal source being clearly identified on the package or in the advertisement. Although we did not investigate it directly, it is also likely that the conditions a brand must meet to receive the eco-seal would be of differential interest and persuasion for high- versus low-concern consumers. Not only is the number of eco-seals proliferating; there are important variations in sources and formats (e.g., industry association or retailer eco-seals), and such seals are used to signify attributes beyond the environment, such as inclusion/exclusion of ingredients (e.g., gluten free). Given that health, wellness, and consumer well-being are at stake with these seals and the consumer's interpretation of them, public policy issues will only grow in importance.

Limitations and Future Research

Our research is limited in several ways. First, the manipulation of the presence versus the absence of the eco-seal in Study 1 was very subtle, given the eco-seal's placement on the product's package. More than 40% of our participants did not correctly identify their condition in a manipulation check. Making the eco-seal more prominent, either on the package or in the ad itself, may enhance the persuasive impact of this cue; thus, prominence is an important factor to be investigated in future studies. More generally, it seems likely that consumers with high levels of environmental concern would be more likely to notice an eco-seal. Consistent with this idea, in the Study 1 manipulation check, we found a nonsignificant ($p > .12$) tendency for HEC participants to be more likely to correctly note the presence of an eco-seal. Hence, environmental concern could affect both attention to and evaluation of the eco-seal. In addition, we investigated two contextual cues—brand familiarity and ad appeal—that might affect how consumers interpret the eco-seal. Future research could examine the impact of other contextual variables, such as editorial content adjacent to the ad, price, or retail outlet.

Second, in Study 2, our explanation of the eco-seal source was more salient than in many naturally occurring advertising situations. Future research should investigate the impact of different depictions of the eco-seal and its source, along with repeated exposure in different environments such as Web sites, news articles, and offline and online word-of-mouth communications. This will be especially important as consumers have increasingly easy access to product information at their fingertips with mobile devices, which may, in some instances, reduce ambiguity of environmental information or add to information overload.

Third, our studies also had low variability on product category involvement and demographic characteristics, including age of study participants, who were primarily undergraduate college students. Although the results are limited to low-involvement products, we can speculate that the vigilance associated with persuasion knowledge might be even more evident when consumers process ads for high-involvement products promoted on the basis of green attributes. Because some surveys show age-related differences in environmental attitudes and behaviors (see Mintel 2012), we can speculate that greater heterogeneity in demographic characteristics of study participants might widen the differences across high versus low environmental concern conditions. Generalizability will be increased by future studies on high-involvement products that are promoted on the basis of green attributes and are evaluated by adult participants with greater variability in environmental concern and demographics such as age.

Given the effects of prevention-focused appeals, future research might extend prevention into appeals on the basis of fear versus more subtle or diffuse emotions such as anxiety, or fear of possible harm versus anger regarding actual (past) harm (e.g., the Exxon *Valdez* oil spill, coal mining; Miller and Sinclair 2009). While we provide some evidence about consumer inference making, the congruency, or "fit," between the ad appeal and specific claims related to the product or the brand's image may play an important role in inference making and attitude formation. Consumers often infer that green products are less effective (see Chang 2011), and so it will be important for future eco-seal research to investigate the impact of consistency in ad appeal, beliefs, and brand image on attitude formation. With the proliferation of eco-seals, these and other research questions will be of importance to advertising theory, practice, and public policy.

REFERENCES

Aaker, Jennifer L., and Angela Y. Lee (2001), "'I' Seek Pleasures and 'We' Avoid Pains: The Role of Self-Regulatory Goals in Information Processing and Persuasion," *Journal of Consumer Research,* 28 (1), 33–49.

Aiken, Leona S., and Stephen G. West (1991), *Multiple Regression: Testing and Interpreting Interactions,* Thousand Oaks, CA: Sage.

Arquitt, Steven P., and T. Bettina Cornwell (2007), "Micro-Macro Linking Using System Dynamics Modeling: An Examination of Eco-Sealing Effects for Farmed Shrimp," *Journal of Macromarketing,* 27 (3), 243–255.

Beltramini, Richard F., and Edward R. Stafford (1993), "Comprehension and Perceived Believability of Seals of Approval Information in Advertising," *Journal of Advertising,* 22 (3), 3–13.

Boulding, William, and Amna Kirmani (1993), "A Consumer-Side Experimental Examination of Signaling Theory: Do Consumers Perceive Warranties as Signals of Quality?" *Journal of Consumer Research,* 20 (June), 111–123.

Bounds, Gwendolyn (2009), "What Do Labels Really Tell You? As Eco-Seals Proliferate, So Do Doubts," *Wall Street Journal* (April 2), D1.

Bustillo, Miguel (2009), "Wal-Mart to Assign New 'Green' Ratings," *Wall Street Journal* (July 16), B1.

Carlson, Les, Stephen J. Grove, and Norman Kangun (1993), "A Content Analysis of Environmental Advertising Claims: A Matrix Method Approach," *Journal of Advertising,* 22 (3), 27–39.

Chaiken, Shelly, and Yaacov Trope (1999), *Dual-Process Theories in Social Psychology,* New York: Guilford.

Chang, Chingching (2011), "Feeling Ambivalent About Going Green: Implications for Green Advertising Processing," *Journal of Advertising,* 40 (4), 19–31.

Cone Trend Tracker (2011), "Americans Value Honesty over Perfection in Environmental Marketing," available at www.conecomm.com/2011-green-gap-blog-post/ (accessed March 24, 2011).

Dean, Dwane H., and Abhijit Biswas (2001), "Third-Party Organization Endorsement of Products: An Advertising Cue Affecting Consumer Prepurchase Evaluation of Goods and Services," *Journal of Advertising,* 30 (4), 41–57.

Fitzsimons, Gavan J. (2008), "Death to Dichotomizing," *Journal of Consumer Research,* 35 (1), 5–8.

Forehand, Mark R., and Sonia Grier (2003), "When Is Honesty the Best Policy? The Effect of Stated Company Intent on Consumer Skepticism," *Journal of Consumer Psychology,* 13 (3), 349–356.

Friestad, Marian, and Peter Wright (1994), "The Persuasion Knowledge Model: How People Cope with Persuasion Attempts," *Journal of Consumer Research,* 21 (June), 1–31.

Hayes, Andrew F. (2012), "PROCESS: A Versatile Computational Tool for Observed Variable Mediation, Moderation, and Conditional Process Modeling," white paper, Ohio State University, available at www.afhayes.com/public/process2012.pdf (accessed February 8, 2013).

———, and Kristopher J. Preacher (2011), "Indirect and Direct Effects of a Multicategorical Causal Agent in Statistical Mediation Analysis," working paper, Ohio State University.

Higgins, E. Tory (1997), "Beyond Pleasure and Pain," *American Psychologist,* 52 (December), 1280–1300.

Hoyer, Wayne D., and Stephen P. Brown (1990), "Effects of Brand Awareness on Choice for a Common, Repeat-Purchase Product," *Journal of Consumer Research,* 17 (September), 141–148.

Kees, Jeremy, Scot Burton, and Andrea Heintz Tangari (2010), "The Impact of Regulatory Focus, Temporal Orientation, and Fit on Consumer Responses to Health-Related Advertising," *Journal of Advertising,* 39 (1), 19–34.

Kirmani, Amna, and Rui (Juliet) Zhu (2007), "Vigilant Against Manipulation: The Effect of Regulatory Focus on the Use of Persuasion Knowledge," *Journal of Marketing Research,* 64 (November), 688–701.

MacInnis, Deborah J., Christine Moorman, and Bernard J. Jaworski (1991), "Enhancing and Measuring Consumers' Motivation, Opportunity, and Ability to Process Brand Information from Ads," *Journal of Marketing,* 55 (October), 32–55.

MacKenzie, Scott B., and Richard A. Spreng (1992), "How Does Motivation Moderate the Impact of Central and Peripheral Processing on Brand Attitudes and Intentions?" *Journal of Consumer Research,* 18 (4), 519–529.

Miller, Barbara, and Janas Sinclair (2009), "Community Stakeholder Responses to Advocacy Advertising: Trust, Accountability, and the Persuasion Knowledge Model (PKM)," *Journal of Advertising,* 28 (2), 37–51.

Mintel Report (2011), "Green Marketing, U.S. 2011, Moving Beyond Eco-Friendly," available at http://academic.mintel.com/sinatra/oxygen_academic/search_results/show&/display/id=543141/ (accessed March 16, 2012).

———— (2012), "Marketing to the Green Consumer, U.S. April 2012," available at http://academic.mintel.com/sinatra/oxygen/display/?no_redirect&id=590323/ (accessed June 7, 2012).

Mohr, Lois A., Dogan Eroglu, and Pam S. Ellen (1998), "The Development and Testing of a Measure of Skepticism Toward Environmental Claims in Marketers' Communications," *Journal of Consumer Affairs,* 32 (1), 30–55.

Neff, Jack (2009), "Laundry Business Embraces Risk: Clorox Doubles Spending to Pit GreenWorks Detergent Against Tide," *Advertising Age* (June 29).

Obermiller, Carl (1995), "The Baby Is Sick, The Baby Is Well: A Test of Environmental Communication Appeals," *Journal of Advertising,* 24 (2), 55–70.

Petty, Richard E., and John T. Cacioppo (1986), *Communication and Persuasion: Central and Peripheral Routes to Attitude Change,* New York: Springer.

Preacher, Kristopher J., Derek D. Rucker, and Andrew F. Hayes (2007), "Assessing Moderated Mediation Hypotheses: Theory, Methods, and Prescriptions," *Multivariate Behavioral Research,* 42 (1), 185–227.

Rockwood, Kate (2010), "Will Wal-Mart's 'Sustainability Index' Actually Work?" *Fast Company* (February 1), available at www.fastcompany.com/node/1518194/print/ (accessed March 14, 2012).

Rosenbloom, Stephanie (2009), "At Wal-Mart, Labeling to Reflect Green Intent," *New York Times* (July 16), B1.

SC Johnson (2012), "Greenlist™ Fact Sheet," available at www.scjohnson.com/en/press-room/fact-sheets/09-10-2009/Greenlist-Fact-Sheet.aspx (accessed March 19, 2012).

Shrum, L. J., John A. McCarty, and Tina M. Lowrey (1995), "Buyer Characteristics of the Green Consumer and Their Implications for Advertising Strategy," *Journal of Advertising,* 24 (Summer), 71–82.

Simmons, Carolyn J., Barbara A. Bickart, and Lauranne Buchanan (2003), "Leveraging Equity Across the Brand Portfolio," *Marketing Letters,* 11 (3), 210–220.

Sung, Yongjun, and Sejung Marina Choi (2011), "Increasing Power and Preventing Pain: The Moderating Role of Self-Construal in Advertising Message Framing," *Journal of Advertising,* 40 (1), 71–85.

Weiner, Bernard (1986), *An Attributional Theory of Motivation and Emotion,* New York: Springer.

Zhao, Xinshu, John G. Lynch, Jr., and Qimei Chen (2010), "Reconsidering Baron and Kenny: Myths and Truths About Mediation Analysis," *Journal of Consumer Research,* 37 (2), 197–206.

Zmuda, Natalie (2010), "Coca-Cola Goes Completely Green at Olympics in Ambitious Eco-Friendly Push," *Advertising Age* (February 1), available at http://adage.com/article/news/coca-cola-completely-green-vancouver-winter-olympics/141839/ (accessed March 16, 2012).

APPENDIX 1

Study 1: Examples of Target Ad

A. Known Brand with Eco-Seal (on Bottle Neck)

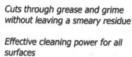

B. Unknown Brand Without Eco-Seal

APPENDIX 2

Measures and Reliabilities

Construct, items, and source	Study 1 α	Study 2 α
Attitude toward the ad (three Likert scale items):	.97	.96

My overall attitude toward the advertisement for _____ is:
   Negative/Positive
   Unfavorable/Favorable
   Bad/Good

	Study 1 α	Study 2 α
Brand attitudes (six semantic differential items):	.90	.92

Overall, [brand] is:
   Low quality/High quality
   Unappealing/Appealing
   Something I dislike very much/Something I like very much
   Unpleasant/Pleasant
   Negative/Positive
   Unfavorable/Favorable

	Study 1 α	Study 2 α
Purchase intentions (three semantic differential items):	.95	.94

How likely is it that you would purchase [brand]?
   Very unlikely/Very likely
   Definitely would not/Definitely would
   Improbable/Probable

	Study 1 α	Study 2 α
Environmental concern (five semantic differential items; Mohr, Eroglu, and Ellen 1998):	.93	.93

Environmental issues are:
   Unimportant/Important
   Something that does not really matter to me/ . . . really matters to me
   Not personally relevant/Personally relevant
   Uninvolving/Involving
   Of little concern to me/Of great concern to me

	Study 1 α	Study 2 α
Manipulation check: SmartCheck attitudes (four semantic differential items):	n.a.	.94

Overall, the SmartCheck™ Certification is:
   Unfavorable/Favorable
   Negative/Positive
   One that I do not like very much/One that I like very much
   Bad/Good

	Study 1 α	Study 2 α
Manipulation check: SmartCheck trust (four semantic differential items):	n.a.	.89

Overall, the SmartCheck™ Certification is:
   Biased/Not biased
   Deceptive/Not deceptive
   Unbelievable/Believable
   Unconvincing/Convincing

Notes: n.a. = not available.

All items were measured on seven-point scales.

APPENDIX 3

Study 2: Examples of Target Ad

A. Promotion Appeal and Manufacturer Eco-Seal

Keeping You Healthy
The Natural Way

So you can continue to enjoy what life has to offer!

Kills germs to prevent illness

All natural and alcohol free

Great fresh fragrance

Easy-to-use spray bottle with no-mess flip-top cap

> **Our Company** created the environmental criteria for the **SmartCheck**™ ✓ program, so that you can feel good about what you're buying. **SmartCheck**™ ✓ is our Company's assurance that this product uses better ingredients for the environment and human health.

B. Prevention Appeal and Government Agency Eco-Seal

Protecting You From Illness
The Natural Way

So you can avoid missing out on what life has to offer!

Kills germs to prevent illness

All natural and alcohol free

Great fresh fragrance

Easy-to-use spray bottle with no-mess flip-top cap

> The **US Consumer Products Safety Commission** created the environmental criteria for the **SmartCheck**™ ✓ program, so that you can feel good about what you're buying. **SmartCheck**™ ✓ is the US Consumer Product Safety Commission's assurance that this product uses better ingredients for the environment and human health.

SUSTAINABLE MARKETING AND SOCIAL MEDIA

A Cross-Country Analysis of Motives for Sustainable Behaviors

Elizabeth Minton, Christopher Lee, Ulrich Orth, Chung-Hyun Kim, and Lynn Kahle

ABSTRACT: Increased spending and demand for sustainable advertising necessitates research to understand better how to encourage sustainable thought and behavior effectively, especially in the understudied areas of social media and cross-cultural research. This study, which includes respondents from the United States, Germany, and South Korea (total $n = 1,018$) who completed an online survey about usage of Facebook and Twitter, examines motives for sustainable behaviors. Kelman's (1958) functional motives, which correspond to the three major philosophies of psychology, were used as the theoretical foundation for this study. For all countries, involvement motives lead to recycling behaviors and green transportation use, but only for the United States and Germany do involvement motives lead to antimaterialistic views and organic food purchase. Collectivist South Korea has the highest level of social media involvement and of sustainable behaviors except in recycling, where Germany leads. Motives are complex, demanding careful analysis from advertisers who plan to deliver green advertisements over social media.

Interest in green marketing is rapidly increasing. According to a recent study by *Environmental Leader,* 82% of companies plan to increase spending on green marketing (Tillinghast 2010). In addition, 74% of these companies planning to increase green-marketing spending plan to do so using the Internet, while only 50% plan to market green advertisements via print media (Tillinghast 2010). In spite of this planned increase in spending on green marketing online, many consumers prefer green-marketing messages through traditional media (e.g., magazines or product labels) versus online media such as Facebook and Twitter (Trevino 2011). However, the rapid increase in use of social media by both consumers and marketers across the globe (Barnhill 2011) signals a need for research looking at the role of these new media in green advertising campaigns.

From a consumer perspective, the spending power of consumers with sustainability and environmental concerns consists of more than $230 billion (Burst Media 2010). It is interesting to note that more than one-third of consumers look to the Internet as a primary source for green products, whereas television and family/friends combined account for just one-quarter of consumers' sources for green product information (Burst Media 2010). In addition, 82% of consumers recognize green claims in advertising, and 43% of consumers trust these green claims to be true (Burst Media 2010). Regardless of whether there is a true change in consumer demand for green products and services or rather companies just desire to integrate the green and sustainable buzzwords into marketing campaigns to have similar strategies as competitors, research shows that spending on green marketing is on the rise (Tillinghast 2010). Therefore, an understanding of consumer receptiveness to green advertisements, specifically in an online environment with the expected increased spending on online advertisements, is particularly useful for the future success of businesses.

By nature, social media strongly center on relationships that are influenced by culture—both individual relationships (i.e., values) and how consumers view themselves (individualist versus collectivist). Therefore, cross-cultural issues need to be taken into account when researching social media. The Green Brands Study conducted by WPP Brands found that developed countries, such as the United States and the United Kingdom, are less likely to pay a premium for green goods in comparison to developing countries, such as China, which place a much higher value on green goods (Longsworth 2011). This willingness to pay a premium for green goods likely translates into interest in green advertising, suggesting differences among countries in attention afforded to and desire for green advertising.

Cross-cultural differences in demand for green goods and green advertising may also vary by advertising medium used. Specifically with social media, large variations between countries exist with the length of time spent on social media. In Russia, for example, the average time spent on social media per month is 10.3 hours (ComScore 2011). In comparison, in the United States, the average time spent on social media per month is just 5.2 hours (ComScore 2011). Even Indonesia, a less developed country, has an average time spent on social media per month of 4.6 hours (ComScore 2011). These figures indicate that around the globe, social media are frequently used, but cross-cultural differences in usage are present.

These cross-cultural differences in social media usage suggest a need to consider advertising media (specifically new media, such as social media, which have been understudied) along with cross-cultural differences in research on green advertising. Therefore, the purposes of this paper are to observe consumer commitment to sustainability in social media while incorporating cross-cultural differences in this commitment and to relate this information to consumer motives and advertising practices.

CONCEPTUAL DEVELOPMENT

Sustainability

Sustainability has become a buzzword used by individuals and businesses alike to convey a sense of caring about the environment, and it is often used interchangeably with other terms such as *green* or *environmentally friendly* (Peattie 1995). One of the first commonly accepted definitions of sustainability comes from the United Nations; it described sustainability as "development that meets the needs of the present without compromising the ability of future generations to meet their own needs" (Brundtland 1987).

Measurement of sustainability is often morphed into many different forms for various research studies. For example, Thøgersen (2010) uses organic food consumption as a means for assessing sustainable behaviors. Banbury, Stinerock, and Subrahmanyan (2011) used subjective personal introspections and found consumers defining sustainable consumption as reducing overall purchases and consumption, producing more than is consumed, using public transportation, living in smaller homes, reducing purchase of single-serving packages, consuming organic foods, using energy-efficient light bulbs, and using low-flow shower heads.

Advertising messages promoting sustainable goods or services are often labeled as green advertising. Zinkhan and Carlson specifically define green advertising as "promotional messages that may appeal to the needs and desires of environmentally concerned consumers" (1995, p. 1). Green advertising has the potential to evoke various responses in consumers; however, previous research suggests that consumers are reluctant to participate in sustainable behaviors (Zinkhan and Carlson

1995). Instead, consumers adopt sustainable viewpoints to be socially acceptable but may not follow through with sustainable behaviors (Zinkhan and Carlson 1995). This (dis)connection between attitudes and behaviors could be related to conspicuous consumption (i.e., are the green advertisements for products or services that a consumer's peers can easily see the consumer conspicuously consuming?) as well as level of internalization of the sustainable attitudes.

In addition, Chang (2011) finds that consumer response to green ads is complex. Green advertisers making high-effort green claims are more likely to evoke feelings of discomfort and disbelief among consumers that are ambivalent to sustainability; however, this research was not conducted within a context of any particular advertising medium, so differences in evoked feelings may differ based on advertising medium used. For example, Chaudhuri and Buck (1995) show that print media are more likely to evoke analytic or rational responses in comparison to electronic media that evoke more emotional and affective responses due to differences in the intrinsic (e.g., print) versus extrinsic (e.g., electronic) nature of the advertising media. Although very little research on green advertising observes differences in consumer response to green advertisements based on the advertising medium used, foundational research by McLuhan (1994/1964) suggests that the medium used can greatly influence the message conveyed.

Individual difference variables also affect consumer participation in sustainable behaviors and resulting response to green advertisements. For example, research shows that there is no significant difference in participation in sustainable behaviors between males and females, although females trend toward having greener shopping habits than males (Diamantopoulos et al. 2003). Age negatively correlates with environmental knowledge (i.e., the older a consumer, the less environmental knowledge he or she is likely to have), although older consumers are more likely to recycle (Diamantopoulos et al. 2003). This previous research suggests that age is an important variable to consider in green advertising research because young and old consumers may have different definitions for what green and sustainability represent. It is important to note that consumers across the globe may not respond in the same way to green advertisements. Thøgersen (2010) found that a country's political regulation, financial support for sustainability initiatives, and national labeling systems played a large part in a consumer's consumption level of sustainable products.

Levels of Attitude Commitment and Motivation

Attitudes toward behaviors can be influenced through normative pressures and other tangible and nontangible motivations. For advertisers, an understanding of the influencers of attitude development is important for designing effective advertisements. Kelman (1958) identified levels of attitude commitment to describe the underlying motivations for participation and support of behaviors. Attitude commitment ranges from compliance or responsibility (participating in a behavior through force, such as laws) to identification (participation for advancing complex interpersonal goals) to internalization (no motivation beyond self-definition needed to participate in a behavior). These motives are interesting in part because they correspond to the three major philosophies of psychology: behaviorism, psychoanalysis, and humanism. Each motive implies different activation and change conditions.

Although Kelman (1958) identifies three specific levels of attitude commitment (compliance or responsibility, identification, and internalization), Kahle, Kambara, and Rose (1996) expanded on these attitude commitment levels to distinguish between public and private attitude influencers, creating seven levels of attitude commitment, still ranging from compliance to internalization. The expanded attitude commitment levels are compliance (as a result of control), obligation (private form of compliance representing a societal need), camaraderie (normative pressures), identification with winning/success (desiring pride through success), self-defining experience (private form of identification representing internal identification), unique/self-expressive experience (self-definition), and internalization (no motivation needed). Others have found evidence consistent with this typology (e.g., Lu et al. 2012).

Sustainability-related advertising would benefit from an understanding of what level of attitude commitment consumers adopt to create better targeted advertisements based on consumer wants and needs. Viscusi, Huber, and Bell (2011) find that governmental policies significantly influence participation in recycling, suggesting that many consumers participate in sustainable practices by means of compliance (following the policies) or identification with winning/success (when receiving a monetary reward for recycling). In addition, Bamberg, Hunecke, and Blöbaum (2007) find that perceived guilt and social norms significantly influence use of public transportation, signifying an obligation level of attitude commitment. An understanding of consumers' level of attitude commitment for sustainable behaviors provides advertisers with valuable information as to how to design advertisements (e.g., if normative pressures are effective for encouraging recycling, then advertisements could be created with messages conveying a sense of social pressure to recycle).

Intermingling of Sustainability, Social Media, Culture, and Advertising

Social media and advertising are both parts of integrated marketing communication. Social media provide avenues for broad reach, allow for interactivity, and often come with little cost (Kahle and Valette-Florence 2012). In addition, social media are beneficial for advertisers because consumers self-select into lifestyle groups that make targeted marketing much easier (Kahle and Valette-Florence 2012). In this sense, marketers have easy access to consumers interested in a lifestyle incorporating sustainability by looking to sustainability groups on social media, searching for sustainability-related feeds, and creating ads that display when sustainability-related posts are made. These reasons and others have contributed to the rapid rise of using social media for advertising and marketing communications. Furthermore, social media have the potential to be a more credible advertising tool due to their personal characteristics (e.g., interactions, networking, interpersonal relations); therefore, social media could be a more appropriate platform for green advertising and social campaigns via these electronic word of mouth (eWOM) modes of indirect communication rather than commercial advertising and marketing (Hung, Li, and Tse 2011). The Persuasion Knowledge Model (PKM) states that consumers are experienced and knowledgeable in the mechanisms of marketing and persuasion processes (Friestad and Wright 1994), but Hung, Li, and Tse (2011) suggest that social media are perceived as less persuasive than traditional marketing communications, thereby creating a need for research specifically addressing social media advertising.

Some may contend that social media are not, in fact, advertising, but Tuten and Solomon (2012) state that social media are definitely advertising, and even more important, a marketing platform. Advertisers must respond to consumers' shift to online communication and embrace social media as new advertising media. Tuten and Solomon state that social media are effective advertising media whether the "focus is to improve customer service, maintain customer relationships, inform consumers of our benefits, promote a brand or related special offer, develop a new product, or influence brand attitudes" (2012, p. 14). Barker et al. (2008) add that social media advertising is nevertheless different from traditional advertising because traditional advertising focuses on one-way communication with control (i.e., controlling all content that the consumer receives), whereas social media advertising focuses on two-way communication with contributions (i.e., what can the advertiser contribute to the consumer and how can the consumer contribute to the advertiser?).

This interactive nature of social media allows marketers to not only passively observe consumers using social media, but also to actively develop dialogue with consumers to understand their wants and needs better. For example, Whole Foods Market recently posted on several social media outlets, including Facebook and Twitter, that the company would no longer be selling seafood on the red-rated list (unsustainable) as determined by Blue Ocean Institute and Monterey Bay Aquarium. Thus, Whole Foods Market could passively monitor posts on Twitter and Facebook about the ban on red-rated seafood as well as actively engage in discussion with consumers regarding the new change. In contrast, traditional print or television media only allow for a passive one-way interaction with consumers. In social media, this interactivity, defined as two or more communication parties acting on each other or the medium (Liu 2002), allows for instantaneous feedback about consumer lifestyle traits, such as consumers' preferences toward recycling or other sustainable behaviors (Kahle and Valette-Florence 2012). In contrast, other advertising media are slower, one-way communication forms.

Consumers nevertheless interact with social media differently depending on individual difference variables. For example, consumers with an interdependent view of self and low psychological well-being are more likely to use social media to connect with others (Hoffman, Novak, and Stein 2012). Consumers with an independent view of self and high psychological well-being, however, are more likely to use social media to interact with content, and are therefore more likely to interact with sustainability advertising and other mass media content (Hoffman, Novak, and Stein 2012).

In spite of prior research on sustainability from a general social marketing perspective (Peattie and Peattie 2009), new research is needed specifically addressing the relationship between sustainability and advertising on social media. McLuhan's (1994/1964) famous saying, "the medium is the message," purports that each communication medium provides a different message in the way that the message is sent over the medium. Following suit with McLuhan's research, the relationship between sustainability and social media needs to be further investigated because prior research on sustainability-focused marketing campaigns investigates other communication media (e.g., television or print) with different characteristics and message mechanisms. Advertisers are aware of the need to understand trends among traditional and emerging media in an effort to reach younger generations of consumers (La Ferle, Edwards, and Lee 2000). Advertising research should keep up with this emphasis on emerging media trends in practice by understanding social media's role in developing effective advertising.

In addition, social media provide a new context for understanding persuasive advertising. Shrum (2004) states that the lines between entertainment and persuasion are becoming increasingly blurred, thereby providing an interesting context for social media research due to the mixture of entertainment, interactivity, and persuasion found in social media. Traditional advertising-based (persuasion) approaches have often failed to change consumer attitudes and behavior (e.g., smoking, unhealthy eating, sustainable consumption). This paper builds on previous advertising research and explores social media's potential (as a soft-persuasion tool) to better understand and target consumer motives with targeted advertising.

Therefore, the purpose of this paper is to assess consumer commitment to sustainability, specifically in the social marketing context, while incorporating a cross-cultural perspective.

This cross-cultural perspective for social media research is necessary due to possible communication and cultural differences among countries resulting in variations in understanding (Papacharissi and Yuan 2011).

Hypotheses

Three countries are examined: Germany, South Korea, and the United States. South Korea is considered a more collectivist country than the United States and Germany, considered more individualistic (Hofstede 2001; Triandis et al. 1988). According to Hofstede (2001), a collectivist culture stresses belonging and relationships, whereas an individualistic culture emphasizes privacy and independence. Given the emphasis on "social" media, which is collectivist by nature of the phrase, the following is hypothesized:

Hypothesis 1: Social media will play a more prominent role in South Korea, a collectivist culture, than in the United States or Germany, which are individualistic cultures.

Each type of medium has its own unique characteristics. Twitter tends to be more public than Facebook, given the prevalence of public profiles and ability to search public tweets. In contrast, Facebook relationships tend to be embedded in more complex and enduring social interactions (i.e., close family and friends). As such, Hughes et al. (2011) found that consumers who desire openness tend to use Twitter, whereas consumers who are seeking information and who wish to fulfill social needs have a preference for Facebook. Therefore, the following is hypothesized:

Hypothesis 2: Different social media (i.e., Twitter and Facebook) will invoke different motives and communication patterns, with Facebook showing more elaborated, social motivations.

Each type of sustainable behavior has its own complex history and causes. Kollmuss and Agyeman (2002) suggested that the relationship between sustainable attitudes and behaviors is strongest when only small cost or effort is necessary. For example, even if a consumer has a positive attitude toward sustainability, he or she may only follow through on the behavior if the sustainable good is low cost or sustainable action is convenient. Therefore, the following is hypothesized:

Hypothesis 3: The pattern of motivations for engaging in sustainable behaviors will vary from one type of behavior to another.

METHOD

Respondents and Procedures

Respondents were chosen from one advanced country in each of the Northern Hemisphere's three continents. Countries

TABLE I
Demographic Profiles of Respondents by Country (Mean Values)

	United States	Germany	South Korea
Age	34	27	33
Female	64%	64%	43%
Received college degree	20%	56%	74%
Single	91%	92%	50%
Primary shopper	80%	84%	71%
Works full time	63%	40%	71%
Twitter usage*	5.1%	5.0%	54.8%
Facebook usage*	86.6%	88.3%	77.7%

* Use social medium at least once per month.

with advanced levels of technology development were desired that would perhaps be leaders showing where other countries may follow. The total of 1,018 respondents includes (1) 337 respondents from the United States collected via Amazon. com's Mechanical Turk service, which is valued for academic research (Buhrmester, Kwang, and Gosling 2011; Paolacci, Chandler, and Ipeirotis 2010); (2) 358 respondents from Germany collected via UniPark, a comparable German Internet survey organization; and (3) 323 respondents from South Korea collected via EZ Survey (a company of Embrain and the leading online survey company in South Korea). The opt-in sampling system was chosen to limit participants to active Internet users, thereby causing the response rate to become less germane. In the United States, 86.6% of respondents use Facebook at least once a month, and 5.1% of respondents use Twitter at least once a month. Similarly, in Germany, 88.3% of respondents use Facebook at least once a month, and 5.0% of respondents use Twitter at least once a month. In contrast, in South Korea, 77.7% of respondents use Facebook at least once a month, and 54.8% of respondents use Twitter at least once a month.

Respondents had an average age of 32, 57% were female, 62% had received a college degree, 44% were single, 79% were primary shoppers, and 38% worked full time (see Table 1 for demographic profiles by country). An online survey was completed by each participant in his or her native language. In South Korea and Germany, the questions were translated and backtranslated until a panel of three multilingual experts each agreed that all items were as comparable as possible. The survey took an average of 6 minutes, 18 seconds, to complete, and respondents were compensated financially.

Measures

The survey contained questions regarding the respondent's sustainable behaviors, use of social media, and attitude commitment levels (Kahle, Kambara, and Rose 1996) relating to sustainable expression on social media, as well as basic demographic variables. (See Table 2 for attitude commitment questions, Table 3 for sustainable behavior questions from the survey, and Table 4 for descriptive statistics of these variables.) Survey questions were measured on a nine-point Likert-type scale ranging from "strongly disagree" to "strongly agree."

For the level of attitude commitment, the data file was randomly split into two equal halves; exploratory factor analysis (EFA) was conducted on the first half and confirmatory factor analysis (CFA) was conducted on the second half. The EFA was conducted through principle axis factoring with promax rotation using 14 attitude commitment variables that were adapted from Kahle, Kambara, and Rose (1996). Three factors (responsibility, involvement, and internalization) were identified, which explained 77% of the variability in attitude commitment. These three levels approximately correspond to Kelman's (1958) three levels, but do not replicate the more complex Kahle, Kambara, and Rose (1996) constructs. It is likely that the factor analysis produced only three factors similar to Kelman's (1958) three levels because Kahle, Kambara, and Rose's (1996) expanded attitude commitment levels involved private and public forms of attitude commitment. By their nature, social media are public; therefore, in measuring social media motives, consumers would likely only be engaging with public motives. The three identified factors represent (1) responsibility to support sustainability on social media, (2) a need to be involved and associated with sustainability on social media, and (3) internalized attitudes about supporting sustainability on social media as a means of self-definition and self-expression. The CFA was conducted using LISREL 8.8 (Jöreskog and Sörbom 1996), had relatively good model fit, and confirmed the factor structure in the EFA (see Table 5 for results of the EFA and CFA for attitude commitment). Evidence of good internal consistency is provided by composite reliability and coefficient α. Composite reliability is a LISREL-generated estimate of internal consistency analogous

TABLE 2

Survey Items for Levels of Attitude Commitment (Adapted from Kahle, Kambara, and Rose [1996] to Sustainability and Social Media)

Construct	Items
Compliance	1. I only follow sustainable companies on [this social media site] because it fills my news feed with sustainable news, making me appear a more sustainable person. 2. I'd be more likely to visit [this social media site] if friends and relatives were to see me interacting with sustainable companies.
Obligation	1. People have an obligation to support sustainability organizations or causes on [this social media site]. 2. [This social media site] represents my friends and me, and our values for sustainability.
Camaraderie	1. I'd be more likely to visit [this social media site] if I knew it contained interesting postings relating to sustainability. 2. I'd be more likely to visit [this social media site] if there were more sustainability-related activities that allowed me to contribute to the spirit of the site.
Identification with winning/success	1. I'd be more likely to visit [this social media site] consistently if it had better coverage of sustainable issues than other media. 2. I'd be more likely to visit [this social media site] if it won awards as a sustainable business.
Self-defining experience	1. When I participate in discussion on [this social media site], I imagine myself influencing sustainability in the future. 2. I feel a sense of accomplishment when [this social media site] helps to encourage sustainable behaviors.
Unique, self-expressive experience	1. [This social media site] allows me to share ways that I am uniquely sustainable. 2. Viewing sustainable companies and ads on [this social media site] is more enjoyable than off [this social media site].
Internalization	1. I consider myself more knowledgeable about sustainability than most other people on [this social media site]. 2. [This social media site] is a good place to follow my favorite sustainable companies

Note: [This social media site] was substituted for both Facebook and Twitter in two separate attitude commitment inventories in this study.

TABLE 3

Sustainable Behavior Survey Items

Construct	Items
Recycling	1. I regularly recycle newspapers. 2. I regularly recycle cans and bottles.
Organics	1. I regularly purchase organic fruits. 2. I regularly purchase organic vegetables.
Transportation	1. When available, I take public transit rather than driving my own car. 2. When purchasing a car, I specifically look for an energy-efficient model.
Antimaterialism	1. I seek to reduce the overall number of purchases I make to help the environment. 2. Buying more than I need hurts the environment.
Charitable organizations/causes	1. I volunteer time to organizations and causes that support sustainability. 2. I donate money to organizations and causes that support sustainability.

to coefficient α (Fornell and Larcker 1981). Also included in Table 5 are the average variance extracted (AVE) estimates, which assess the amount of variance captured by a construct's measure relative to measurement error, and the correlations (φ estimates) among the latent constructs in the model. AVE estimates of .50 or higher indicate validity for a construct's measure (Fornell and Larcker 1981). All constructs achieved this criterion.

For sustainable behaviors, the same split data file was used to conduct an EFA on the first half and a CFA on the second half. The EFA was conducted through principle axis factoring with promax rotation using 13 sustainability variables that were

TABLE 4
Means and Standard Deviations for Attitude Commitment and Sustainable Behaviors

Attitude commitment variables

	Facebook	Twitter
Compliance1	2.56 (2.02)	4.14 (2.35)
Compliance2	2.82 (2.33)	4.44 (2.47)
Obligation1	3.52 (2.31)	4.64 (2.33)
Obligation2	3.22 (2.31)	4.65 (2.40)
Camaraderie1	3.22 (2.49)	4.80 (2.50)
Camaraderie2	3.40 (2.54)	4.91 (2.39)
IDwWin1	3.29 (2.46)	4.90 (2.45)
IDwWin2	3.27 (2.43)	4.72 (2.37)
SelfDef1	3.39 (2.53)	4.82 (2.40)
SelfDef2	3.69 (2.54)	4.91 (2.35)
SelfExp1	3.52 (2.48)	4.89 (2.30)
SelfExp2	2.86 (2.22)	4.37 (2.24)
Internal1	3.68 (2.31)	4.48 (2.18)
Internal2	3.33 (2.34)	4.68 (2.23)

Sustainable behavior variables

	United States	Germany	South Korea	Overall
Recycle1	7.22 (2.72)	7.46 (2.55)	7.06 (1.86)	7.25 (2.42)
Recycle2	7.70 (2.33)	7.91 (2.15)	7.31 (1.67)	7.65 (2.09)
Organic1	3.98 (2.58)	4.01 (2.59)	4.97 (1.70)	4.30 (2.38)
Organic2	3.97 (2.58)	4.01 (2.58)	4.96 (1.72)	4.30 (2.38)
Transportation1	4.99 (2.91)	5.21 (2.82)	6.59 (2.16)	5.57 (2.75)
Transportation2	6.75 (2.33)	6.91 (2.27)	7.19 (1.39)	6.95 (2.06)
Materialism1	4.21 (2.57)	4.18 (2.50)	5.67 (1.63)	4.66 (2.38)
Materialism2	5.95 (2.61)	6.12 (2.54)	5.81 (1.88)	5.96 (2.38)
Charity1	2.01 (1.89)	1.89 (1.78)	4.25 (1.93)	2.68 (2.15)
Charity2	2.31 (2.24)	2.22 (2.19)	4.22 (1.95)	2.88 (2.32)

Notes: $N = 1,018$.

For a description of all attitude commitment variables, see Table 2. For a description of all sustainable behavior variables, see Table 3.

All variables were measured on a nine-point Likert-like scale ranging from "strongly disagree" to "strongly agree."

TABLE 5
Measurement Model Results: Attitude Commitment*

	EFA results		
Variable name	Factor 1 (Responsibility)	Factor 2 (Involvement)	Factor 3 (Internalization)
Compliance1	.864		
Compliance2	.885		
Obligation1	.676		
Obligation2	.820		
Camaraderie1		.918	
Camaraderie2		.940	
IDwWin1		.915	
IDwWin2		.792	
SelfDef1			.777
SelfDef2			.819
SelfExp1			.817
SelfExp2			.747
Internal1			.536
Internal2			.782

Percent of variance explained: 77%

	CFA fit				
	χ^2	df	CFI	RMSEA	SRMR
Measurement model	430.31	74	.98	.097	.03

	Internal consistency		
	Composite reliability	Average variance extracted	Cronbach's α
Responsibility	.918	.738	.915
Involvement	.953	.837	.952
Internalization	.909	.628	.908

Notes: EFA = exploratory factor analysis; CFA = confirmatory factor analysis; CFI = comparative fit index; RMSEA = root mean square error of approximation; SRMR = standardized root mean residual.

* The data set was randomly split into two equal halves. EFA was conducted on the first half, and CFA was conducted on the second half.

developed for the purposes of this research. Six factors were identified that explained 82% of the variability in respondent sustainability. These six factors were expected to be grouped together because each factor is composed of two questions relating to the same concept (e.g., recycling newspapers and recycling cans or purchasing organic fruits and purchasing organic vegetables). The CFA was conducted using LISREL 8.8, had relatively good model fit, and confirmed the factor structure in the EFA (for results of the EFA and CFA for sustainable behaviors, see Table 6). Evidence of adequate internal consistency is provided by composite reliability and coefficient α. Also included in Table 5 are the AVE estimates, and all but two constructs achieved the .50 AVE criterion (i.e., .30 for the

two indicators of transportation and .46 for the two indicators of antimaterialism).

Results

Structural equation modeling (SEM) was used to test the relationship between level of attitude commitment to social media motives and sustainable behaviors (see Figure 1 for a path diagram). The overall fit for the full model (i.e., all countries, all social media) is good with CFI (comparative fit index) (.98), RMSEA (root mean square error of approximation) (.07), and SRMR (standardized root mean residual) (.05) values, all being well within the recommended cutoffs suggested by Hu

TABLE 6
Measurement Model Results: Sustainable Behaviors[a]

	EFA results				
Variable name	Factor 1 (Recycling)	Factor 2 (Organics)	Factor 3 (Transportation)	Factor 4 (Antimaterialism)	Factor 5 (Charity)
Recycle1	.832				
Recycle2	.839				
Organic1		.984			
Organic2		.975			
Transportation1			.574		
Transportation2			.548		
Materialism1				.668	
Materialism2				.717	
Charity1					.952
Charity2					.716

Percent of variance explained: 82%

	CFA fit				
	χ^2	df	CFI	RMSEA	SRMR
Measurement model	92.67	25	.97	.073	.05

	Internal consistency		
	Composite reliability	Average variance extracted	Cronbach's α[b]
Recycling	.743	.593	.730
Organics	.977	.955	.978
Transportation	.453	.293	.451
Antimaterialism	.624	.462	.598
Charity	.825	.704	.823

Notes: EFA = exploratory factor analysis; CFA = confirmatory factor analysis; CFI = comparative fit index; RMSEA = root mean square error of approximation; SRMR = standardized root mean residual.

[a] The data set was randomly split into two equal halves. EFA was conducted on the first half, and CFA was conducted on the second half.

[b] More accurately, this is a Pearson's *r* correlation because there are only two variables per construct.

and Bentler (1999)[1] (see Table 7). The χ^2 is significant for the full model, but this result is most likely due to the large sample size of 1,018 and artificial inflation of the χ^2 values (Bagozzi 2010; Steiger 2007). In the full model, attitude commitment at the responsibility level significantly leads to organic food purchase (t = 3.39), antimaterialistic views (t = 3.44), contributions to sustainable charities (t = 5.26), and decreased green transportation use (t = −1.90). Attitude commitment at the involvement level only significantly leads to increased green transportation use (t = 4.52). Attitude commitment at the internalization level significantly leads to antimaterialistic views (t = 2.27), contributions to sustainable charities (t = 5.12), and increased green transportation use (t = 1.91). Therefore, the pattern of motivations for engaging in sustainable behaviors is different for each behavior, thereby supporting H3. Additional analysis shows that age, gender, income, marital status, and employment status are significant predictors of level of attitude commitment, with consumers who are significantly younger (t = 1.82), female (t = 8.58), less wealthy (t = −2.33), married (t = 5.49), and not employed full time (t = −2.41) more likely to hold a responsibility level of attitude commitment. However, many of these relationships between level of attitude commitment and sustainable behaviors may be confounded by country or type of social medium. Therefore, individual SEM models were run to test for differences between type of social medium (Facebook, Twitter) and country (United States, Germany, South Korea).

FIGURE 1
Conceptual Model

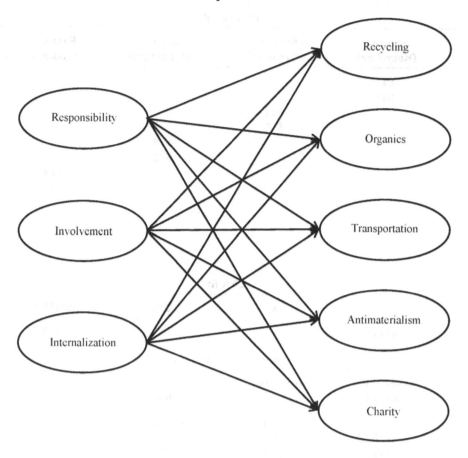

Country Differences

Before assessing individual country differences, cross-national measurement equivalence was assessed following the procedures recommended by Steenkamp and Baumgartner (1998). Results across the three countries reveal sufficient support for configural, metric, and scalar equivalence based on (1) good overall fit (χ^2[120] = 1515, p < .001, RMSEA = .10, CFI = .95) for configural equivalence; (2) slight change in fit indices ($\Delta\chi^2$[10] = 301, p < .001, RMSEA Δ = .01, CFI Δ = .01) for metric invariance; and (3) good overall fit (χ^2[156]) = 1,816, p < .001, RMSEA = .098, CFI = .94) and slight change in fit indices ($\Delta\chi^2$[26] = 301, p < .001, RMSEA Δ = .01, CFI Δ = .01) for scalar invariance (constraining loadings and intercepts). Together, these results provide reasonable fit to the aggregate data, and therefore, the estimated coefficients for each country can be validly examined to reveal the specific relationships by country for each construct.

Motives for participating in sustainable behaviors were then tested between countries (United States, Germany, South Korea) and compared to a full model (all countries) using SEM. (The results for the overall fit of the structural models are presented in Table 7.) The χ^2 is significant for all models, but this finding is most likely due to the large sample size of 1,018 (and at least 300 for each country) and artificial inflation of the χ^2 values (Bagozzi 2010; Steiger 2007). Overall model fit for all models is good, with CFI and SRMR falling within the recommended cutoffs suggested by Hu and Bentler (1999), but RMSEA falling outside of these cutoffs. However, Browne and Cudeck (1993) suggest that RMSEA values less than or equal to .10 can produce adequate model fit. Following these guidelines, all models provide at least adequate model fit.

As expected, South Korea, a collectivist country, exhibited motivation patterns for sustainable behaviors that differed from those in the United States and Germany, which are individualistic cultures, thereby providing partial support for H1. For the United States, Germany, and South Korea alike, the responsibility level of attitude commitment significantly leads to organic food purchase (United States, t = 2.28; Germany, t = 2.88; South Korea, t = 6.61), antimaterialistic views (United States, t = 3.96; Germany, t = 4.32; South Korea, t = 6.79), and contributions to sustainable charities (United States, t = 3.94; Germany, t = 3.70; South Korea, t = 3.52). However, for the United States and Germany, the involvement

TABLE 7
Structural Model Results: Country Comparison

	χ^2	df	CFI	RMSEA	SRMR
	Fit				
Model 1: All countries	235.93	40	.98	.07	.05
Model 2: United States	444.50	40	.95	.10	.05
Model 3: Germany	409.85	40	.95	.09	.05
Model 4: South Korea	417.82	40	.97	.09	.03

Completely standardized path estimates and (t-values)

	Model 1 (All countries)		Model 2 (United States)		Model 3 (Germany)		Model 4 (South Korea)	
Recycling								
Responsibility → Recycling: γ_{11}	−.03	(−.38)	−.07	(−1.38)	−.01	(−.30)	.02	(.26)
Involvement → Recycling: γ_{12}	.03	(.39)	.20	(3.91)	.16	(3.36)	.13	(2.28)
Internalization → Recycling: γ_{13}	.01	(.14)	.04	(.88)	.01	(.31)	−.04	(−.56)
Organics								
Responsibility → Organics: γ_{21}	.24	(3.39)	.11	(2.28)	.13	(2.88)	.38	(6.61)
Involvement → Organics: γ_{22}	.07	(.96)	.10	(2.14)	.11	(2.49)	−.07	(−1.33)
Internalization → Organics: γ_{23}	.03	(.48)	.03	(.63)	−.02	(−.33)	.14	(2.40)
Transportation								
Responsibility → Transportation: γ_{31}	−.20	(−1.90)	−.10	(−1.40)	−.10	(−1.59)	−.06	(−.71)
Involvement → Transportation: γ_{32}	.47	(4.52)	.21	(3.20)	.28	(4.26)	.43	(4.54)
Internalization → Transportation: γ_{33}	.19	(1.91)	.15	(2.27)	.19	(2.87)	−.02	(−.23)
Antimaterialism								
Responsibility → Antimaterialism: γ_{41}	.27	(3.44)	.22	(3.96)	.23	(4.32)	.43	(6.79)
Involvement → Antimaterialism: γ_{42}	.07	(.95)	.15	(2.82)	.16	(3.07)	−.05	(−.94)
Internalization → Antimaterialism: γ_{43}	.17	(2.27)	.10	(1.99)	.14	(2.80)	.29	(4.61)
Charity								
Responsibility → Charity: γ_{51}	.33	(5.26)	.20	(3.94)	.18	(3.70)	.21	(3.52)
Involvement → Charity: γ_{52}	.05	(.73)	.03	(.67)	−.05	(−1.11)	.05	(.87)
Internalization → Charity: γ_{53}	.31	(5.12)	.21	(4.43)	.30	(6.39)	.25	(4.08)

Notes: CFI = comparative fit index; RMSEA = root mean square error of approximation; SRMR = standardized root mean residual.

See Figure 1 for models.

All χ^2 statistics were significant at the .01 level; *t*-values of 1.65 or greater are significant at the .05 level, and *t*-values of 2.33 or greater are significant at the .01 level.

level of attitude commitment significantly leads to recycling (United States, $t = 3.91$; Germany, $t = 3.36$), organic food purchase (United States, $t = 2.14$; Germany, $t = 2.49$), green transportation use (United States, $t = 3.20$; Germany, $t = 4.26$), and antimaterialistic views (United States, $t = 2.82$; Germany, $t = 3.07$). In comparison, for South Korea, the involvement level of attitude commitment significantly leads to only recycling ($t = 2.28$) and green transportation use ($t = 4.54$). Finally, for both the United States and Germany, the internalization level of attitude commitment significantly leads to green transportation use (United States, $t = 2.27$; Germany

$t = 2.87$), antimaterialistic views (United States, $t = 1.99$; Germany, $t = 2.80$), and contributions to sustainable charities (United States, $t = 3.94$; Germany, $t = 3.70$). For South Korea, the internalization level of attitude commitment significantly leads to organic food purchase ($t = 2.40$), antimaterialistic views ($t = 4.61$), and contributions to sustainable charities ($t = 4.08$).

Social media motives for participating in sustainable behaviors are distinctly different between countries and in comparison to an all-country model. Separate motive models by country reveal significant relationships between involvement and recycling behaviors, involvement and organic food purchase, and involvement and antimaterialistic views that were shown to be nonsignificant in the all-country model. Therefore, research in social media motives and social media advertising would generally benefit from a cross-cultural analysis.

With regard to specific sustainable behaviors, there are significant differences between countries in recycling behaviors, $F(2, 1012) = 3.67$, $p = .026$; organic food purchases, $F(2, 1013) = 19.73$, $p < .001$; green transportation use, $F(2, 1006) = 18.31$, $p < .001$; antimaterialistic views, $F(2, 1011) = 10.68$, $p < .001$; and contributions to sustainable charities, $F(2, 1013) = 154.16$, $p < .001$. Respondents from South Korea consistently participate in more sustainable behaviors than respondents from the United States or Germany, with the exception of recycling, where German respondents are the most frequent recyclers.

Social Media Differences

Before assessing individual differences in type of social media, measurement equivalence was assessed following the procedures recommended by Steenkamp and Baumgartner (1998) and Byrne and Stewart (2006). Results across the two types of social media reveal sufficient support for configural, metric, and scalar equivalence based on (1) adequate overall fit ($\chi^2[80] = 1236$, $p < .001$, RMSEA = .12, CFI = .95) for configural equivalence; (2) adequate overall fit ($\chi^2[85] = 1276$, $p < .001$, RMSEA = .12, CFI = .95) for metric invariance; and (3) adequate overall fit ($\chi^2[98] = 1276$, $p < .001$, RMSEA = .11, CFI = .95) for scalar invariance (constraining loadings and intercepts). Together, these results provide adequate fit to the aggregate data, and therefore, the estimated coefficients for each type of social medium can be validly examined to reveal the specific relationships by social media type for each construct.

Motives for participating in sustainable behaviors were then tested between social media (Facebook and Twitter) and a full model (all social media) using SEM. (The results for the overall fit of the three structural models are presented in Table 8.) The χ^2 is significant for all models, but this result is most likely due to the large sample size of 1,018 and artificial inflation of the χ^2 values (Bagozzi 2010; Steiger 2007). Overall model fit for all models is good, with CFI and SRMR falling within the recommended cutoffs suggested by Hu and Bentler (1999), but RMSEA falling outside of these cutoffs. However, after following the Brown and Cudeck (1993) suggestion that RMSEA values should be less than or equal to .10, only the Twitter model falls outside of the recommended guidelines for RMSEA.

As expected, Facebook and Twitter exhibited different motivation patterns for sustainable behaviors, thereby providing partial support for H2. For Facebook, the responsibility level of attitude commitment significantly leads to organic

food purchase ($t = 3.45$), antimaterialistic views ($t = 3.31$), contributions to sustainable charities ($t = 4.03$), and decreased green transportation use ($t = -2.05$). In contrast, for Twitter, the responsibility level of attitude commitment significantly leads to organic food purchase ($t = 3.39$), antimaterialistic views ($t = 2.52$), and contributions to sustainable charities ($t = 2.57$). For the involvement level of attitude commitment, motivations are the same for Facebook and Twitter, which significantly leads to green transportation use (Facebook, $t = 3.84$; Twitter, $t = 3.58$). Finally, for Facebook, the internalization level of attitude commitment significantly leads to green transportation use ($t = 2.30$), antimaterialistic views ($t = 2.75$), and contributions to sustainable charities ($t = 6.99$). For Twitter, however, the internalization level of attitude commitment significantly leads only to antimaterialistic views ($t = 2.94$) and contributions to sustainable charities ($t = 5.46$).

With regard to specific sustainable behaviors, there are significant differences between heavy users (at least once per week) of Facebook and Twitter in organic food purchases ($t[918] = -2.23$, $p = .026$), green transportation use ($t[918] = -3.752$, $p < .001$), antimaterialistic attitudes ($t[918] = -2.04$, $p = .042$), and contributions to sustainable charities ($t[918] = -8.67$, $p < .001$). Compared with heavy Twitter users, heavy Facebook users are significantly less likely to participate in all sustainable behaviors.

DISCUSSION

Findings show significant differences in social media motives for sustainability among countries and type of social medium. Thus, advertisers using social media should be cautious in creating blanket advertising plans to cover all countries and all social media. Instead, advertisers should target distinct sets of motives that apply to each country (e.g., targeting involvement motives for Germany and the United States to encourage organic food purchase) and to each social medium (e.g., targeting internalization motives for Facebook to encourage green transportation use).

More specifically, South Korea is the most collectivist or social of the three countries surveyed. Respondents from South Korea showed the most activity in social media and sustainability. It is interesting to note that South Korean respondents used Twitter substantially more than respondents from the United States or Germany. Dholakia (2006) confirms that South Koreans have high levels of technological adoption for both genders, even when comparing South Korea to other countries with a higher gross domestic product and suggests that these high adoption rates are due to successful use of public policies. In addition, Dholakia (2006) shows that general Internet use is highest for South Koreans (males = 15.9 hours per week, females = 12.1 hours per week), in contrast to consumers from the United States (males = 13.1 hours per week,

TABLE 8
Structural Model Results: Facebook and Twitter Comparison

			Fit		
	χ^2	df	CFI	RMSEA	SRMR
Model 1: All social media	235.93	40	.98	.07	.05
Model 2: Facebook	383.70	40	.97	.09	.06
Model 3: Twitter	535.02	40	.96	.11	.06

Completely standardized path estimates and (t-values)

	Model 1 (All social media)		Model 2 (Facebook)		Model 3 (Twitter)	
Recycling						
Responsibility → Recycling: γ_{11}	−.03	(−.38)	−.10	(−1.35)	.14	(1.52)
Involvement → Recycling: γ_{12}	.03	(.39)	.03	(.44)	.01	(.11)
Internalization → Recycling: γ_{13}	.01	(.14)	−.05	(−.67)	−.01	(−.11)
Organics						
Responsibility → Organics: γ_{21}	.24	(3.39)	.23	(3.45)	.29	(3.39)
Involvement → Organics: γ_{22}	.07	(.96)	.07	(.99)	.09	(1.12)
Internalization → Organics: γ_{23}	.03	(.48)	.04	(.66)	.07	(.84)
Transportation						
Responsibility → Transportation: γ_{31}	−.20	(−1.90)	−.21	(−2.05)	.08	(.72)
Involvement → Transportation: γ_{32}	.47	(4.52)	.39	(3.84)	.39	(3.58)
Internalization → Transportation: γ_{33}	.19	(1.91)	.22	(2.30)	−.12	(−1.14)
Antimaterialism						
Responsibility → Antimaterialism: γ_{41}	.27	(3.44)	.24	(3.31)	.23	(2.52)
Involvement → Antimaterialism: γ_{42}	.07	(.95)	.07	(1.04)	.11	(1.27)
Internalization → Antimaterialism: γ_{43}	.17	(2.27)	.19	(2.75)	.25	(2.94)
Charity						
Responsibility → Charity: γ_{51}	.33	(5.26)	.23	(4.03)	.22	(2.57)
Involvement → Charity: γ_{52}	.05	(.73)	.08	(1.48)	−.05	(−.65)
Internalization → Charity: γ_{53}	.31	(5.12)	.38	(6.99)	.43	(5.46)

Notes: CFI = comparative fit index; RMSEA = root mean square error of approximation; SRMR = standardized root mean residual.

See Figure 1 for models. All χ^2 statistics were significant at the .01 level; t-values of 1.65 or greater are significant at the .05 level, and t-values of 2.33 or greater are significant at the .01 level.

females = 10.1 hours per week) and Germany (males = 12.4 hours per week, females = 10.7 hours per week). Therefore, the higher technology adoption rates in South Korea may have led South Koreans to be early adopters of Twitter, perhaps leaving consumers in the United States and Germany to adopt this social medium more highly in the near future.

South Korea's overall social media use is greater than that of the United States or Germany, thereby partially supporting H1 that social media will play a more prominent role in South Korea. The evidence from this study is consistent with the observation that the more collective a society is, all other things being equal, the more sustainable its motivations and activities will be. However, arguably the most important find-ing from this study (and in support of H3) is that the pattern of motives for sustainability on social media is more complex than expected, thereby stressing caution to advertisers involved in any way with green marketing on social media. Responsibility motives consistently lead to organic food purchase, antimate-rialistic views, and contributions to sustainable charities for all countries. Responsibility invokes behaviorism as its primary change mechanism, where rewards and punishments shape behavior. Changing simple rewards can change patterns of motivation. In fact, a long history of social engineering shows that mild rewards can indeed motivate many sustainable behaviors (e.g., Kahle and Beatty 1987). These findings have large implications for green advertising. Advertisers involved in the organic food market, social marketing campaigns to decrease materialism, or with sustainability-related charities should identify ways to reward consumers on social media for participating in sustainable behaviors. For example, a company selling organic foods could reward consumers with a coupon for a free organic food product after every 10 times a consumer uploads a receipt to the company's Facebook page showing purchase of the company's organic food product. Or a company could reward a customer with a free sustainable product sample after the customer follows the company on Twitter.

Involvement motives feature distinctly different patterns of behaviors among countries. In all countries, consumers with involvement motives are significantly more likely to recycle and use green transportation. However, involvement motives for consumers from the United States and Germany also significantly lead to organic food purchase and antimaterialistic views. It is particularly interesting that all countries associate involvement motives rather than responsibility motives with recycling and green transportation use. This means that consumers have moved past a stage of needing to be rewarded for recycling behaviors and green transportation use; they would rather feel involved with other consumers and with companies as encouragement to recycle and use green transit. Given that green advertising can be defined as promoting a green lifestyle with or without highlighting a product or service (Banerjee, Gulas, and Iyer 1995), green advertisers can capitalize on these findings by creating advertising campaigns where the consumer feels that he or she is doing a part in sustaining the future of the world. For example, a company could send a message out on social media that the company uses 50% recycled parts in making final products and tell consumers that by recycling, the consumer is taking a part in making more recycled goods and sustaining the planet. In addition, for advertisers involved in the transportation industry (e.g., city buses, energy-efficient cars), these findings suggest that consumers want to feel involved before committing to using sustainable transit. An energy-efficient car company could easily invoke this motive by posting ideas for new cars and seeking consumer feedback on social media, thereby involving the consumer in the design process. Specifically for the United States and Germany, both responsibility and involvement motives lead to organic food purchase and antimaterialistic views, suggesting that advertisers desiring to influence these behaviors can target either the motives of responsibility (e.g., rewards) or involvement (e.g., being part of a larger sustainable group).

Internalization, the highest level of attitude commitment, also exhibited different relationships to behaviors among countries. Respondents from all countries saw internalization motives as significantly leading to antimaterialistic views and contributions to sustainable charities. Only South Korean participants associated internalized motives with organic

food purchases, and only participants from the United States and Germany associated internalized motives with green transportation use. In South Korea, it is likely that internalized motives do not lead to green transportation use because using public transit is more of a necessity and a way to fit in with the community than a personal choice toward sustainability. Also, it is particularly interesting to note that both responsibility and internalization motives, but not involvement motives, lead to contributions to sustainable charities for all countries. This finding shows that donations of time and money to sustainable charities are coming about from two means—either the consumer feels obligated to support a company and desires a reward (e.g., a free T-shirt) the company will give in response to a contribution or the consumer internally supports sustainability and desires to support the company with no reward in return desired. Sustainable charities could benefit by targeting each of these groups. For consumers with internalized motives, charities need to ensure that they have a social media presence where consumers can find the company and make a contribution. For consumers with responsibility motives, charities should provide rewards to encourage charitable contributions (e.g., a bumper sticker, hat, or a post on the consumer's social media page thanking them for donating). Ironically, internalized motives are probably used to influence consumers more often than these motives are actually exhibited by consumers. It is likely that many of the advertisers devising strategies to influence sustainability have a core self-image tied to sustainability that is not found as strongly among the consumers whom advertisers are trying to reach with green advertisements, although further research would be needed to test this theory. To influence sustainable purchase and nonpurchase behaviors effectively, advertisers should take time to identify a target market clearly and appropriately to integrate the motives of this target market into green advertising design.

In terms of social media, Twitter and Facebook presented very different patterns in motivations, as expected from H2. Of all motive levels, the greatest differences between Facebook and Twitter occurred at the responsibility level of motivation. Facebook shows a significant negative relationship between responsibility motives and green transportation use, whereas Twitter shows no significant relationship. Also, although not significant, responsibility motives are negatively associated with recycling on Facebook, but positively associated with recycling on Twitter. Perhaps because communications tend to be longer and relationships more complex on Facebook, it provides more opportunity for extensive, deep social interaction and for motivations to manifest themselves (Tuten and Solomon 2012). Following this line of thought, consumers on Facebook would be more likely to hold involvement motives that relate to these deep social interactions rather than responsibility motives that are purely based on obligation and reward. With its shorter and less-involved communication, Twitter would thus be more likely to have users desiring less involvement and motivated more by responsibility, which is supported by the findings of this study. Between social media and among countries, motives on social media are quite different as to how they relate to sustainable behaviors. Advertisers need to acknowledge these complex relationships to be successful in social media marketing efforts.

CONCLUSION

Social media provide an ideal advertising medium for green advertisers because consumers can self-select into sustainable lifestyle groups. In addition, social media, as advertising media, may be especially important in understanding sustainability and green advertising because sustainability is inherently social. This research provides an initial look into how sustainability motives on social media differ by country and social medium. This research also provides advertisers with details about which motives to target on which social media and in which countries. If they want to achieve maximum advertising effectiveness and encourage consumers to go green, advertisers need to heed caution in developing mass-marketing campaigns blanketing all consumers and instead delve into the specific motives that consumers in different locations hold.

NOTE

1. Hu and Bentler (1999) recommend cutoffs of less than .06 for SRMR, less than .05 (great fit) to .08 (adequate fit) for RMSEA, and less than .95 for CFI.

REFERENCES

Bagozzi, Richard P. (2010), "Structural Equation Models Are Modelling Tools with Many Ambiguities: Comments Acknowledging the Need for Caution and Humility in Their Use," *Journal of Consumer Psychology,* 20 (2), 208–214.

Bamberg, Sebastian, Marcel Hunecke, and Anke Blöbaum (2007), "Social Context, Personal Norms and the Use of Public Transportation: Two Field Studies," *Journal of Environmental Psychology,* 27 (3), 190–203.

Banbury, Catherine, Robert Stinerock, and Saroja Subrahmanyan (2012), "Sustainable Consumption: Introspecting Across Multiple Lived Cultures," *Journal of Business Research,* 65 (4), 497–503.

Banerjee, Subhabrata, Charles Gulas, and Easwar Iyer (1995), "Shades of Green: A Multidimensional Analysis of Environmental Advertising," *Journal of Advertising,* 24 (2), 21–31.

Barker, Melissa S., Donald L. Barker, Nicholas F. Bormann, and Krista E. Neher (2008), *Social Media Marketing: A Strategic Approach,* Mason, OH: South-Western, Cengage Learning.

Barnhill, John (2011), "Internet, Advertising, and Marketing," in *Green Culture: An A-to-Z Guide,* Kevin Wehr and Paul Robbins, eds., Thousand Oaks, CA: Sage.

Browne, Michael W., and Robert Cudeck (1993), "Alternative Ways of Assessing Model Fit," in *Testing Structural Equation Models,* Kenneth A. Bollen and Scott J. Long, eds., Newbury Park, CA: Sage.

Brundtland, Gro H. (1987), *World Commission on Environment and Development: Our Common Future,* Oxford: Oxford University Press.

Buhrmester, Michael, Tracy Kwang, and Samuel D. Gosling (2011), "Amazon's Mechanical Turk: A New Source of Inexpensive, Yet High-Quality, Data?" *Perspectives on Psychological Science,* 6 (1), 3–5.

Burst Media (2010), "Consumers Willing to Spend More Green to Go 'Green,'" available at www.greenmarketing.com/files/2010_01_01.pdf (accessed February 12, 2013).

Byrne, Barbara M., and Sunita M. Stewart (2006), "Teacher's Corner: The MACS Approach to Testing for Multigroup Invariance of a Second-Order Structure: A Walk Through the Process," *Structural Equation Modeling,* 13 (2), 287–321.

Chang, Chingching (2011), "Feeling Ambivalent About Going Green: Implications for Green Advertising Processing," *Journal of Advertising,* 40 (4), 19–31.

Chaudhuri, Arjun, and Ross Buck (1995), "Media Differences in Rational and Emotional Responses to Advertising," *Journal of Broadcasting and Electronic Media,* 39 (1), 109–125.

ComScore (2011), "Average Time Spent on Social Networking Sites Across Geographies," available at www.comscore-datamine.com/2011/06/average-time-spent-on-social-networking-sites-across-geographies/ (accessed February 12, 2013).

Dholakia, Ruby R. (2006), "Gender and IT in the Household: Evolving Patterns of Internet Use in the United States," *Information Society,* 22 (4), 231–240.

Diamantopoulos, Adamantios, Bodo B. Schlegelmilch, Rudolf R. Sinkovics, and Greg M. Bohlen (2003), "Can Socio-Demographics Still Play a Role in Profiling Green Consumers? A Review of the Evidence and an Empirical Investigation," *Journal of Business Research,* 56 (6), 465–480.

Fornell, Claes, and David F. Larcker (1981), "Evaluating Structural Equation Models with Unobservable Variables and Measurement Error," *Journal of Marketing Research,* 18 (1), 39–50.

Friestad, Marian, and Peter Wright (1994), "The Persuasion Knowledge Model: How People Cope with Persuasion Attempts," *Journal of Consumer Research,* 21 (1), 1–31.

Hoffman, Donna L., Thomas P. Novak, and Randy Stein (2012), "Flourishing Independents or Languishing Interdependents: Two Paths from Self-Construal to Identification with Social Media," Social Science Research Network, available at http://ssrn.com/abstract=1990584/ (accessed February 12, 2013).

Hofstede, Geert (2001), *Culture's Consequences: Comparing Values, Behaviors, Institutions, and Organizations Across Nations,* Thousand Oaks, CA: Sage.

Hu, Li-tze, and Peter M. Bentler (1999), "Cutoff Criteria for Fit Indexes in Covariance Structure Analysis: Conventional Criteria Versus New Alternatives," *Structural Equation Modeling: A Multidisciplinary Journal,* 6 (1), 1–55.

Hughes, David J., Moss Rowe, Mark Batey, and Andrew Lee (2011), "A Tale of Two Sites: Twitter Vs. Facebook and the Personality Predictors of Social Media Usage," *Computers in Human Behavior,* 28 (2), 561–569.

Hung, Kineta, Stella Y. Li, and David K. Tse (2011), "Interpersonal Trust and Platform Credibility in a Chinese Multibrand Online Community," *Journal of Advertising,* 40 (3), 99–112.

Jöreskog, Karl G., and Dag Sörbom (1996), *LISREL 8 User's Reference Guide,* Lincolnwood, IL: Scientific Software.

Kahle, Lynn R., and Sharon E. Beatty (1987), "Cognitive Consequences of Legislating Postpurchase Behavior: Growing Up with the Bottle Bill," *Journal of Applied Social Psychology,* 17 (9), 828–843.

———, and Pierre Valette-Florence (2012), *Marketplace Lifestyles in an Age of Social Media: Theory and Method,* Armonk, NY: M.E. Sharpe.

———, Kenneth M. Kambara, and Gregory M. Rose (1996), "A Functional Model of Fan Attendance Motivations for College Football," *Sport Marketing Quarterly,* 5 (4), 51–60.

Kelman, Herbert C. (1958), "Compliance, Identification, and Internalization: Three Processes of Attitude Change," *Journal of Conflict Resolution,* 2 (1), 51–60.

Kollmuss, Anja, and Julian Agyeman (2002), "Mind the Gap: Why Do People Act Environmentally and What Are the Barriers to Pro-Environmental Behavior?" *Environmental Education Research,* 8 (3), 239–260.

La Ferle, Carrie, Steven M. Edwards, and Wei-Na Lee (2000), "Teens' Use of Traditional Media and the Internet," *Journal of Advertising Research,* 40 (3), 55–65.

Liu, Yuping, and L. J. Shrum (2002), "What Is Interactivity and Is It Always Such a Good Thing? Implications of Definition, Person, and Situation for the Influence of Interactivity on Advertising Effectiveness," *Journal of Advertising,* 31 (4), 53–64.

Longsworth, Annie (2011), "Green Brands Survey," Cohn & Wolfe; Landor Associates; Penn, Shoen, & Berland; Etsy Environmental Partners, available at www.cohnwolfe.com/en/ideas-insights/white-papers/green-brands-survey-2011/ (accessed February 12, 2013).

Lu, Zhi, Lynn R. Kahle, Sang M. Lee, and Sing-Young Lee (2012), "Football Fans' Contrasting Motivations: China, S. Korea, and the USA," *Asia Pacific Journal of Innovation and Entrepreneurship,* 6 (1), 9–32.

McLuhan, Marshall (1994/1964), *Understanding Media: The Extensions of Man,* Cambridge: MIT Press.

Paolacci, Gabriele, Jesse Chandler, and Panagiotis G. Ipeirotis (2010), "Running Experiments on Amazon Mechanical Turk," *Judgment and Decision Making,* 5 (5), 411–419.

Papacharissi, Zizi, and Elaine Yuan (2011), "What If the Internet Did Not Speak English? New and Old Language for Studying Newer Media Technologies," in *The Long History of New Media: Technology, Historiography, and Contextualizing Newness,* David W. Park, Nicholas W. Jankowski, and Steve Jones, eds., New York: Peter Lang.

Peattie, Ken (1995), *Environmental Marketing Management: Meeting the Green Challenge,* London: Pitman.

———, and Sue Peattie (2009), "Social Marketing: A Pathway to Consumption Reduction?" *Journal of Business Research,* 62 (2), 260–268.

Shrum, L. J. (2004), *The Psychology of Entertainment Media: Blurring the Lines Between Entertainment and Persuasion,* Mahwah, NJ: Lawrence Erlbaum.

Steenkamp, Jan-Benedict, and Hans Baumgartner (1998), "Assessing Measurement Invariance in Cross-National Consumer Research," *Journal of Consumer Research,* 25 (1), 78–107.

Steiger, James H. (2007), "Understanding the Limitations of Global Fit Assessment in Structural Equation Modeling," *Personality and Individual Differences,* 42 (5), 893–898.

Thøgersen, John (2010), "Country Differences in Sustainable Consumption: The Case of Organic Food," *Journal of Macromarketing,* 30 (2), 171–185.

Tillinghast, Tig (2010), "Customers Reward Marketing and Advertising That Employs 'Green' Messages, According to New Report from Environmental Leader," Business Wire, available at www.businesswire.com/news/home/20100107005422/en/Customers-Reward-Marketing-Advertising-Employs-%E2%80%9CGreen%E2%80%9D-Messages/ (accessed February 12, 2013).

Trevino, Marcella B. (2011), "Communication, Global, and Regional," in *Green Culture: An A-to-Z Guide,* Kevin Wehr and Paul Robbins, eds., Thousand Oaks, CA: Sage.

Triandis, Harry C., Robert Bontempo, Marcelo J. Villareal, Masaaki Asai, and Nydia Lucca (1988), "Individualism and Collectivism: Cross-Cultural Perspectives on Self-Ingroup Relationships," *Journal of Personality and Social Psychology,* 54 (2), 323–338.

Tuten, Tracy, and Michael Solomon (2012), *Social Media Marketing,* Englewood Cliffs, NJ: Prentice Hall.

Viscusi, W. Kip, Joel Huber, and Jason Bell (2011), "Promoting Recycling: Private Values, Social Norms, and Economic Incentives," *American Economic Review,* 101 (3), 65–70.

Zinkhan, George M., and Les Carlson (1995), "Green Advertising and the Reluctant Consumer," *Journal of Advertising,* 24 (2), 1–6.

THE EFFECTIVENESS OF BENEFIT TYPE AND PRICE ENDINGS IN GREEN ADVERTISING

Marla B. Royne, Jennifer Martinez, Jared Oakley, and Alexa K. Fox

ABSTRACT: This study assesses consumer perceptions of advertising messages for two proenvironmental products by examining the effectiveness of environmental versus personal benefit appeals and .99 versus .00 price endings. The authors borrow from Prospect Theory and Mental Accounting Theory to explain consumers' perceptions of psychological pricing and product attributes. In addition, the moderating role of environmental skepticism is assessed as it relates to the effectiveness of environmentally friendly advertisements. Results indicate that consumers feel that some products advertised with environmental appeals are more costly, but are not perceived as lower quality as compared with products advertised with personal benefits. Findings also indicate a price ending × appeal interaction for two different products, but the effects vary between the products. Finally, environmental skepticism is found to moderate perceptions of the message appeal. Implications are provided.

Consumer concern about the environment has increased considerably in recent years (Chitra 2007) and the development of green products and the concomitant use of green advertising continue to grow. The number of environmentally friendly products available for consumer purchase increased from about 2,700 to 4,700 between 2009 and 2010 (Terrachoice 2010), a growth rate of more than 73%. Other evidence indicates that green advertising has grown exponentially during the last two decades. From September 2006 to August 2007, the equivalent of nearly $26.9 million was spent on advertising containing the words "CO2," "carbon," "environmental," "emissions," or "recycle" (Futerra 2008). Moreover, 5% of the full-page ads placed in *The Atlantic, National Geographic, National Review,* and *Time* during the January 2005–June 2011 time frame were considered "green" (Svoboda 2011).

Despite this vast growth in both green products and green advertising, along with indications that consumption of such

products reached an all-time high (Saad 2007), about 41% of consumers indicate they do *not* buy green products because of their perceived inferiority (Pickett-Baker and Ozaki 2008). This inconsistency is likely a function of consumers having both positive and negative evaluations about green products (Chang 2011).

If green products are to become well accepted in the marketplace, it is critical to understand the specific factors, or combination of factors, that should be included in advertising developed to promote such products. One important question is whether the inclusion of the environmental benefits of an eco-friendly product in an ad influences consumer perceptions of the product. Research on this issue can inform firms seeking to design optimum advertising messages for their environmentally friendly products. Moreover, as Vlosky, Ozanne, and Fontenot (1999) note, marketers must carefully set prices for green products while considering consumers' sensitivity to cost. Although some research shows that consumers are willing to pay more for green products (Chen 2008; Laroche, Bergeron, and Barbaro-Forleo 2001; Royne, Levy, and Martinez 2011), to our knowledge, no studies exist that consider consumer response to specific types of pricing approaches in the advertising of green products.

There is much to learn in this area. Considerable research has demonstrated that consumer attitudes and buying behavior for green products represent a paradox. On the surface, a large number of U.S. consumers claim that they are environmentally concerned (Osterhus 1997; Ottman 2011; Shrum, McCarty, and Lowrey 1995). Yet this concern does not clearly translate into purchasing behavior for green products (Pickett-Baker and Ozaki 2008). While many firms have launched new products in response to the shifting concern for the environment and sustainability, market share for most green products remains low (Luchs et al. 2010).

The purpose of this research is to extend the understanding of consumer perceptions of advertising messages for proenvironmental products by examining the effectiveness of two types of benefit appeals along with psychological pricing strategies and their role in perceptions of the environmentally friendly product. Although considerable literature has examined the effects of .99 price endings, research investigating the influence of this ending within the context of advertising message appeals is quite limited, yet very much needed (Choi, Lee, and Ji 2012). To better explain consumer perceptions of product benefits and different price endings, we borrow from Prospect Theory (Kahneman and Tversky 1979) and Mental Accounting Theory (Thaler 1985) to guide our research. Study 2 extends Study 1 by further examining the use of .99 price endings and benefit types, but also investigates the moderating role of environmental skepticism in the perceptions of these types of advertisements for an environmentally friendly product.

BACKGROUND

Environmental concern has reemerged as an important topic in both the popular press and academic literature, but current discussion is focused primarily on sustainability. Although sustainability may be a relatively new business strategy, its underlying concepts are not. In fact, environmental concern was first identified as a popular issue in 1962, when Rachel Carson published *Silent Spring* (Carson 1962). Banerjee and McKeage (1994) noted the emergence of environmental concern following the first observance of Earth Day in 1970, which brought environmental destruction into the spotlight. Heightened media attention surrounding air and water pollution, ozone depletion, and other environmental issues led to increased legislation (Landler, Schiller, and Smart 1991), new products created to appeal to those with a concern for the environment (Dillingham 1990), and substantial increases in firms' spending on green advertising (Iyer and Banerjee 1992).

Adults have shown concern for environmental issues since the 1970s (Dunlap 2002). In 1991, about 90% of consumers responding to a popular press poll claimed they were concerned about how the products they purchase affect the environment (Cramer 1991). More recent research indicates that 91% of consumers feel that if they don't take care of our planet, future generations will suffer (Mohan 2011). The same report indicates that 78% of consumers believe more than ever that buying green is a way to consider their values and ethics in their shopping choices (Mohan 2011). These consumers are what Ottman (1992) defines as "environmentally conscious," or "those who actively seek out products perceived as having relatively little impact on the environment."

Growing environmental awareness and concern has led to an increased number of individuals who proactively engage in using environmentally friendly products in their daily lives (Kalafatis et al. 1999). As a result, firms are recognizing the advantages of environmentally friendly marketing strategies (Luo and Bhattacharya 2006), and there has been a proliferation of green marketing and advertising to serve those consumers (Kalafatis et al. 1999). In fact, about 60% of executives consider climate change an important issue when developing and marketing new products (McKinsey and Company 2008). Specifically, many consumer product marketers tailor advertising messages to environmentally concerned consumers. However, little research has documented how consumers actually react to the use of environmental benefits in advertisements. Moreover, despite reports of consumers' willingness to pay more for an environmentally friendly product, to date, no research has examined the use of pricing strategies in advertisements for environmentally friendly products. Hence, our research considers the type of benefit appeal and the use of psychological price endings on consumer perceptions of green products.

Advertising Appeals

Advertisers face several decisions when developing print advertising, and green advertising is no exception. Banerjee, Gulas, and Iyer (1995) define green advertising as any ad that contains at least one of the following three criteria: (1) explicitly or implicitly addresses the relationship between a product/service and the biophysical environment; (2) promotes a green lifestyle with or without highlighting a product/service; or (3) presents a corporate image of environmental responsibility.

One key decision when promoting an environmentally friendly product is the type of message appeal to use and how to appropriately frame this message. For example, should the message framing highlight the product's environmental benefits or should advertisers provide information about the product's attributes that are more beneficial to the consumer (e.g., value, ease of use)? Some consumers may be perplexed by the many claims of environmentally friendly products that appear to be contradictory (Maronick and Andrews 1999), oversimplified (Morris, Hastak, and Mazis 1995), or exaggerated (Mayer, Scammon, and Gray-Lee 1993). Some evidence suggests that the efficacy of advertising messages that tout proenvironmental benefits may be context-specific. That is, when the use of a product is aligned to a need for a gentle effect (e.g., baby shampoo), it will be perceived more positively than when the need is for strength and durability (e.g., automobile tires) (Luchs et al. 2010). In short, framing the advertising message based on the consumers' greatest perceived gain is essential. Therefore, we further explore these issues through the lens of Prospect Theory.

Prospect Theory proposes that individuals value gains and losses differently based on whether the choice is displayed in a risk-averse or risk-seeking manner, and that attitudes toward risks concerning gains may be very different from their attitudes concerning losses (Kahneman and Tversky 1979). Several researchers have defined the framing effect in the context of choice under uncertainty (Kahneman and Tversky 1979; Puto 1987; Thaler 1985; Tversky and Kahneman 1981). Generally, framing is observed when buyers alter their choice among alternatives in response to changes in the frame of reference of these alternatives (Berger and Smith 1998).

Prospect Theory in advertising has traditionally assessed how consumers perceive messages framed in terms of either gains or losses. Several studies have extended Prospect Theory to consider similar, but less strict, framing effects. For example, Salminen and Wallenius (1993) tested the decision-making process by giving participants two options for a particular decision: (1) a positive anchor point, and (2) an additional perceived gain. These choices, therefore, represent varying degrees of positivity as opposed to the more traditional one positive and one negative option. Participants chose alternative 2 as significantly more appealing, supporting Prospect Theory; although the first alternative was still positive, participants changed their initial choice based on the perceived gain offered in option 2. Berger and Smith (1998) studied Prospect Theory in advertising to assess consumer reactions through an experiment with three ads utilizing different message frames: product attributes, price frames, or a message framed in terms of product outcome. Results of this study indicated that in contrast to product attributes or price information, framing an advertisement in terms of buyer outcome has greater influence on purchase judgment, as long as the framing is in a positive valence. Extending the work of Berger and Smith (1998) in applying Prospect Theory to advertising, the current study examines the effect of product attribute framing (personal benefit versus environmental benefit) on the overall product judgment, such as product quality.

Advertising message appeals are generally based on consumers' motivations for purchase. Although consumers' goals may differ in their buying decisions (Bettman, Luce, and Payne 1998), there tends to be cognitive consistency in matching risks (both financial and nonfinancial) to reward (Murphy and Ennis 1986). The perceived quality of a product is of likely concern in this process. When individuals have no experience or knowledge of an item, they tend to develop an evoked set that is predicated on both informational cues in the product claims and some lower-level attributes that might include packaging and price (Zeithaml 1988). Only product attributes that are judged by the individual as important are considered in the evaluative process. In the case of an environmentally friendly product with additional attributes that benefit the consumer in personal ways, the consumer could perceive either functional or symbolic benefits (Keller 1993). These perceptions subsequently converge to determine the value of the product (Zeithaml 1988). In the case of a product that has benefits to both the consumer and the greater good (i.e., the

environment), much of what we know about consumer judgments surrounding quality and price may be confounded.

Marketers understand that an ad must appeal to the intended consumer for that consumer to gain interest in the advertised product, perceive that product in a positive manner, and, ultimately, create a desire to purchase that product. Hence, advertisements use a variety of benefits to appeal to the intended target consumer. These benefits can be financial (saving the consumer money), temporal (providing time savings and efficiency), or environmental (geared toward altruistic consumers), to name a few. An understanding of which benefits to use when advertising an environmental product is particularly important because although consumers often desire products with environmental benefits (Carlson, Grove, and Kangun 1993), their motivations may stem from different areas.

Research shows that environmental consumerism is not keeping pace with the increasing number of consumers who report they are "very concerned about the environment" (Roper Consulting 2010). This may be due, in part, to the perceived inferiority of green products. Ottman (1998) found that 41% of people believe that green products do not work as well as conventional products, and a number of environmentally friendly products have been spotlighted in the media because of quality-related concerns (e.g., Appell 2007; Phillips 2008). It has also been noted that consumers often feel confused about the environmental claims in advertisements (Mayer, Scammon, and Gray-Lee 1993). Adding to the difficulty in advertising and selling green products is the perception that such products are more expensive. Roper's Green Gauge Report (2010) reports that 74% of consumers say that green products cost more than traditional products. Based on these general beliefs permeating the literature, and because Prospect Theory suggests that consumers view known personal gains as risk averse and more positive while viewing environmental gains as riskier, we believe that consumers will respond differently to ads including an environmental benefit appeal as compared with a personal benefit appeal. Hence, we offer the following hypotheses:

Hypothesis 1: The perceived quality of an advertised product will be lower when the advertisement uses an environmental benefit appeal than when it uses a personal benefit appeal.

Hypothesis 2: The perceived price of an advertised product will be higher when the advertisement uses an environmental benefit appeal than when it uses a personal benefit appeal.

Psychological Price Endings

Also affecting consumer perceptions is the advertised selling price of a product. Consumers may use price as a heuristic for determining quality, but the extent to which they do will hinge on other quality cues that are present (Zeithaml 1988).

Research over the years shows that the "just below" .99 price ending signals a low price appeal (Bliss 1952; Harper 1966; Schindler 2003), perceptions of a more discounted price (Freling et al. 2010; Schindler and Kibarian 2001), and a lower-quality image (Freling et al. 2010). This may be based on the belief that nine-ending prices are used more often for discount prices than for regular prices (Huston and Kamdar 1996) and the perception that lower-priced retailers use nine-ending prices (Stiving 2000). Moreover, such effects are based on the idea that consumers distort the perceptions of .99 price endings and view them as perceptually lower prices than the true value. As a result, they are construed more favorably than the .00 round number ending (Lambert 1975; Nagle and Holden 1995).

Ironically, Schindler (2001) found that products in the marketplace with the .99 price ending were *not* actually lower in price than products with the .00 price ending; moreover, products with the .99 price ending were perceived to be of both favorable and unfavorable quality (Schindler and Kibarian 2001). This discrepancy may be related to the image of a retailer with either a favorable or unfavorable quality image and not directly related to the price ending given to an individual product. This suggests that other factors such as the message may also affect the perception of the .99 price ending, a finding supported by Choi, Lee, and Ji (2012). Hence, there is reason to believe that the price ending will interact with the appeal type.

Various explanations have been postulated to explain psychological pricing. For example, Schindler and Kirby (1997) suggest that rounding down requires less cognitive effort than rounding up. Another argument is that consumers pay less attention to the last two digits of a price (Basu 1997; Bizer and Schindler 2005; Stiving and Winer 1997). However, to better understand the reasons behind the effectiveness of psychological pricing, it is important to examine how the cognitive accessibility of numbers may play a role in comparing a given price with its perceived reference price. Accessibility, in this context, is defined as the ease with which an individual can retrieve a mental representation of a number or set of numbers (Fazio et al. 1982).

In multiple studies where individuals made numerical estimates, respondents consistently demonstrated a proclivity for generating values that ended in 0 (e.g., Dehaene and Mehler 1992; Hornik, Cherian, and Zakay 1994; Hultsman, Hultsman, and Black 1989; Huttenlocher, Hedges, and Bradburn 1990; Schindler and Wiman 1989; Tarrant and Manfredo 1993). Moreover, when consumers were asked to recall prices for various products, their mental formulations generally ended in 0 (Schindler and Wiman 1989). The propensity for recalling numbers with .00 endings speaks to the prevailing accessibility of this number over others from a cognitive perspective. It also suggests that prices ending

in .00 are a likely ending for a reference price (Schindler and Kirby 1997).

Borrowing from the idea of framing within Prospect Theory (Kahneman and Tversky 1979), this tendency toward accessibility of .00 endings could play a pivotal role in assessing value. That is, consumers would likely perceive a price ending in .99 as a financial gain over an easily assessed reference price ending in .00. Although this amount represents a nominal numerical value, the S-shaped curve of gains and losses in Prospect Theory indicates that the way consumers evaluate gains and losses is not linear. This means that a .05 reduction could create a perception of a significant gain when tied to a $5 starting point compared with a .05 reduction on a higher stated price. Moreover, small and immediate gains tend to have a disproportionately larger positive effect on perceived outcomes compared with subsequent units of gain that accumulate (Schindler and Kirby 1997). Mental Accounting Theory (Thaler 1985) further builds on this concept by demonstrating that prices that are lower than reference prices tend to create a perception of a positive transaction utility for the consumer. Thaler (1985) also showed that when consumers evaluate the outcomes of purchase transactions, segregating individual perceived gains creates a more positive outcome as opposed to accumulating the gains into one single amount. This seems to be the path that most retailers have chosen with consumers; there is well-documented evidence of a preponderance of .99 price endings (Schindler and Kibarian 1996).

Empirical evidence suggests that a .99 price ending is generally associated with a discounted price (a perceived gain by the consumer) and lower quality (Schindler 1991, 2001; Schindler and Kibarian 1996), while a .00 ending is generally associated with a higher price and higher quality (Schindler, Parsa, and Naipaul 2011; Stiving 2000). Moreover, as noted, environmentally friendly products are generally believed to be more expensive (e.g., Roper Consulting 2010). We believe that the additive effects of the .00 price ending with the environmental benefit appeal (no financial gain combined with general beliefs about the expensive nature of environmentally friendly products) will result in a higher perceived price than when the product is advertised with a .99 price ending and an environmental benefit appeal, or when it is advertised with a .00 ending and a personal benefit appeal. Moreover, we expect that the ad featuring a .99 price ending and a personal benefit appeal will produce a lower product price perception than the .99 price ending with the environmental appeal or the .00 ending paired with the personal benefit appeal. Hence, we propose the following interaction effects:

Hypothesis 3a: Products featured in ads with .00 price endings that emphasize environmental benefits will be perceived as more expensive than those featured in ads with .99 price endings that emphasize environmental benefits or those featured in ads with .00 price endings that emphasize personal benefits.

Hypothesis 3b: Products featured in ads with .99 price endings that emphasize personal benefits will be perceived as less expensive than those featured in ads with .99 price endings that emphasize environmental benefits or those featured in ads with .00 price endings that emphasize personal benefits.

Similarly, if environmental products are perceived as lower quality and the .99 ending is also indicative of a lower-quality product and a financial gain, this combination should result in an overall lower level of perceived quality than a product advertised with personal benefits and a .99 ending, or a product advertised with environmental benefits and a .00 ending. Conversely, a product advertised with personal benefits and a .00 ending should result in a higher level of perceived quality than a product advertised with personal benefits and a .99 ending, or a product advertised with environmental benefits and a .99 ending. Specifically, we propose the following:

Hypothesis 4a: Products featured in ads with .99 endings that emphasize environmental benefits will be perceived as lower in quality than products advertised with personal benefits paired with a .99 ending, or products advertised with environmental benefits paired with a .00 ending.

Hypothesis 4b: Products featured in ads with .00 endings that emphasize personal benefits will be perceived as higher in quality than products advertised with personal benefits paired with a .99 ending, or products advertised with environmental benefits paired with a .00 ending.

STUDY 1

Method

To test the proposed hypotheses, we developed a 2 × 2 experimental design with benefit type (environmental or personal) and price appeal (.99 or .00) as the two factors. The product used in Study 1 was an environmentally friendly liquid body wash, an increasingly popular product among consumers that now accounts for 40% of the total soap, bath, and shower market (Thau 2011); in addition, liquid body wash sales are expected to increase by 35% between 2009 and 2014 (Thau 2011). Although body wash is popular among female consumers, revenue for men's formulas increased from 17% of the liquid body soap market in 2005 to 28% of its share in 2008 (Newman 2009), indicating that body wash is a relevant product for both male and female consumers. College students likely play an important role in this escalating market share, with an increasing number of body wash brands specifically targeting young men and women. For example, an advertisement for body wash in Stanford University's campus newspaper, *The*

Daily Stanford, specifically targeted male students by extolling the efficacy of body wash in attracting the opposite sex (Safire 2007). To maintain realism, we used an actual product with its real brand name, but to ensure that knowledge of the brand did not influence perceptions, the last item on the questionnaire assessed the participants' existing knowledge of the product; this item was subsequently included in our model as a control variable.

An existing advertisement for another green product was used as the basis for developing the stimuli. The color advertisement depicted the image of the item as well as copy describing its key benefits. In one ad, the pro-environmental benefits of the product were stressed, while the second ad emphasized personal benefits. Psychological pricing was manipulated by presenting each product in the ad as priced with either a .99 or .00 ending.

Manipulation Check

To ensure that the latent benefit manipulation (environmental versus personal) was successful, a manipulation check was conducted well before the execution of the actual study (Perdue and Summers 1986). This allowed us to demonstrate that the messages aligned with each ad were indeed perceived as having either environmental or personal benefits. The product was shown with one of the two message strategies, which was accomplished by changing verbiage in the ads.

A total of 57 students each responded to a two-item scale assessing the level of both personal benefits and environmental benefits in one of the two ads. *T*-test results indicated that the ad with the environmental benefits was perceived as containing significantly more environmental benefits than the ad with personal benefits ($t = 4.70$, $p < .001$), and the ad with personal benefits was perceived as having significantly more personal benefits than the ad containing environmental benefits ($t = -4.99, p < .001$), indicating that each message strategy had the desired effect of communicating either proenvironmental benefits or personal benefits.

Sample and Procedure

Subjects were recruited from upper-division business classes and given a small amount of extra credit in exchange for their participation. Students were randomly assigned to one of four treatments to accommodate the 2 (benefit appeal) × 2 (price ending) study design. Participants were provided with a booklet that contained three ads: one of the four test ads and two filler ads unrelated to the product of interest. In all four conditions, the test ad was in the middle of the two others. Subjects were instructed to look at the ad for as long as they wished and then complete the questionnaire at their own pace. They were also told not to look back at the ads while

TABLE I
MANCOVA Results: *F*-tests

	Wilks's λ	Perceived price	Perceived quality
Body wash			
Independent variable			
Price ending	.437	.010	.787
Benefit appeal	1.06	1.21	1.44
Prior knowledge	.224	.07	.44
Price × benefit	4.84**	4.90**	6.27**
Car wash			
Independent variable			
Price ending	1.33	.393	2.15
Benefit appeal	5.37***	7.41***	4.16**
Prior knowledge	.163	.05	.264
Price × benefit	2.69*	5.21**	.421

Note: MANCOVA = multivariate analysis of covariance.

* *p* < .10.

** *p* ≤ .05.

*** *p* < 01.

completing the questionnaire. The questionnaire began with a thought-listing procedure and was followed by simple measures to assess participants' perceptions of quality and price, as well as their previous knowledge of the product. Demographic information was also collected. Cell sizes ranged from 19 to 22, for a total sample size of 84 students. The final sample was 37.3% female; 72.5% were ages 18 to 25, 22.5% were 26 to 35, 3.8% were 36 to 45, and 1.3% were 46 to 55.

Measures

To assess perceived price and perceived quality, we used single-item measures that included one item from Schindler and Kibarian's (2001) study of .99 price endings. Because our goal was to ascertain participants' simple assessments of quality and perceptions of expensiveness, we chose to use a single item measure based on Bergkvist and Rossiter (2007), who argued that for many constructs consisting of a concrete singular attribute, it is preferable to use single-item measures. This is consistent with others (e.g., Burke and Edell 1986; Burton and Lichtenstein 1988; Drolet and Morrison 2011; Park and Young 1986) who claim that the use of single-item measures in marketing and advertising research is appropriate. For perceived quality, participants responded to the question, "How would you rate the quality of XYZ product?" The seven-point

scale had "low quality" and "high quality" as the endpoints. For perceived price, participants responded to the statement "The price of XYZ product is . . . ," with "inexpensive" and "expensive" as the endpoints of a seven-point scale. The last question asked the participants, "Prior to this study, how familiar were you with XYZ product?" A seven-point scale with the endpoints "not familiar at all" and "very familiar" was included.

Analysis and Results

Because of the potential correlation between the two dependent measures, we utilized MANCOVA (multivariate analysis of covariance). Benefit type and price ending were the two factors, with perceived price and perceived quality as the dependent measures. Prior knowledge was included as a control variable. As indicated in Table 1, neither the main effect for price ending nor the benefit appeal is significant at the multivariate level ($p > .10$) or the univariate level ($p > .10$). Hence, neither H1 nor H2 is supported. However, the price × benefit interaction is significant at both the multivariate (Wilks's λ, $F = 4.84$, $p < .05$) and the univariate level for both perceived price ($F = 4.90$, $p = .05$) and perceived quality ($F = 6.27$, $p < .05$). As indicated in Table 2 and Figure 1, the ad with the environmental appeal and the .00 ending produces the highest

TABLE 2
Descriptive Statistics

Benefit appeal	Price ending	Cell size	Perceived price means	Perceived quality means
		Body wash		
Environmental	.00	22	6.11	5.03
	.99	19	5.33	4.45
Personal	.00	20	4.99	3.69
	.99	22	5.70	4.91
		Car wash		
Environmental	.00	22	4.08	3.52
	.99	21	4.68	4.13
Personal	.00	22	3.92	3.13
	.99	22	2.86	3.36

perceived price. H3 predicted that products featured in ads with .00 endings that emphasize environmental benefits would be perceived as more expensive than an ad with environmental benefits and a .99 price ending or an ad with personal benefits and a .00 price ending. Perceived price for the environmental appeal by .00 price ending product = 6.11, which is significantly different from the ad with personal benefits and the .00 ending ($M = 4.99$, $t = 2.19$, $p < .05$), but is not significantly different from ads emphasizing environmental benefits and a .99 price ending ($M = 5.33$, $t = 1.62$, $p > .10$). Hence, H3a is partially supported.

The perceived price of the product advertised with personal benefits and the .99 ending ($M = 5.70$) did not differ significantly from the perceived price of the product featured with environmental benefits and a .99 ending ($M = 5.33$, $t = 1.65$, $p = .10$), or the perceived price of the product advertised with personal benefits and the .00 ending ($M = 4.99$, $t = 1.75$, $p = .09$). Hence, H3b is not supported.

H4a posited that a product advertised with .99 endings and environmental benefits will result in lower-quality perceptions ($M = 4.45$) than personal benefit ads with a .99 ending ($M = 4.91$) or environmental benefit ads with a .00 ending ($M = 5.03$). As shown in Figure 1, the means are in the predicted direction; however, the differences are not significant ($p > .05$). H4b proposed that a product advertised with .00 endings and personal benefits will be perceived as having higher quality than a product advertised with personal benefits and a .99 price ending ($M = 4.91$) or an environmental benefit appeal paired with a .00 ending ($M = 5.03$). As indicated in Figure 1, the ad with a .00 price ending and personal benefits actually results in the lowest level of perceived quality ($M = 3.69$), and this combination is significantly different

from the perceived quality of the product advertised with environmental appeals and the .00 price ending ($M = 5.03$, $t = 2.64$, $p < .05$), which actually produced the highest-quality perceptions. Hence, H4 is not supported.

Discussion

Our results from Study 1 indicate that the product advertised with an environmental appeal and a .00 price ending produced the highest-quality perceptions and the highest-perceived price, while the ad with the personal benefit appeal and a .99 price ending ranked slightly lower on these measures, but not at a significantly different level. Moreover, the general pattern of the treatment means suggests that consumers may be equating higher perceived price with higher perceived quality. It is interesting to note that our results show that there was no significant difference between the two treatments utilizing the .99 price ending for both dependent variables, but the effect of the .00 price ending does differ based on the type of appeal used. To further investigate our findings, we used a second product in a second study to test our four hypotheses. In addition, we sought to assess the potential moderating role of environmental skepticism on the perceptions of price and quality.

STUDY 2

Environmental Skepticism

As noted, despite the popularity of the environmental movement and the recent increase in consumer environmental concern, green products, and green advertising, the actual purchasing of green products and patronage of green firms is

FIGURE 1
Interaction Effects: Body Wash Product

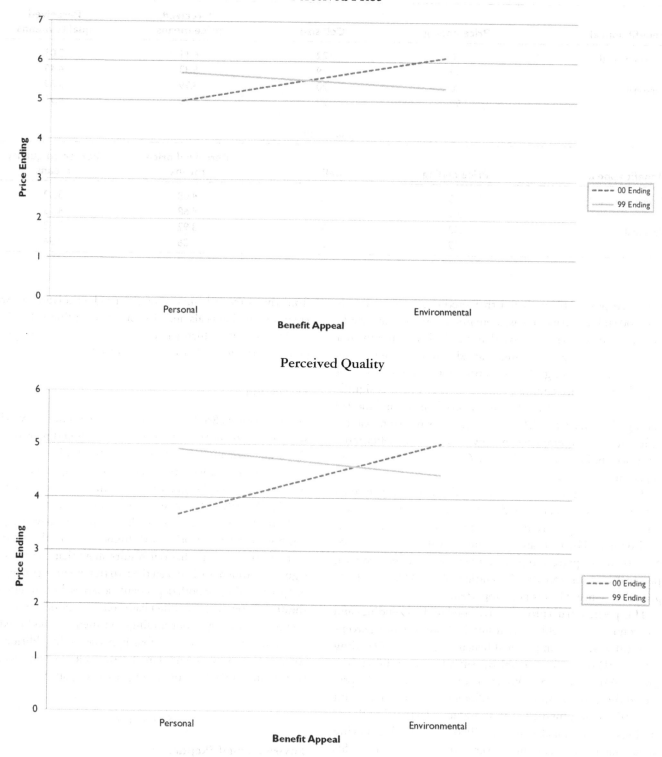

Perceived Price

Perceived Quality

not representative of the level of self-professed environmental concern by consumers (Gregory and Di Leo 2003; Mayer, Scammon and Gray-Lee 1993; Shrum, McCarty, and Lowrey 1995). In fact, many consumers still view green product claims with skepticism.

There have been numerous reports of customer dissatisfaction with some green products. For example, after the market release of compact fluorescent light bulbs (CFL), news reports claimed these bulbs contained a level of mercury that posed a potential health hazard to consumers (Appell 2007). When Wal-Mart changed the shape of their large milk containers to a square form to reduce storage and shipping costs, customers found the items clumsy and difficult to use (Phillips 2008). Toyota was forced to halt advertisements for their hybrid car, the Prius, in the United Kingdom after it was determined that its environmental efficiency was exaggerated (Marketing Week 2007). Moreover, the Federal Trade Commission (FTC) has expressed concern that general marketing claims of environmentally friendly benefits can be misleading because they leave the consumer with the impression that the product poses no harm to any element of the environment, which is almost never the case (Walker 2011).

Perhaps because of these reports, there is a distinct segment of highly skeptical consumers who intentionally avoid considering any product that references proenvironmental benefits. One study estimated this segment to be about 10% of the population and coined the term the "Never-Greens" based on their unwavering skepticism toward environmental conditions (Edwards 2008).

Skepticism toward advertising is often grounded in Friestad and Wright's (1994) Persuasion Knowledge Model (PKM). Friestad and Wright (1994) determined that consumers have varying levels of knowledge about persuasion attempts by others. The PKM posits that consumers assess the persuasion techniques of selling messages and may cope with high levels of persuasion knowledge through learned consumer skepticism. Advancing this framework further, Obermiller and Spangenberg (1998) found that consumers who possess high levels of ad skepticism might be impossible to persuade because of their disbelief of the stated claim. Applying this theoretical framework to the general notion of environmental skepticism suggests that consumers with very high levels of environmental skepticism would be difficult to persuade with advertisements emphasizing the environmental benefits of an eco-friendly product.

A consumer's level of environmental skepticism may also affect his or her response to a particular price ending. Baumgarner and Steiner (2007) argued that consumers are not homogeneous in their beliefs about odd- and even-priced products. Since consumers vary in their degree of environmental skepticism and because consumers' level of environmental

skepticism would likely affect their responses to the environmental benefit appeal, we pose the following hypotheses:

Hypothesis 5: Environmental skepticism will moderate the relationship between benefit appeal and perceived quality. More specifically, when ads include environmental benefits, (a) lower levels of environmental skepticism will result in higher levels of perceived quality, and (b) higher levels of environmental skepticism will result in lower levels of perceived quality.

Hypothesis 6: Environmental skepticism will moderate the relationship between benefit appeal and perceived price. More specifically, when ads include environmental benefits, (a) higher levels of environmental skepticism will result in higher levels of perceived product price, and (b) lower levels of environmental skepticism will result in lower levels of perceived product price.

Sample and Procedure

For Study 2, we used a car wash product. We chose a car wash product for several reasons. First, in Study 1, we used a product that a person uses on his or her body; for Study 2, we wanted a product that was used on a possession (an object), but was somewhat similar to the product used in Study 1. Furthermore, although men do use body wash, it is a product used more by women. In Study 2, we chose a product that is also used by both sexes, but may be used more by men. In 2010, the automobile wax, polish, and wash market was valued at $83 million (McCracken, Cimilluca, and Byron 2010). Although car care products are often thought of as male-dominated purchases, 78% of female drivers feel that regular preventive vehicle maintenance is important (Paradise 2004). Moreover, 49% of students at national universities keep cars at college (Hopkins 2011), indicating that car wash products are very relevant for many college students. Finally, the data was collected on a university campus where 91% of students keep cars on campus (*U.S. News & World Report* 2011), in part because many of the students who attend the university are commuter students.

The same basic ad from the first study was used except that the wording was slightly changed to reflect the type of wash. Once again, we used a real product, so the brand name was also different. A separate sample of 87 students was randomly assigned to one of four groups to accommodate the 2 (benefit appeal) × 2 (price ending) study design. Cell sizes ranged from 19 to 22, and we followed the same process used in the first study. That is, subjects first viewed three different print ads for as long as they wished and then completed the questionnaire at their own pace. Questions were the same as in Study 1 except the product type and name were adjusted as appropriate. In addition, to measure environmental skepticism, we adapted

TABLE 3
Means for Main Effects

Dependent variable	Body wash	
	Perceived price	Perceived quality
Benefit		
Environmental	5.69	4.76
Personal	5.38	4.26
Price ending		
.99	5.60	4.67
.00	5.48	4.35

Dependent variable	Car wash	
	Perceived price	Perceived quality
Benefit		
Environmental	4.39	3.83
Personal	3.38	3.25
Price ending		
.99	3.77	3.33
.00	4.02	3.75

Mohr, Eroglu, and Ellen's (1998) four-item measure of consumer skepticism; a seven-point Likert scale was used.

Two items were discarded after reliability and validity analyses; the resulting coefficient α was .69. The two items were "Most environmental claims on package labels or in advertising are intended to mislead rather than to inform consumers," and "Because environmental claims are exaggerated, consumers would be better off if such claims on package labels or in advertising were eliminated."

Demographic information was also collected. The sample for the second study was 56.3% female; 81.6% were ages 18 to 25, 12.6% were 26 to 35, 1.1% were 36 to 45, 3.4% were 46 to 55, and 1.1% were 56 to 65.

Analysis and Results

As in the first study, a manipulation check was conducted in advance of the study with two separate samples of ($n = 30$ and $n = 28$) of student participants. Again, each sample responded to the two questions on environmental and personal benefits for one of the two product ads. Results indicated that the ad with the environmental benefits was perceived as containing significantly more environmental benefits than the ad with personal benefits ($t = 2.25, p < .05$), and the ad featuring personal benefits was perceived as having significantly more personal benefits than the ad containing environmental benefits ($t = -3.621, p < .01$), indicating that each message strategy had the desired

effect of communicating either proenvironmental benefits or personal benefits.

We then proceeded with the same analysis used for the first study. Once again, a MANCOVA was conducted, with benefit appeal and price ending as the independent variables and perceived quality and perceived price as the dependent variables; prior knowledge was again included as a control variable. The benefit appeal was significant at both the multivariate (Wilks's λ, $F = 5.37, p < .01$) and univariate levels (perceived price, $F = 7.41, p < .01$; perceived quality, $F = 4.16, p < .05$). H1 predicted that quality would be perceived as lower for the product featured with environmental benefits, but our results indicated the opposite. The mean for perceived quality when environmental benefits were used ($M = 3.83$) was significantly higher than the mean for perceived quality when personal benefits were used ($M = 3.25$, $t = -1.936, p = .056$). Hence, H1 is not supported. Univariate results indicate that the appeal type also has a significant effect on perceived price ($F = 7.647, p < .01$). The means (shown in Table 3) indicate that the product featured in an ad with environmental benefits was perceived as significantly more expensive ($M = 4.39$) than an ad with personal benefits ($M = 3.38, t = -3.57, p < .01$). Hence, H2 is supported for the car wash product.

The interaction effect was significant at the .07 multivariate level (Wilks's λ, $F = 2.65$) and at the univariate level for perceived price ($F = 5.21, p < .05$). H3a predicted that products featured in ads with .00 endings emphasizing environmental benefits ($M = 4.08$) would be perceived as more expensive than when advertised with environmental benefits and a .99 ending ($M = 4.68$) or personal benefits with a .00 ending ($M = 3.92$). The lack of significant differences in the predicted direction indicates that H3a is not supported for the car wash product.

H3b proposed that products featured in ads with a .99 price ending and a personal benefits appeal would be perceived as less expensive than the product advertised with a .99 price ending and an environmental benefit appeal, or a product in an ad featuring a .00 price ending and personal benefits. Because the mean for the former ($M = 2.86$) is significantly lower than the two other conditions ($M = 4.68, t = 3.57, p < .001; M = 3.92$, $t = 2.07, p < .05$), respectively, H3b is fully supported. This significant interaction effect is shown in Figure 2.

H4a and 4b postulated a benefit appeal $\times$ price ending interaction effect on perceived quality. However, because the interaction effect of appeal and price ending on perceived quality is nonsignificant ($p > .05$), H4 is not supported.

To test H5 and H6, which posited that environmental skepticism would moderate the effect of benefit type on perceived quality and perceived price, we followed the process recommended by Fitzsimons (2008), Fitzsimons, Chartrand, and Fitzsimons (2008), and Aiken and West (1991) for ex-

FIGURE 2
Interaction Effects: Car Wash Product

Perceived Price

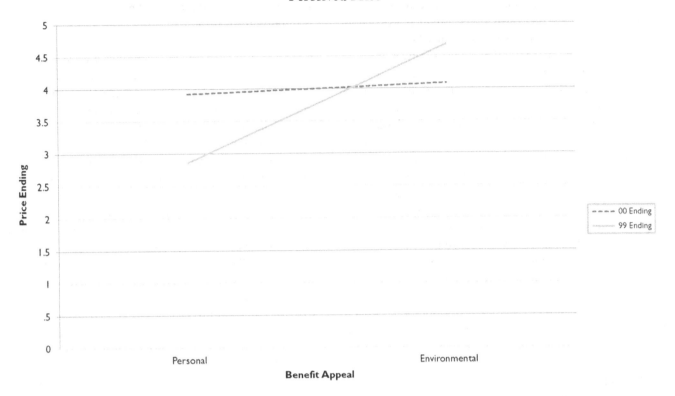

amining an interaction between a continuous variable and a categorical variable. First, perceived quality was regressed on benefit appeal and environmental skepticism, as well as the interaction between the two independent variables. Both the predictor and moderator variables were mean centered for inclusion in the interaction prior to the analysis. The overall model was significant ($F = 3.18$, $p < .05$). As per Fitzsimons, Chartrand, and Fitzsimons (2008), we then conducted the regression analysis at 1 standard deviation below and 1 standard deviation above the mean to understand the interaction effect. At both the low and mean levels, environmental skepticism moderated the effect of the benefit appeal on perceived price. At low levels of skepticism, benefit appeal was positively related to perceived quality ($\beta = 1.14$, $t = 2.86$, $p < .01$). Similarly, at mean levels of environmental skepticism, this same relationship also held ($\beta = .57$, $t = 2.0$, $p < .05$). At high levels of environmental skepticism, however, the moderator was not significant ($t = .0443$, $p > .10$). Because environmental appeals were dummy coded at the higher value for individuals who were less skeptical or moderately skeptical toward the environment, the use of environmental appeals resulted in higher levels of perceived quality. Hence, H5a is supported, but H5b is not.

To test H6, the process was repeated with message appeal and environmental skepticism and the interaction between the two as predictor variables and perceived price as the dependent variable. Regression results indicate that the model is significant at the .058 level ($F = 2.58$). To better understand this interaction effect, we then conducted a spotlight analysis as per Fitzsimons, Chartrand, and Fitzsimons (2008) at one standard deviation below and one standard deviation above the mean.

Results of this analysis suggest that the benefit type has a positive effect on perceived price at lower levels of environmental skepticism ($\beta = 1.23$, $t = 2.33$, $p < .05$), as well as mean levels of skepticism ($\beta = 1.02$, $t = 2.72$, $p < .01$). That is, when environmental skepticism is low or moderate, environmental benefits are perceived as more expensive. While this demonstrates that environmental skepticism plays a moderating role in the effect of benefit on price, it is not in the direction we hypothesized.

GENERAL DISCUSSION AND IMPLICATIONS

Our findings offer initial insight and implications for environmentally oriented advertising. First, H1, which posited that a product advertised with an environmental appeal will be perceived as being of lower quality than a product advertised with a personal benefit appeal, was not supported for either product. While past findings have purported that many consumers may perceive conventional products as superior in quality to a green alternative (Ottman 1998), it appears that the perceived quality level of products advertised with eco-friendly attributes is not necessarily lower. Hence, from a perceived quality standpoint, advertisers should not be hesitant about using proenvironmental advertising appeals because eco-friendly products may not be burdened with the image of having low efficacy or as being a less desirable substitute as some past research has demonstrated. This shift in consumer tastes and preferences could possibly be due to growing concerns about sustainability, personal health, or the realization of the negative effects that the presence of harmful chemicals can have on one's daily activities, increasing the perceived risk associated with *not* using environmentally friendly products. Another potential explanation is that the 400+ green certification systems now in place (Bogdan 2010) have increased consumers' quality perceptions of green products. If so, then these positive perceptions may suggest that consumers now see these products as a "gain" for the environment, which may raise the consumer's overall assessment of the product.

The support of H2 (which tested price level perceptions of environmental benefits versus personal benefits) in Study 2 demonstrates the proclivity of consumers to assume that some green products are more expensive and to expect higher prices when products are advertised with environmentally oriented appeals. Taken together with the lack of significance for the benefit main appeal, this suggests that while consumers feel they need to pay more for some products that help the environment, they do not necessarily have to sacrifice quality. Again, this may suggest that environmental benefits are a gain for the customer, but that they need to pay more to receive that gain.

It is also possible that the perception of product efficacy when using a proenvironmental appeal may be more complex than originally conceptualized. In Study 2, it appears that the ad emphasizing the product's environmental benefits created the perception of a higher price as compared with a message that focused on personal benefits. This implies that advertisers may need to use caution when positioning an environmentally friendly product. If the target market is more affluent, an environmental appeal for certain products may be effective. For the price-conscious consumer, however, the use of personal appeals may be more appropriate.

Furthermore, despite their limited disposable income, students may be willing to pay more for products that are believed to be environmentally friendly because the millennial generation places considerable importance on environmental issues (LOHAS 2012). This possibility is supported by Gurău (2012), who suggests that millennials' purchase patterns can be interpreted as a form of self-expression; hence, these consumers may be willing to spend more to communicate what is important to them.

Consumer choices for products that are positioned as environmentally friendly may be highly diverse and address a wide variety of consumer needs. One may assume that in the broad domain of "green buying," consumers hold a broad range of beliefs and attitudes about the efficacy of any given product based on its product category and usage. In support of this concept, Luchs et al. (2010) found that one heuristic consumers used in evaluating products was whether it possesses "soft" attributes for products such as baby shampoo, or "hard" attributes for products such as automobile tires. The authors found contrasting positive and negative perceptions of the price of these products when they were presented as either an environmentally friendly or a standard version of these items. The body wash product used in the current study would likely evoke a similar sentiment as baby shampoo because it is something applied to one's own skin. It is possible that the car wash product might be considered differently than the body wash product because it is applied to an object instead of a person. Hence, the perceived gain may be stronger for the body wash product. However, consumers are growing increasingly knowledgeable about the importance of avoiding harsh detergents on their automobiles due to the potential damage it can cause to the car's exterior (Shutovich 2000). Thus, a key finding of this study is that consumer perceptions of eco-friendly products appear to be contextual.

Our finding regarding price perceptions for both products stands in contrast to one of our hypotheses and previously held views about green products. As noted, when prices end in .00 versus .99, the former is often considered a heuristic for quality and the latter for value. This idea points to a general belief that retailers price their items with an odd ending (e.g., .99, .95) to communicate that the item is a "bargain" or a good value. Conversely, when a price ends in .00, the business is sending a subtle but distinct message that the commodity is of high quality (Lamb, Hair, and McDaniel 2010; Schindler, Parsa, and Naipaul 2011).

While the phenomenon known as "odd-ending" pricing has been documented in past research, there may be a contextual element to it. That is, it may not be a heuristic that can be applied universally to all consumer evaluations of price. For example, when an individual has low knowledge or little experience with a product, he or she may tend to use price as a heuristic for judging quality (Monroe and Krishnan 1985; Peterson and Wilson 1985; Zeithaml 1988). Assuming that consumers use such heuristics to evaluate unknown products, the propensity to rely on this may well override the attraction of the .99 price ending.

Another possibility is the potential for a .00 price ending to create a situation that would require additional cognitive processing. Since the accepted paradigm for low value consumer goods might be an odd-ending price, consumers may not want to expend the cognitive resources necessary to consider this product in their evoked set, particularly in light of the overall low value of the purchase. This again suggests that the commonly accepted heuristic for pricing at odd or even endings is not generalizable to all products. That is, while an SUV priced at $80,000 may infer higher quality than one priced at $79,995, the same may not be necessarily true for a bottle of shampoo priced at $8 when contrasted with one priced at $7.95. For low-priced goods such as the products used in this study, the .00 price ending may cause consumers to dismiss the price itself from the purchasing decision, given the large number of substitutes generally available for such goods. An examination of whether this difference exists for other types of products warrants further investigation.

An explanation for the inconsistent psychological pricing results may lie in varying levels of consumer expertise on the added attribute of proenvironmentalism to both products. Alba and Hutchinson defined consumer expertise as "the ability to perform product-related tasks successfully" (1987, p. 411), which includes activities such as decision making, purchasing, and interaction with salespeople. Consumers typically possess different levels of expertise about product attributes. In addition, the decision rules involved in the evaluation of those attributes vary in complexity. As products become more complex, the decision rules also become more intricate through increased familiarity and no longer hinge on a single piece of information (Alba and Hutchinson 1987).

When the attribute of environmentalism is linked to any given product, irrespective of whether or not it is the main benefit claim of the ad, it adds a dimension of complexity to the evaluation process. Given the differing levels of consumer expertise that likely exist with this attribute, a variety of decision rules might be invoked. As noted, the Persuasion Knowledge Model (Friestad and Wright 1994) tells us that consumers tend to filter persuasive claims through a knowledge structure that may discount some elements of those claims. According to the PKM, an individual evaluates the veracity of information by comparing it with past experiences and congruency with expectations (Friestad and Wright 1994). This presents the distinct possibility that the cognitive effect of framing and perceived gain from .99 pricing supported by Prospect Theory (Kahneman and Tversky 1979) might be disrupted in some situations. That is, as consumers apply more complex decision rules to product evaluations that include popular issues such as environmentalism, they may not respond as expected to framing and the traditional view of an individual gain.

It is interesting to note that in the first study, the interaction effects for perceived price interact similarly for quality; that is, results indicate that perceptions of high price go hand in hand with perceptions of high quality. Moreover, for the body wash product, response to the .99 price ending did not seem to matter based on the appeal. However, the opposite seems true for the car wash product where the .00 price ending for both appeals generates the same response for perceived price, but response to the .99 ending varies based on the particular appeal used. These conflicting results are congruent with Luchs et al. (2010), who noted that the effectiveness of advertisements with pro-environmental benefits may be context-specific; what is effective for one type of environmentally friendly product may not be effective for another.

The perceived gain based on the price also seems to vary based on the product. Our products differed in characteristics of their use (e.g., a product used on a person versus a product used on an object) and their brand names. In fact, the prefix "eco" is part of the brand name for the body wash, but not for the car wash. Hence, it is possible that some of our findings may be attributable to these product disparities. However, because this study did not directly test the differences across the two product types, further research utilizing other product types and brand names is warranted.

Our results indicate that environmental skepticism moderated the relationships between the benefit appeal and perceptions of quality and price. More specifically, those subjects who exhibited low or moderate levels of environmental skepticism viewed products advertised with environmental appeals as higher quality. However, high levels of environmental skepticism did not affect quality perceptions of the benefit appeal. Perhaps this indicates that consumers compartmentalize perceptions of the effect of green products on the environment when there is a direct benefit to the consumer. Moreover, we found that the lower and mean levels of environmental skepticism moderated the benefit-perceived price relationship. While this relationship was in the opposite direction as predicted, it is consistent with the rest of our findings that demonstrate that perceived price and perceived quality seem to be congruent with the environmentally oriented benefit appeal.

LIMITATIONS, FUTURE RESEARCH, AND CONCLUSIONS

Although this study generated some interesting and important findings, limitations must be noted. First, only two products of relatively low involvement were examined. Environmentally friendly products and product claims are now prevalent in a wide variety of both high- and low-involvement products, and, as noted, consumers may not perceive quality in the same way for commodity and luxury goods. Therefore, future research should include a wider range of products to establish the contextual boundaries for the different types of appeals.

Another limitation was the use of a student sample, restricting generalizability. However, the use of students in testing theory is fairly well documented (Calder, Phillips, and Tybout 1981; Thomas 2011). Moreover, items used in the study were from product categories that are relevant for the student population. In addition, millennials are the largest generational group since the baby boomers (Smith 2012), and green consumption is an integral part of the college experience because these students are generally eager to enroll in environmental studies courses and assume active roles in campus sustainability initiatives (LOHAS 2012). Given their sizable buying power and strong attitudes toward the environment, these consumers are an important group to study. Nevertheless, a cross-sectional sample should be used in future research to enhance external validity.

To our knowledge, however, this is the first study to assess advertising appeals and price endings in the environmental advertising arena, and our findings begin the process of understanding the use of relatively common advertising approaches effectively in green advertising. Our results indicate that some of the commonly accepted paradigms about environmental products are evolving and that psychological pricing strategies might behave differently for products that may have an effect on long-term sustainability. By studying a broader base of consumers along with a wider range of products, more clarity on how green products are perceived and evaluated by consumers can be discerned. For example, under what specific conditions does a personal appeal perform better than an environmental appeal? What motivations drive consumer perceptions of these appeals? Are there ways to counter the effects of environmental skepticism? Answers to such research questions could have profound implications for advertisers because they would shape how advertisements for environmentally friendly products should be positioned to achieve the most success.

REFERENCES

Aiken, Leona S., and Stephen G. West (1991), *Multiple Regression: Testing and Interpreting Interactions*, Thousand Oaks, CA: Sage.

Alba, Joseph W., and J. Wesley Hutchinson (1987), "Dimensions of Consumer Expertise," *Journal of Consumer Research*, 13 (4), 411–454.

Appell, David (2007), "Toxic Bulbs," *Scientific American*, 297 (4), 30–32.

Banerjee, Bobby, and Kim McKeage (1994), "How Green Is My Value: Exploring the Relationship Between Environmentalism and Materialism," in *Advances in Consumer Research*, vol. 21, Chris T. Allen and Deborah Roedder John, eds., Provo, UT: Association for Consumer Research, 147–152.

Banerjee, Subhabrata, Charles S. Gulas, and Easwar Iyer (1995), "Shades of Green: A Multidimensional Analysis of Environmental Advertising," *Journal of Advertising*, 2 (Summer), 21–31.

Basu, Kaushik (1997), "Why Are So Many Goods Priced to End in Nine? And Why This Practice Hurts the Producers," *Economics Letters*, 54 (1), 41–44.

Baumgartner, Bernhard, and Winfried J. Steiner (2007), "Are Consumers Heterogeneous in Their Preferences for Odd and Even Prices? Findings from a Choice-Based Conjoint Study," *International Journal of Research in Marketing*, 24 (4), 312–323.

Berger, Paul D., and Gerald E. Smith (1998), "The Impact of Prospect Theory Based Framing Tactics on Advertising Effectiveness," *Omega: International Journal of Management Science*, 26 (5), 593–609.

Bergkvist, Lars, and John R. Rossiter (2007), "The Predictive Validity of Multiple-Item Versus Single-Item Measures of the Same Constructs," *Journal of Marketing Research*, 44 (2), 175–184.

Bettman, James R., Mary Frances Luce, and John W. Payne (1998), "Constructive Consumer Choice Processes," *Journal of Consumer Research*, 25 (3), 187–217.

Bizer, George Y., and Robert M. Schindler (2005), "Direct Evidence for Ending-Digit Drop-Off in Price Information Processing," *Psychology and Marketing*, 22 (October), 771–783.

Bliss, Perry (1952), "Price Determination at the Department Store Level," *Journal of Marketing*, 17 (July), 37–46.

Bogdan, Lea (2010), "ECO Labels 101: Green Certifications Explained," Inhabitat, available at www.inhabitat.com/2010/04/06/demystifying-eco-labels/ (accessed February 27, 2012).

Burke, Marian C., and Julie A. Edell (1986), "Ad Reactions over Time: Capturing Changes in the Real World," *Journal of Consumer Research*, 13 (1), 114–118.

Burton, Scot, and Donald R. Lichtenstein (1988), "The Effect of Ad Claims and Ad Context on Attitude Toward the Advertisement," *Journal of Advertising*, 17 (1), 3–11.

Calder, Bobby J., Lynn W. Phillips, and Alice M. Tybout (1981), "Designing Research for Application," *Journal of Consumer Research*, 8 (2), 197–207.

Carlson, Les, Stephen J. Grove, and Norman Kangun (1993), "A Content Analysis of Environmental Advertising Claims: A Matrix Method Approach," *Journal of Advertising*, 22 (3), 27–39.

Carson, Rachel (1962), *Silent Spring*, Boston: Houghton Mifflin.

Chang, Ching Ching (2011), "Feeling Ambivalent About Going Green," *Journal of Advertising*, 40 (4), 19–31.

Chen, Yu-Shan (2008), "The Positive Effect of Green Intellectual Capital on Competitive Advantages of Firms," *Journal of Business Ethics*, 77 (3), 271–286.

Chitra, K. (2007), "In Search of the Green Consumers: A Perceptual Study," *Journal of Services Research*, 7 (1), 173–191.

Choi, Jungsil, Kiljae Lee, and Yong-Yeon Ji (2012), "What Type of Framing Message Is More Appropriate with Nine-Ending Pricing?" *Marketing Letters*, 23 (3), 603–614.

Cramer, Jerome (1991), "The Selling of Green," *Time* (September 16), 48.

Dehaene, Stanislas, and Jacques Mehler (1992), "Cross-Linguistic Regularities in the Frequency of Number Words," *Cognition*, 43 (April), 1–29.

Dillingham, Susan (1990), "Hawking Consumer Goods with the Environmental Pitch," *Insight* (March 26), 40–42.

Drolet, Aimee L., and Donald G. Morrison (2001), "Do We Really Need Multiple-Item Measures in Service Research?" *Journal of Service Research*, 3 (February), 196–204.

Dunlap, Riley E. (2002), "An Enduring Concern: Light Stays Green for Environmental Protection," *Public Perspective*, 13 (September/October), 10–14.

Edwards, Jim (2008), "Forget the Environment Say the 'Never Greens,'" *Brandweek*, 49 (27), 8–11.

Fazio, Russell H., Jeaw-Mei Chin, Elizabeth C. McDonel, and Steven J. Sherman (1982), "Attitude Accessibility, Attitude-Behavior Consistency, and the Strength of the Object-Evaluation Association," *Journal of Experimental Social Psychology*, 18 (July), 339–357.

Fitzsimons, Gavan J. (2008), "Death to Dichotomizing," *Journal of Consumer Research*, 35 (June), 5–8.

Fitzsimons, Gráinne, Tanya L. Chartrand, and Gavan J. Fitzsimons (2008), "Automatic Effects of Brand Exposure on Motivated Behavior: How Apple Makes You 'Think Different,'" *Journal of Consumer Research*, 35 (June), 21–35.

Freling, Traci, Leslie Vincent, Robert Schindler, David M. Hardesty, and Jason Rowe (2010), "A Meta-Analytic Review of Just-Below Pricing Effects," in *Advances in Consumer Research*, vol. 37, Margaret C. Campbell, Jeff Inman, and Rik Pieters, eds., Provo, UT: Association for Consumer Research, 618–620.

Friestad, Marian, and Peter Wright (1994), "The Persuasion Knowledge Model: How People Cope with Persuasion Attempts," *Journal of Consumer Research*, 21 (1), 1–31.

Futerra (2008), "The Greenwash Guide," available at www.futerra.co.uk/downloads/Greenwash_Guide.pdf (accessed March 1, 2012).

Gregory, Gary D., and Michael Di Leo (2003), "Repeated Behavior and Environmental Psychology: The Role of Personal Involvement and Habit Formation in Explaining Water Consumption," *Journal of Applied Social Psychology*, 33 (6), 1261–1296.

Gurău, Calin (2012), "A Life-Stage Analysis of Consumer Loyalty Profile: Comparing Generation X and Millennial Consumers," *Journal of Consumer Marketing*, 29 (2), 103–113.

Harper, Donald V. (1966), *Price Policy and Procedure*, New York: Harcourt, Brace and World.

Hopkins, Katy (2011), "10 Least Car-Friendly Universities," U.S. News & World Report, available at www.usnews.com/education/best-colleges/the-short-list-college/articles/2011/10/27/10-least-car-friendly-universities (accessed June 10, 2012).

Hornik, Jacob, Joseph Cherian, and Dan Zakay (1994), "The Influence of Prototypic Values on the Validity of Studies Using Time Estimates," *Journal of the Market Research Society*, 36 (April), 145–147.

Hultsman, Wendy Z., John T. Hultsman, and David R. Black (1989), "'Response Peaks' as a Component of Measurement Error: Assessment Implications for Self-Reported Data in Leisure Research," *Journal of Leisure Research*, 21 (4), 310–315.

Huston, John, and Nipoli Kamdar (1996), "$9.99: Can 'Just-Below' Pricing Be Reconciled with Rationality?" *Eastern Economic Journal*, 22 (2), 137–145.

Huttenlocher, Janellen, Larry V. Hedges, and Norman M. Bradburn (1990), "Reports of Elapsed Time: Bounding and Rounding Processes in Estimation," *Journal of Experimental Psychology: Learning, Memory, and Cognition*, 16 (March), 196–213.

Iyer, Easwar, and Bobby Banerjee (1992), "Anatomy of Green Advertising," in *Advances in Consumer Research*, vol. 20, L. McAlister and M. Rothschild, eds., Provo, UT: Association for Consumer Research, 494–501.

Kalafatis, Stavros P., Michael Pollard, Robert East, and Markos H. Tsogas (1999), "Green Marketing and Azjen's Theory of Planned Behaviour: A Cross-Market Examination," *Journal of Consumer Marketing*, 16 (5), 441–460.

Kahneman, Daniel, and Amos Tversky (1979), "Prospect Theory: An Analysis of Decision Under Risk," *Econometrica*, 47 (2), 263–292.

Keller, Kevin Lane (1993), "Conceptualizing, Measuring, and Managing Customer-Based Brand Equity," *Journal of Marketing*, 57 (January), 1–22.

Lamb, Charles W., Joseph F. Hair, and Carl McDaniel (2010), *MKTG 4*, Mason, OH: South-Western.

Lambert, Zarrel V. (1975), "Perceived Price as Related to Odd and Even Price Endings," *Journal of Retailing*, 51 (3), 13–22.

Landler, Mark, Zachary Schiller, and Tim Smart (1991), "Suddenly Green Marketers Are Seeing Red Flags," *Business Week* (February 25), 74–75.

Laroche, Michel, Jasmin Bergeron, and Guido Barbaro-Forleo (2001), "Targeting Consumers Who Are Willing to Pay More for Environmentally Friendly Products," *Journal of Consumer Marketing*, 18 (6), 503–520.

Lifestyles of Health and Sustainability (LOHAS) (2012), "We Are All Green Consumers: Now and for the Future," available at www.lohas.com/content/we-are-all-green-consumers-now-and-future/ (accessed June 10, 2012).

Luchs, Michael G., Rebecca Walker Naylor, Julie R. Irwin, and Rjagopal Raghunathan (2010), "The Sustainability Liability: Potential Negative Effects of Ethicality on Product Preference," *Journal of Marketing*, 74 (5), 18–31.

Luo, Xueming, and C. B. Bhattacharya (2006), "Corporate Social Responsibility, Customer Satisfaction, and Market Value," *Journal of Marketing*, 70 (4), 1–18.

Marketing Week (2007), "Toyota Pulls Prius Ads After Exaggerating CO_2 Benefits" (July 7), available at www.marketingweek.co.uk/toyota-pulls-prius-ad-after-exaggerating-co2-benefits/2056556.article/ (accessed June 10, 2012).

Maronick, Thomas J., and Craig J. Andrews (1999), "The Role of Qualifying Language on Consumer Perceptions of Environmental Claims," *Journal of Consumer Affairs*, 33 (2), 297–320.

Mayer, Robert N., Debra L. Scammon, and Jason W. Gray-Lee (1993), "Will the FTC Guidelines on Environmental Marketing Affect the Hue of Green Marketing? An Audit of Claims on Product Labels," in *Proceedings of the 1993 Marketing and Public Policy Conference,* Mary Jane Sheffert, ed., East Lansing, MI: Michigan State University Press, 19–30.

McCracken, Jeffrey, Dana Cimilluca, and Ellen Byron (2010), "Clorox Is Moving Toward Sale of Auto Brands STP, Armor All," *Wall Street Journal,* April 9, available at http://online.wsj.com/article/SB100014240527023048301045751723 50977746476.html (accessed June 10, 2012).

McKinsey and Company (2008), "How Companies Think About Climate Change: A McKinsey Global Survey," available at www.nyu.edu/intercep/lapietra/ClimateChangeAttitudes.pdf (accessed February 27, 2012).

Mohan, Anne Marie (2011), "Green Consumerism Is on the Rise, Poll Shows," Greener Package, available at www.greenerpackage.com/green_marketing/green_consumerism_rise_poll_shows/ (accessed March 1, 2012).

Mohr, Lois A., Dogan Eroglu, and Pam Scholder Ellen (1998), "The Development and Testing of a Measure of Skepticism Toward Environmental Claims in Marketers' Communications," *Journal of Consumer Affairs,* 32 (1), 30–55.

Monroe, Kent B., and R. Krishnan (1985), "The Effects of Price on Subjective Product Evaluations," in *Perceived Quality,* Jacob Jacoby and Jerry C. Olson, eds., Lexington, MA: Lexington Books, 209–232.

Morris, Louis A., Manoj M. Hastak, and Michael B. Mazis (1995), "Consumer Comprehension of Environmental Advertising and Labeling Claims," *Journal of Consumer Affairs,* 29 (2), 328–350.

Murphy, Patrick E., and Ben M. Ennis (1986), "Classifying Products Strategically," *Journal of Marketing,* 50 (July), 24–42.

Nagle, Thomas T., and Reed K. Holden (1995), *The Strategy and Tactics of Pricing: A Guide to Profitable Decision Making,* 2nd ed., Englewood Cliffs, NJ: Prentice-Hall.

Newman, Andrew A. (2009), "Adding a Masculine Edge to Body Wash," *New York Times,* September 7, available at www.nytimes.com/2009/09/08/business/media/08adco.html?_r=1/ (accessed June 10, 2012).

Obermiller, Carl, and Eric R. Spangenberg (1998), "Development of a Scale to Measure Consumer Skepticism Toward Advertising," *Journal of Consumer Psychology,* 7 (2), 159–186.

Osterhus, Thomas L. (1997), "Pro-Social Consumer Influence Strategies: When and How Do They Work?" *Journal of Marketing,* 61 (4), 16–29.

Ottman, Jacquelyn A. (1992), "Green Marketing," *Journal of Business Strategy,* 13 (4), 3–7.

——— (1998), *Green Marketing: Opportunity for Innovation,* New York: McGraw-Hill.

——— (2011), *The New Rules of Green Marketing,* San Francisco: Berrett-Koehler.

Paradise, Andrew (2004), "Women on the Move: A Look at Today's Female Motorist," Automotive Aftermarket Industry Association, available at www.aftermarket.org/Resources/MR/FemaleMotoristExecSum.aspx (accessed June 13, 2012).

Park, C. Whan, and S. Mark Young (1986), "Consumer Response to Television Commercials: The Impact of Involvement and Background Music on Brand Attitude Formation," *Journal of Marketing Research,* 23 (1), 11–24.

Perdue, Barbara C., and John O. Summers (1986), "Checking the Success of Manipulations in Marketing Experiments," *Journal of Marketing Research,* 23 (4), 317–326.

Peterson, Robert A., and William R. Wilson (1985), "Perceived Risk and Price-Reliance Schema and Price Perceived-Quality-Mediators," in *Perceived Quality,* Jacob Jacoby and Jerry C. Olson, eds., Lexington, MA: Lexington Books, 247–268.

Phillips, David (2008), "Square Jugs and Carbon Footprinting," *Dairy Foods,* 109 (9), 10.

Pickett-Baker, Josephine, and Ritsuko Ozaki (2008), "Pro-Environmental Products: Marketing Influence on Consumer Purchase Decision," *Journal of Consumer Research,* 25 (5), 281–293.

Roper Consulting (2010), "Green Gauge Report 2010," New York.

Royne, Marla B., Marian Levy, and Jennifer Martinez (2011), "The Public Health Implications of Consumers' Environmental Concern and Their Willingness to Pay for an Eco-Friendly Product," *Journal of Consumer Affairs,* 45 (2), 329–343.

Saad, Lydia (2007), "Americans See Environment as Getting Worse," Gallup, available at www.gallup.com (accessed January 16, 2012).

Safire, William (2007), "On Language," *New York Times* (December 16).

Salminen, Pekka, and Jyrki Wallenius (1993), "Testing Prospect Theory in a Deterministic Multiple Criteria Decision-Making Environment," *Decision Sciences,* 24 (2), 279–294.

Schindler, Robert M. (1991), "Symbolic Meanings of a Price Ending," in *Advances in Consumer Research,* vol. 18, Rebecca H. Holman and Michael R. Solomon, eds., Provo, UT: Association for Consumer Research, 794–801.

——— (2001), "Relative Price Level of 99-Ending Prices: Image Versus Reality," *Marketing Letters,* 12 (3), 239–247.

——— (2003), "The 99 Price Ending as a Signal of a Low-Price Appeal," in *Advances in Consumer Research,* vol. 20, Punam Anand Keller and Dennis W. Rook, eds., Valdosta, GA: Association for Consumer Research, 270.

———, and Thomas M. Kibarian (1996), "Increased Consumer Sales Response Through Use of 99-Ending Prices," *Journal of Retailing,* 72 (2), 187–199.

———, and ——— (2001), "Image Communicated by the Use of 99 Endings in Advertised Prices," *Journal of Advertising,* 30 (4), 95–99.

———, and Patrick N. Kirby (1997), "Patterns of Rightmost Digits Used in Advertised Prices: Implications for Nine-Ending Effects," *Journal of Consumer Research,* 24 (2), 192–201.

———, and Alan R. Wiman (1989), "Effect of Odd Pricing on Price Recall," *Journal of Business Research,* 19 (November), 165–177.

———, H. G. Parsa, and Sandra Naipaul (2011), "Hospitality Managers' Price-Ending Beliefs: A Survey and Applications," *Cornell Hospitality Quarterly,* 52 (4), 421–428.

Shrum, L. J., John A. McCarty, and Tina M. Lowrey (1995), "Buyer Characteristics of the Green Consumer and Their Implications for Advertising Strategy," *Journal of Advertising,* 24 (2), 71–82.

Shutovich, Christina A. (2000), "Breaking Tradition Through Education," *Aftermarket Business,* 110 (4), 102.

Smith, Taken Katherine (2012), "Longitudinal Study of Digital Marketing Strategies Targeting Millennials," *Journal of Consumer Marketing,* 29 (2), 86–92.

Stiving, Mark (2000), "Price-Endings When Prices Signal Quality," *Management Science,* 46 (12), 1617–1629.

———, and Russell S. Winer (1997), "An Empirical Analysis of Price Endings with Scanner Data," *Journal of Consumer Research,* 24 (1), 57–67.

Svoboda, Michael (2011), "Advertising Climate Change: A Study of Green Ads, 2005–2010," Yale Forum on Climate Change & the Media, available at www.yaleclimatemedia-forum.org/2011/07/advertising-climate-change-a-study-of-green-ads-2005-%E2%80%93-2010/ (accessed March 15, 2012).

Tarrant, Michael A., and Michael J. Manfredo (1993), "Digit Preference, Recall Bias, and Nonresponse Bias in Self-Reports of Angling Participation," *Leisure Sciences,* 15 (July–September), 231–238.

Terrachoice (2010), "The Sins of Greenwashing," available at http://sinsofgreenwashing.org/findings/greenwashing-report-2010/ (accessed March 15, 2012).

Thaler, Richard (1985), "Mental Accounting and Consumer Choice," *Marketing Science,* 4 (3), 199–214.

Thau, Barbara (2011), "Will Body Wash or Soap Get You Cleaner?" Daily Finance, available at www.dailyfinance.com/2011/05/03/savings-experiment-will-body-wash-or-soap-get-you-cleaner/ (accessed June 10, 2012).

Thomas, Rodney W. (2011), "When Student Samples Make Sense in Logistics Research," *Journal of Business Logistics,* 32 (3), 287–290.

U.S. News & World Report (2011), "2012 Best Colleges," available at http://colleges.usnews.rankingsandreviews.com/best-colleges/ (accessed June 10, 2012).

Vlosky, Richard P., Lucie K. Ozanne, and Renée J. Fontenot (1999), "A Conceptual Model of U.S. Consumer Willingness-to-Pay for Environmentally Certified Wood Products," *Journal of Consumer Marketing,* 16 (2), 122–140.

Walker, Jean-Cyril (2011), "It's Not Easy Being Green: Environmental Advertising in Light of the FTC's Proposed Guides," *Surface Mount Technology* (July), 50–56.

Zeithaml, Valarie A. (1988), "Consumer Perceptions of Price, Quality, and Value: A Means-End Model and Synthesis of Evidence," *Journal of Marketing,* 52 (July), 2–22.

APPENDIX

Experimental Advertisements

IS THE DEVIL IN THE DETAILS?

The Signaling Effect of Numerical Precision in Environmental Advertising Claims

Guang-Xin Xie and Ann Kronrod

ABSTRACT: Numerical information is an important feature in green advertising claims. In four experiments, the authors examine the extent to which numerical precision signals the competence of an advertised company. The results suggest that consumers who are low in advertising skepticism tend to perceive the advertised company as more competent when presented with precise numbers, which are considered more informative and scientific. Highly skeptical consumers are less likely to be affected by numerical precision. Furthermore, the moderation effect of advertising skepticism can be mitigated by consumer topic knowledge about the advertised environmental issue: Highly skeptical but less knowledgeable consumers are also susceptible to numerical precision.

An important characteristic of environmental advertising (i.e., "green advertising") is its association with scientific research findings (Carlson, Grove, and Kangun 1993; Chan 2000; Zinkhan and Carlson 1995). Emerging from quantitative measurement of the impact of human activities on the environment, green advertising claims are oftentimes substantiated with numerical information (Nakajima 2001). Such numerical information may be particularly pertinent to claims about proenvironmental product attributes because of the specificity about the quantifiable environmental benefits and the scientific connotations. To our knowledge, however, no prior work has examined the effect of numerical information in green advertising, especially with regard to the level of precision.

The present research addresses this void in the literature, exploring the extent to which numerical precision signals an advertised company's competence. In four experiments, we find that consumer skepticism toward advertising in general (hereafter referred to as "ad skepticism") moderates the positive effect of numerical precision on perception of company competence. Consumers who are low in ad skepticism (hereafter referred to as "low skeptics") tend to consider the advertised company as more competent when the numerical information is more precise (e.g., 19.42% versus 20%). In contrast, those who are high in ad skepticism (hereafter referred to as "high skeptics") are not affected by numerical precision. We find that perceived trustworthiness of green advertising claims mediates the observed effect. Furthermore, the moderating

effect of ad skepticism can be mitigated when consumers lack topic knowledge about the environmental issue featured in an advertisement. In other words, highly skeptical but less knowledgeable consumers are also likely to be susceptible to the signaling effect of numerical precision.

CONCEPTUAL DEVELOPMENT

Signaling Effect of Green Message

Extant research has examined a number of consumer and message characteristics that influence the persuasiveness of green advertising (e.g., Kangun, Carlson, and Grove 1991; Kilbourne 1995; Obermiller 1995; Schuhwerk and Lefkoff-Hagius 1995). Over the past four decades, this literature has evolved from categorizing claims and profiling target consumers (e.g., Kinnear, Taylor, and Ahmed 1974; Murphy, Kangun, and Locander 1978; Shrum, McCarty, and Lowrey 1995; Stafford, Stafford, and Chowdhury 1996) to a comprehensive approach that integrates consumer individual traits with organizational goals (Kotler 2011; Montoro-Rios et al. 2008; Sheth, Sethia, and Srinivas 2011).

More recently, researchers have begun to study the effect of linguistic and semantic implications of environmental messages on consumer perceptions of the advertised products and companies (e.g., Kronrod, Grinstein, and Wathieu 2012; Luchs et al. 2010). This novel venue of research generally suggests that consumers construct the meaning of environmental marketing messages as an effect of their preexisting cognitive schemata (e.g., ethics is associated with gentleness) or expectations (e.g., assertive language implies issue importance).

This project was funded by a Joseph P. Healey Research Grant, University of Massachusetts Boston. The authors thank Tong-Xin Fu for her assistance with graphical design and data collection.

Consumers rely on specific communicational cues in advertising, which can signal unobservable product quality, especially when they do not have adequate information to evaluate product attributes prior to purchase (Kirmani and Rao 2000). Previous studies have documented such positive cues as brand name (Erdem and Swait 2004), advertising expenditure (Kirmani 1997; Kirmani and Wright 1989), sponsorship (Clark, Cornwell, and Pruitt 2002), and product warranty (Boulding and Kirmani 1993; Wiener 1985). The underlying rationale is that consumers make inferences about product quality from these cognitive shortcuts, especially when they are not motivated or they are unable to assess the validity of advertising claims about the product or the company. For example, when a company invests heavily in advertising, a "rational" consumer would assume that the product quality must be good enough for the company to cover the costs and to make profits (Kirmani 1997).

The signaling effect of environmentally friendly product attributes can be particularly pertinent in green advertising. Extant research has documented that green attributes of a product/service have a positive impact on attitudes toward other attributes, and on judgment of the advertised brand (e.g., Miles and Covin 2000; Scammon and Mayer 1995; Schuhwerk and Lefkoff-Hagius 1995; Sen and Bhattacharya 2001). The effect of green claims is not always positive, however. For example, Chernev and Carpenter (2001) found that a superior green attribute can be associated with other relatively "inferior" attributes, because consumers infer that companies are resource limited but remain profit oriented. The more resources that are allocated to green attributes, the less resources there are for other attributes. As a result, the overall perception of product quality becomes less positive. Given the mixed signals of green claims, it is important for companies to formulate advertising messages cautiously. When it comes to the question of whether to introduce numerical information, and more specifically numerical precision, the answer is often not straightforward. Next, we discuss the literature on numerical precision and its effects in green advertising.

Numerical Precision

Green advertising sometimes presents claims about ingredients or features of a product, employing different types of numerical information. In the case of green washing, in particular, advertisers sometimes use ambiguous and misleading numbers that exaggerate environmental benefits. For example, a claim on a package label that reads "50% more recycled content than before" suggests an increase of recycled goods by one half. As the previous recycled content is only 2%, the manufacturer's total increase of recycled content has actually improved by 1%, from 2% to 3%. Although the message is technically true (an improvement from 2% to 3% is indeed

50%), the Federal Trade Commission (FTC) may rule the advertisement deceptive if it creates false impressions (FTC 2012).

Advertisers who intend to emphasize a green attribute of a product face the choice of using more or less precise numbers. In general, to achieve salient presence, advertisers tend to use a simple and clear message. The complexity of a message, as might be the case when employing high numerical precision, may distract consumers from focusing on the claim (Mader 1973) and reduce positive attitude toward the advertised product due to lack of processing fluency (Alter and Oppenheimer 2006; Lee and Labroo 2004; Shah and Oppenheimer 2007). Indeed, King and Janiszewski (2011) found that numerical fluency enhances liking for advertised brand names. However, it is plausible that the enhanced salience of a piece of information presented in a disfluent manner, such as exact numerical information, overcomes the commonly found unpleasant effect of disfluency. This is because disfluency may be more engaging due to the higher processing effort it demands (Diemand-Yauman, Oppenheimer, and Vaughan 2011; Kim, Rao, and Lee 2009; Schwarz 2004). As a result, claims employing more precise numbers (e.g., 19.42%, compared with 20%) may be more salient, elevating the processing effort and resulting in higher attention and possibly stronger persuasiveness.

Echoing this dilemma, previous research on the effect of numerical information suggests mixed results. Wei (2003) suggests that using general terms with nonprecise numerical information may imply deficient subject knowledge and avoidance of responsibility on the part of the source. It was also found that oversimplification signals lack of competence or seriousness (Burke 1954; Suau-Jiménez 2005). In contrast, when dealing with numbers, some people have a preference for approximation, using more vague numerical expressions and consistently choosing more round numbers (Cummins, Sauerland, and Solt 2012; Sigurd 1988).

Taken together, the literature remains inconclusive with regard to the preferred level of numerical precision, especially the appropriate employment of precise numbers in advertising. Ample evidence supports simplification, such as the research on fluency and conversational norms. But competing arguments (e.g., those about the positive effects of disfluency) advocate numerical precision in contexts that may use less familiar terms, such as environmentally friendly product attributes. One possible reason for this inconsistency may be that consumers generally tend to be skeptical about advertisers' intentions and the truthfulness of advertising claims. It is likely that, when facing numerical precision, consumers are torn between believing the seriousness of an advertised company that is able to provide detailed numerical information and their inherent skepticism, which leads them to believe the precise numbers are part of a selling gimmick, not representative of the truth.

We next extend our discussion to the effect of ad skepticism in relation to numerical precision.

Advertising Skepticism and Numerical Precision

Ad skepticism is a tendency to disbelieve the informational claims of advertising in general (Obermiller and Spangenberg 1998). Prior studies suggest that ad skepticism is a relatively stable individual difference that can influence trust toward advertising messages (e.g., Boush, Friestad, and Rose 1994; Darke and Ritchie 2007; Ford, Smith, and Swasy 1990; Hardesty, Carlson, and Bearden 2002). In particular, Obermiller, Spangenberg, and MacLachlan (2005) found that high skeptics tend to suspect informational appeals in the advertisement more than low skeptics. In other words, highly skeptical consumers tend to discredit informative claims in advertising. It is also possible that such high skeptics are less sensitive to nuance in numerical precision. Whether presented with a round number (e.g., 10, 50, 200) or a more exact number (e.g., 9.8, 51.2, 203), they disbelieve the integrity of the number and therefore are less persuaded by the advertising claim. This may result in no alteration to their beliefs about the company's seriousness or credibility. Following this reasoning, we predict that the effectiveness of numerical precision in green advertising can be moderated by ad skepticism: The more skeptical consumers discount advertising claims, so the signaling effect of precision becomes less salient. For those consumers who attend to and believe the numeric information, the effectiveness of numerical precision can be ascribed to the perceptions that more precise numbers are more scientific and informative. Formally, we hypothesize that:

Hypothesis 1a: For consumers who are low in ad skepticism, more precise numerical information signals more positive perception of an advertised company's competence than less precise numerical information. For consumers who are high in ad skepticism, in comparison, the signaling effect of numerical precision is expected to be attenuated. This difference will be mediated by perceived trustworthiness of the advertising claims: The more skeptical consumers are, the less likely they are to trust the advertised information, which in turn, reduces the signaling effect of numerical precision.

Hypothesis 1b: More precise numbers will be perceived as more scientific and informative, which mediates the effect of numerical precision on perceived competence of an advertised company.

Skepticism, Topic Knowledge, and Effectiveness of Numerical Precision

Is there no way to persuade high skeptics? Do high skeptics always disbelieve precision in numerical claims? Drawing on literature linking consumer knowledge and ad skepticism, we

speculate that some consumers might be less knowledgeable about the advertised environmental issues, which may mitigate the moderating effect of ad skepticism.

Conceptually, ad skepticism reflects general suspicion toward advertising. Topic knowledge is more specific about the advertised product or service. We speculate that topic knowledge may interact with general ad skepticism, which in turn affects consumer susceptibility to numerical precision. Friestad and Wright (1994) argue that consumer knowledge about the topic of persuasion, as well as tactics of persuasion, influence the outcome of persuasive attempts. The effect of such knowledge has been well documented in quite a few empirical studies (e.g., Campbell and Kirmani 2000; DeCarlo 2005; Forehand and Grier 2003; Main, Dahl, and Darke 2007). Specifically, valid topic knowledge can reinforce or elevate distrust toward advertising claims, which then adversely affects perceptions of the company's credibility and competence (Boush, Friestad, and Rose 1994). On the flip side, the lack of topic knowledge may attenuate the effect of ad skepticism. For example, although many consumers understand what sodium is, it is perhaps less common knowledge that reduced usage of sodium citrate in detergent helps protect the environment. If an advertising claim stresses a certain percentage of reduced sodium citrate, less knowledgeable consumers are less likely to reject the claim as untrue immediately after the moment of exposure. As a result, more precise numerical information is more likely to be attended to and factored into the process of making inferences about the advertised company's competence, even among high skeptics.

Furthermore, research on scarcity of information suggests that in the absence of essential information (e.g., personal experience with the product), more readily available information is perceived as more valuable and is more likely to be utilized (Kivetz and Simonson 2000). Indeed, green advertising often employs technical terms that are less familiar to ordinary consumers (Lord 1994). It is plausible that some environmental claims represent such a case of lower consumer topic knowledge. Consequently, the numerical precision in the advertisement becomes more relevant in constructing an impression about an advertised company. In short, we predict that consumer topic knowledge can mitigate the moderation effect of ad skepticism on perceived competence of the advertised company, when the more or less precise numerical information is presented in the green claims. Formally, we hypothesize that:

Hypothesis 2: Consumers' topic knowledge about an advertised environmental issue will influence the moderation effect of ad skepticism. While more knowledgeable and highly skeptical consumers are expected to be less affected by the signaling effect of numerical precision, less knowledgeable and highly skeptical consumers are expected to be more likely to be influenced by

FIGURE 1
Conceptual Model

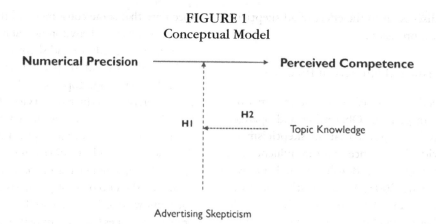

numerical precision, which will result in more positive perceptions of an advertised company's competence.

Our conceptual theorizing is illustrated in Figure 1. We suggest that ad skepticism moderates the effect of numerical precision on perceived competence of the advertised company: More precise numbers are expected to positively affect the perceptions of consumers low in ad skepticism, but not those high in ad skepticism. This moderation effect varies, depending on consumers' topic knowledge of the advertised proenvironment issues/attributes.

OVERVIEW OF METHOD

Study 1a and Study 1b were conducted to test H1a and H1b, suggesting that ad skepticism moderates the effect of numerical precision on company perception. Study 1a employs two print ads that differ only in the numerical precision of the claim (10% versus 10.2%). Study 1b uses text-only claims with four levels of numeric precision (19%, 19.2%, 19.24%, and 20%). Employing a different product, Study 2 replicates the effect demonstrated in Study 1a, showing its consistency for smaller but more precise numbers (19.41% versus 20%). Study 3 supports H2, suggesting that high skeptics may also be influenced by numerical precision in cases where they perceive themselves as less knowledgeable about the advertised green aspect of the product.

STUDY 1a

The purpose of Study 1a was to test the hypothesis that numerical precision elicits more positive perceptions of the company's competence among low skeptics, but does not affect high skeptics. We employed a one-factor (more versus less precise numbers) between-subject experimental design, with ad skepticism as an individual difference measurement. A total of 132 respondents were recruited from an online panel

to participate in this online experiment (56 males; 76 females; average age, 36.2).

Method

Stimuli

We created a fictitious print advertisement promoting an environmentally friendly aspect of a car (i.e., reduction of carbon emissions). The advertisement consisted of a simple picture of a car and an accompanying catchphrase. We manipulated numerical precision by varying the numerical information in the catchphrase: "Introducing the green car, 10% (10.2%) reduction in carbon emission." An example of the advertisement appears in Appendix 1. We used this simple design to avoid introducing potential noise such as visual complexity, layout, and color.

Procedure

Participants were residents living in the United States who had registered as survey respondents at an online public portal Web site. A brief introduction of the survey was posted on the Web site and it became viewable for the registered users. Clicking the link in the introduction directed participants to an online experiment. The participants were randomly assigned to one of the two conditions (i.e., more versus less precise numbers: 10.2% versus 10%). They read the print advertisement and answered the questions that followed.

Measures

Perception of company competence was measured by a five-item scale: "Please indicate the extent to which you think the advertised company is 'competent,' 'effective,' 'efficient,' 'expert,' and 'professional'" (1 = definitely not; 7 = definitely yes; unidimensional, $\alpha = .94$). Participants also rated trustworthiness of the ad on a five-item scale: "Please indicate the extent to which you think the advertisement is 'believable,' 'credible,' 'reliable,' 'trustworthy,' and 'truthful'" (1 = definitely not; 7 = definitely yes; unidimensional, α = .96).

Next, participants rated the degree of numerical precision in the claim: "The number mentioned in the advertisement is 'exact,' 'detailed,' 'precise,' and 'specific'" (1 = definitely not; 7 = definitely yes; unidimensional, α = .87). They were also asked about processing fluency: "The claim of 10% (10.2%) reduction in carbon emission is 'ambiguous,' 'easy to understand,' 'requires an effort to comprehend,' and 'vague'" (1 = definitely not; 7 = definitely yes; unidimensional, α = .84). Then participants rated the degree to which the advertisement promoted an environmentally friendly aspect of the product (1 = definitely not; 7 = definitely yes). Toward the end of the survey, participants reported their general skepticism toward advertising (Obermiller and Spangenberg 1998) on a seven-point scale (1 = strongly disagree; 7 = strongly agree; unidimensional, α = .95). Items in each multiple-item measurement scale were randomly presented to the participants. The means were used to measure the corresponding variables.

Results

Manipulation Check

Participants rated the numerical information as more precise in the 10.2% condition (M = 5.68, SD = 1.36) than in the 10% condition (M = 4.93, SD = 1.44), $F(1, 130)$ = 7.95, p = .006. They also indicated that this car advertisement (regardless of numerical precision condition) promoted an environmentally friendly aspect of the product (M = 5.91, SD = 1.32) compared to the neutral point 4 in the seven-point scale, $t(131)$ = 16.59, p < .001. These two claims did not differ significantly in processing fluency, $F(1, 130)$ = .98, p = .32.

Competence

Given that ad skepticism was a continuous variable, we used regression analysis to test whether skepticism interacted with numerical precision on the perceived competence of the advertised company (Aiken and West 1991). The standardized values of self-reported competence ratings were regressed on the numerical precision (10% versus 10.2%, binary), standardized values of individual differences in ad skepticism (continuous), and the interaction term (continuous). The results suggest that numerical precision alone does not have a significant effect on competence evaluation (β = .12, p = .16). Ad skepticism was not a significant predictor of company perception when the interaction term was added (β = −.07, p = .72). However, the interaction term was significant (β = .42, p = .036). In the 10% condition, advertising skepticism did not predict

competence perception (β = .10, p = .45). In the 10.2% condition, advertising skepticism was a significant predictor of competence perception (β = .48, p = .001).

To illustrate the interaction better, we categorized the participants as high or low skeptics using median split of the ad skepticism. Note that we did not recode the original advertising skepticism scale, so that the higher ratings indicated lower skepticism. Those whose ratings were higher than the median 3.33 were considered low skeptics (M = 4.30, SD = .74); those whose ratings were equal or lower than 3.33 were considered high skeptics (M = 2.20, SD = .80). The between-group mean difference was significant, $F(1, 130)$ = 243.31, p < .001.

We conducted a two-way ANOVA (analysis of variance) representing a 2 (numerical precision: 10% versus 10.2%) × 2 (ad skepticism: high versus low) design on perception of company competence. We found a significant main effect of ad skepticism on company competence: Lower skeptics (M = 5.10, SD = 1.12) rated the company as more competent in the 10.2% condition (M = 4.46, SD = 1.44), compared with high skeptics (M = 4.46, SD = 1.44), $F(1, 128)$ = 6.96, p = .009. The main effect of numerical precision was not significant, $F(1, 128)$ = 1.92, p = .17. As we predicted in H1a, the interaction was significant, $F(1, 128)$ = 8.01, p = .005. Specifically, perception of the company's competence in the 10% condition (M = 4.59, SD = 1.20) and in the 10.2% condition (M = 4.64, SD = 1.52) was not significantly different among high skeptics, $F(1, 61)$ = .75, p = .39. In comparison, perception of company competence was significantly more positive in the 10.2% condition (M = 5.52, SD = .88) than in the 10% condition (M = 4.32, SD = 1.38) among low skeptics, $F(1, 67)$ = 13.47, p < .001. Looking at those results from a different angle, low skeptics (M = 5.66, SD = .88) rated the advertised company as more competent than did high skeptics (M = 4.59, SD = 1.32) in the 10.2% condition, $F(1, 71)$ = 19.71, p < .001. In the 10% condition, high skeptics (M = 4.59, SD = 1.47) and low skeptics (M = 4.66, SD = 1.10) did not differ significantly, $F(1, 57)$ = .01, p = .91. Figure 2 depicts this interaction.

Mediation Analysis

We speculated that perceived trustworthiness would mediate the effect of ad skepticism on consumer perception of company competence. That is, high skeptics tend to distrust the informational claims so that the effect of numerical precision is not salient. In contrast, low skeptics tend to trust the informational claims, so more precise numbers become diagnostic in evaluating company competence. We tested the mediation effect following the procedure suggested by Baron and Kenny (1986). Ad skepticism predicted perception of company competence (β = .31, p < .001) and claim trustworthiness (β = .45, p < .001). When ad skepticism and trustworthiness were both

FIGURE 2
Perception of Company Competence as an Effect
of Ad Skepticism and Numerical Precision (Study 1)

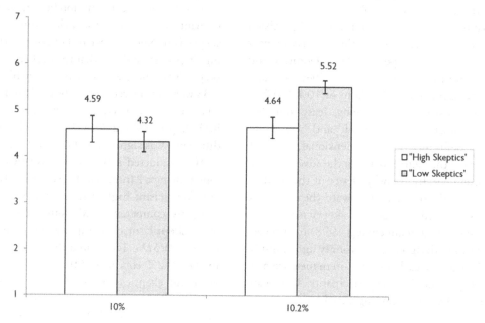

included in the regression to predict competence, the effect of ad skepticism was not significant (β = .09, p = .27), while the effect of trustworthiness was significant (β = .50, $p < .001$). A full mediation was evident, Sobel's t = 3.19, p = .001. H1a was supported. We performed the same mediation test for processing fluency. The results suggest that it was not a significant mediator of the effect of ad skepticism on perception of company competence.

Discussion

Study 1a supports H1a's prediction that ad skepticism moderates the effect of numerical precision on perceived company competence. Low skeptics tend to consider the advertised company as more competent when the numerical information is more precise. High skeptics, in contrast, do not differentiate between more versus less precise numerical information and tend to evaluate a company's competence lower than low skeptics regardless of the information provided in the ad. That is, low skeptics tend to be more susceptible to the signaling effect of numerical precision than high skeptics. Trustworthiness of the green claim mediates the observed effect: High skeptics tend to distrust the information presented in an advertisement. As a result, the signaling effect of numerical precision is mitigated.

Three questions remain, however. First, the evidence is inconclusive as to what inferences consumers draw from precise numbers. Namely, why do more precise numbers signal higher competence? Second, consumers differ in terms of preference and ability of processing numerical information, as the prior research on numeracy suggests (e.g., Peters et al. 2006, 2009; Viswanathan 1997). In this context, do individual differences in numeracy moderate the effect of numerical precision? Third, in our theoretical development, we suggest that numerical information is perceived as more important in advertising green attributes than regular attributes. This assumption has not been tested empirically yet. In Study 1b, we explore the answers to these three questions.

STUDY 1b

The purpose of Study 1b was to test the hypothesis that perceived scientific validity and informativeness mediate the effect of numerical precision on company competence. In this regard, we examined the inferences consumers draw when presented with precise numbers. We also investigated the effects of individual differences in numeracy. In addition, we measured perceived importance of precise numerical information in the advertising of green attributes as compared with utility attributes. We employed a 2 (advertised attribute: utility versus green) × 4 (four numbers: 19%, 19.2%, 19.24%, 20%) between-subject experimental design. Two hundred and thirty-nine respondents were recruited from an online panel to participate in this online experiment (100 males; 138 females; average age, 33.1).

Method

Stimuli and Manipulation

We used text-only claims similar to the catchphrase in Study 1a. The numbers and attributes were modified in order to represent: (1) gradual increase in the degree of numeric exactness (i.e., 20%, 19%, 19.2%, and 19.24%), and (2) green versus utility attributes (i.e., reduced carbon emissions versus reduced interior noise). Specifically, the advertising claim read, "introducing the green [quiet] car: 19% [19.2%, 19.24%, 20%] reduced carbon emissions [reduced interior noise]."

Procedure and Measures

After participants read the advertising claim, they reported the degree to which they perceived the number to be "informative" and "scientific" on a seven-point scale (1 = definitely not; 7 = definitely yes). The other dependent measure scales remained the same as those in Study 1a. We also asked participants about the relative importance of numerical information in advertising green attributes as compared with utility attributes: "How important is it that advertisers use precise numerical information when advertising green attributes of a product (e.g., carbon emissions, hazardous material use), compared with utility attributes of the product (e.g., noise level, color brightness)?" (1 = more important for green attributes; 4 = equally important; 7 = more important for utility attributes). Finally, participants completed the subjective numeracy scale (Fagerlin et al. 2007).

Results

Numerical Precision

A 2 (green versus utility claim) $\times$ 4 (four numbers) ANOVA showed that perceived numerical precision was significantly different across four numeric conditions, $F(3, 231) = 11.48$, $p < .001$. Planned contrasts suggest that 19% ($M = 5.16$, $SD = 1.55$) was more precise than 20% ($M = 4.13, SD = 1.85$), $t(235) = 3.52, p = .001$, whereas 19.2% ($M = 5.42, SD = 1.49$) was not significantly more precise than 19%, $t(235) = .92$, $p = .36$. In addition, 19.24% ($M = 5.73, SD = 1.37$) was more precise than 19%, $t(235) = 2.00, p = .047$, but it was not significantly more precise than 19.2%, $t(235) = 1.08, p = .28$. The main effect of advertised attribute (green versus utility) on numerical precision was not significant, $F(1, 231) = 1.10, p = .30$. The interaction was not significant, $F(3, 231) = .36, p = .78$.

Competence

We ran a 2×4 ANCOVA (analysis of covariance), controlling for the individual difference in numeracy as a covariate. The results indicate that none of the main effects or interaction were significant ($p > .10$). Numeracy as a covariate was significant, $F(1, 230) = 15.86, p < .001$, suggesting that numeracy may directly affect perceptions of a company's competence.

To test the potential moderation effect of numeracy, we used a median-split to categorize participants as high and low in numeracy. We focused on green claims (i.e., reduced carbon emissions) and ran a 2 (high versus low in numeracy) $\times$ 4 (four numbers) between-group ANOVA. The results suggest a significant main effect of numeracy: high-numeracy participants rated the advertised company as more competent ($M = 4.62$, $SD = 1.20$) than the low-numeracy participants ($M = 3.68$, $SD = 1.39$), $F(1, 110) = 17.55, p < .001$. However, the main effect of number ($p = .15$) and the interaction were not significant ($p = .21$).

Mediation Analysis

We suggested in H1b that more precise numbers would be considered more informative and scientific, which would mediate the precision effect on consumer perception of company competence. We tested the mediation effect of "informativeness" and "scientific-ness," respectively. Numerical precision predicted perception of company competence ($\beta = .51, p < .001$), "informativeness" ($\beta = .41, p < .001$), and "scientific-ness" ($\beta = .50, p < .001$). When numerical precision and informativeness were both included in the regression to predict company competence, the effect of numerical precision was significant but weaker ($\beta = .38, p < .001$), while the effect of informativeness remained significant ($\beta = .35$, $p < .001$). A partial mediation was evident, Sobel's $t = 4.61$, $p < .001$. In a similar vein, when numerical precision and "scientific-ness" were both included in the regression to predict company competence, the effect of numerical precision was significant but weaker ($\beta = .35, p < .001$), while the effect of "scientific-ness" remained significant ($\beta = .33, p < .001$). A partial mediation was evident, Sobel's $t = 4.24, p < .001$. H1b was therefore supported.

Importance of Numerical Precision

First, participants indicated that the "reduced carbon emission" claim promoted an environmentally friendly aspect of the product ($M = 5.99, SD = 1.40$) to a greater extent than the "reduced interior noise" claim ($M = 2.26, SD = 1.55$), $F(1, 237) = 381.33, p < .001$. Second, we tested the relative importance of precise numerical information in advertising green attributes versus utility attributes. One-way ANOVA suggested that numerical information was rated as more important in the "reduced carbon emission" condition ($M = 3.97$, $SD = 1.64$) than in the "reduced interior noise" condition ($M = 3.55, SD = 1.64$), $F(1, 237) = 4.09, p = .044$. Last, on average, participants reported that it was more important to use precise numerical information when advertising green attributes than when advertising utility attributes ($M = 3.76$, $SD = 1.65$), compared to the neutral point 4 (equally important), $t(238) = -2.27$, $p = .024$.

Discussion

In Study 1b, we introduced another set of numbers and claims, testing three questions: whether numerical precision is considered more important when advertising green attributes than when advertising utility attributes; whether numeracy as an individual difference moderates susceptibility to numerical precision; and finally, we explored two possible mediators for the effect of precision on perceived company competence. The results provide evidence that precise numbers are perceived as more informative and scientific, which contributes to more positive perceptions of company competence. Furthermore, consumers who are higher in numeracy consider the advertised company as more competent, but numeracy doesn't moderate the effect of precision on perceived company competency. Last, results supported our assumption presented in the beginning of the paper that numerical precision would be perceived as more important in advertising green attributes than in advertising utility attributes.

Combined, the results of Studies 1a and 1b suggest that the effect of numerical precision is more pronounced for low skeptics than for high skeptics. But one question remains: To what extent is the interaction between precision and skepticism context-specific? In other words, is the observed effect bounded by factors such as product category, the specific advertised attribute, the environmental focus of the claim, or using unique numbers? In particular, it is possible that our results can be accounted for by the mere fact that the number 10.2 is slightly but objectively bigger than 10. In Study 2, our goal was to replicate the observed interaction addressing this alternative explanation. We used a different product and focused on two different beneficial attributes.

STUDY 2

We used a 2 (claim focus: more- versus less-focused on environmental issues) × 2 (numerical precision: 19.41% versus 20%) between-subject experimental design, with ad skepticism as an individual difference measurement. A total of 148 respondents in an online panel participated in this online experiment (47 males; 101 females; average age, 34.9).

Method

Stimuli and Manipulation

We created another fictitious print advertisement, changing the product from a car to a mattress. The advertisement con-

sisted of a simple picture of a mattress and an accompanying catchphrase. An example of the ad appears in Appendix 2. The catchphrase was "greener foam, better sleep; 20% (19.41%) soy-infused organic foam" or "better foam, better sleep; 20% (19.41%) high density memory foam." Numerical precision was manipulated by adding two decimal digits to the percentage number (19.41% versus 20%). Mathematically, 19.41% is smaller than 20%, and usually 19.41% would be rounded to 19% rather than 20%.

Procedure and Measures

Participants went through a procedure similar to that used in Study 1a. We measured company competence, claim trustworthiness, the extent to which the advertisement promotes an environmental aspect of the product, and perceived numerical precision. The ad skepticism scale was again placed toward the end of the online survey. We used a median-split to categorize participants as high skeptics and low skeptics.

Results

Manipulation Check

Participants rated the numerical information as more precise in the 19.41% condition ($M = 5.57$, $SD = 1.30$) than in the 20% condition ($M = 5.11$, $SD = 1.44$), $F(1, 146) = 4.23$, $p = .04$. They considered the advertisement as promoting an environmentally friendly aspect of the product to a higher degree in the organic foam condition ($M = 5.95$, $SD = 1.18$) than the higher density condition ($M = 2.19$, $SD = 1.34$), $F(1, 146) = 329.21$, $p < .001$.

Competence

We conducted a 2 (numerical precision: 10% versus 10.2%) × 2 (claim: more- versus less-focused on environmental issue) × 2 (ad skepticism: high versus low) between-subject ANOVA on perception of company competence. The main effect of ad skepticism was significant: Low skeptics rated the company as more competent ($M = 4.59$, $SD = 1.33$) than the high skeptics ($M = 3.82$, $SD = 1.29$), $F(1, 140) = 10.30$, $p = .002$. Replicating the results of Study 1a, the two-way interaction between precision and skepticism was significant, $F(1, 140) = 5.25$, $p = .02$. Low skeptics rated the advertised company as more competent ($M = 4.78$, $SD = 1.29$) than high skeptics ($M = 3.54$, $SD = 1.46$) in the 19.41% condition, $F(1, 72) = 15.21$, $p < .001$. In the 20% condition, high skeptics ($M = 4.10$, $SD = 1.02$) and low skeptics ($M = 4.39$, $SD = 1.37$) did not differ significantly, $F(1, 72) = 1.05$, $p = .31$. None of the other main or interaction effects were significant at the $p = .05$ level.

Discussion

Study 2 provides further evidence that ad skepticism moderates the effect of numerical precision on perceived company competence. It extends the findings of Study 1 in a different product category (mattresses), using a different set of numerical information (19.41% or 20%), where the more precise number is smaller than and more distant from the round number. Study 2 replicates the results in two types of claims: a more environmentally focused claim versus a less environmentally focused claim (soy infusion/density). Our results further support H1a, suggesting that the interaction of ad skepticism and numerical precision holds across different product categories, different numbers, and different attributes.

Next, we test H2, which suggested that there would be boundary conditions for the effect of ad skepticism on consumer perceptions of a company's competence in response to numerical precision. As we found in Study 1a, high skeptics do not tend to trust precise numbers more than round numbers. In H2, we predicted that the low effectiveness of numerical precision on high skeptics could change in the case of low topic knowledge of the advertised issue. This might occur because it becomes harder for high skeptics to completely discount the validity of the precision cues without adequate topic knowledge. In Study 3, we manipulated topic knowledge and tested the effectiveness of numerical precision in the case of high skeptics with low topic knowledge.

STUDY 3

The purpose of Study 3 was to examine the extent to which consumer topic knowledge influences the effect of ad skepticism on susceptibility to numerical precision. We used a 2 (numerical precision: 15% versus 15.32%) × 2 (topic knowledge: high versus low) between-subject experimental design, with ad skepticism as an individual measurement. A total of 180 respondents in an online panel participated in this online experiment (101 males; 79 females; average age, 33.9).

Method

Stimuli and Manipulation

We used the car print ad employed in Study 1a, modifying the numbers and claims. The layout remained the same. The catchphrase was "introducing the green car, 15% (15.32%) higher fuel (thermal) efficiency." We chose 15% rather than 20% or 10% to extend our results to less round percentage numbers (i.e., numbers that do not end with a zero). Topic knowledge about fuel efficiency and thermal efficiency was pretested with another 60 online panel participants (37 males; 23 female; average age, 34.7). They read both claims (text only,

without numbers or pictures: "introducing the green car, with higher fuel/thermal efficiency") in a random order, and then indicated how knowledgeable they were about each claim on a seven-point Likert scale (1 = not knowledgeable at all; 7 = very knowledgeable). The within-subject mean difference was significant: Participants indicated they were more knowledgeable about fuel efficiency ($M = 5.51$, $SD = 1.31$) than thermal efficiency ($M = 2.39$, $SD = 1.58$), $t(56) = 13.45$, $p < .001$.

Procedure and Measures

Participants went through the same procedure that was used in Study 1a. All the dependent measure scales remained the same. In addition, we asked, "How knowledgeable are you about thermal (fuel) efficiency?" on a seven-point Likert scale (1 = not knowledgeable at all; 7 = very knowledgeable). The ad skepticism was measured toward the end of the survey. We used a median-split of the ad skepticism to categorize participants as high and low skeptics.

Results

Manipulation Check

Participants rated the numerical information as more precise in the 15.32% condition ($M = 5.68$, $SD = 1.28$) than in the 15% condition ($M = 4.86$, $SD = 1.63$), $F(1, 178) = 13.92$, $p < .001$. They indicated being more knowledgeable about fuel efficiency ($M = 4.52$, $SD = 1.41$) than about thermal efficiency ($M = 2.43$, $SD = 1.79$), $F(1, 178) = 75.13$, $p < .001$. No confounding effect was found: The level of topic knowledge was not significantly different between 15% and 15.32% conditions, $F(1, 178) = .002$, $p = .96$, and perceived precision was not significantly different between the claim types, $F(1, 178) = .15$, $p = .70$. Manipulations were successful.

Competence

We conducted a 2 (topic knowledge: high versus low) × 2 (advertising skepticism: high versus low) × 2 (numerical precision: 15% versus 15.32%) between-subject ANOVA on perceived company competence. The results suggest that the main effect of ad skepticism was significant: Low skeptics rated the advertised company as more competent ($M = 5.13$, $SD = 1.09$) than high skeptics ($M = 4.41$, $SD = 1.24$), $F(1, 172) = 17.54$, $p < .001$. None of the other main effects or two-way interactions were significant at the $p = .05$ level.

As expected, the three-way interaction was significant, $F(1, 172) = 6.08$, $p = .015$. We interpret the interaction by examining the high versus low topic knowledge conditions separately. When the claim was about fuel efficiency (i.e.,

FIGURE 3

Perception of the Company's Competence as an Effect of Numerical Precision
in the Case of Low Topic Knowledge (Study 3: Thermal Efficiency)

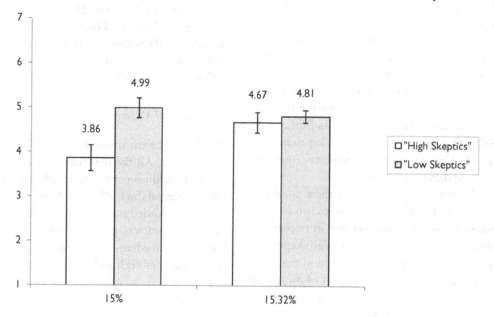

"high topic knowledge"), low skeptics rated the advertised company as more competent ($M = 5.44$, $SD = .92$) than high skeptics ($M = 4.25$, $SD = 1.49$) in the precise number condition (15.32%), $F(1, 41) = 10.51$, $p = .002$. In the 15% condition, high skeptics ($M = 4.74$, $SD = .78$) and low skeptics ($M = 5.20$, $SD = 1.16$) did not differ significantly, $F(1, 43) = 2.13$, $p = .15$. This pattern replicated the moderation effect of ad skepticism in Study 1a and Study 2.

In contrast, when the claim was about thermal efficiency (i.e., "low topic knowledge"), high skeptics ($M = 4.67$, $SD = 1.26$) and low skeptics ($M = 4.81$, $SD = 1.07$) did not differ significantly in the 15.32% condition, $F(1, 42) = .16$, $p = .70$. In the 15% condition, low skeptics rated the advertised company as more competent ($M = 4.99$, $SD = 1.15$) than high skeptics ($M = 3.86$, $SD = 1.18$), $F(1, 46) = 10.67$, $p = .002$ (see Figure 3). That is, when more precise numerical information was presented, less knowledgeable high skeptics rated the advertised company's competence as positively as the low skeptics..

Furthermore, the interaction between topic knowledge and numerical precision was not significant among low skeptics, $F(1, 96) = .88$, $p = .35$. Among high skeptics, however, the interaction was significant, $F(1, 76) = 5.67$, $p = .02$. High skeptics rated the advertised company as more competent in the 15.32% condition ($M = 4.67$, $SD = 1.26$) than in the 15% condition ($M = 3.86$, $SD = 1.18$) when the claim was about thermal efficiency, $F(1, 43) = 4.72$, $p = .04$. When the claim was about fuel efficiency, high skeptics did not consider 15.32% ($M = 4.25$, $SD = 1.49$) and 15% ($M = 4.74$,

$SD = .78$) significantly differently, $F(1, 33) = 1.55$, $p = .22$. H2 was supported.

Discussion

Study 3 suggests that when topic knowledge is low, high skeptics and low skeptics can respond to precise numerical information similarly. In other words, in the case of low knowledge about an environmental aspect of a product, high skeptics also tend to associate more precise numbers with higher competence of the advertised company. Extending the findings of Study 1a, Study 1b, and Study 2, Study 3 reveals a situation where the moderation of ad skepticism on the signaling effect of numerical precision can be attenuated.

GENERAL DISCUSSION

Summary of Results

The current work demonstrates the moderating role of ad skepticism on the signaling effect of numerical precision on consumer perception of an advertised company's competence. We find that when more precise numbers are used in environmental advertising claims (e.g., 19.41%), consumers who are less skeptical tend to trust the advertisement and eventually evaluate the competence of the advertised company more positively, as opposed to using less precise numbers (e.g., 20%). However, high skeptics tend to disbelieve the information presented in advertisements, which makes it harder to convince them of a company's competence, even if more precise numbers are used.

We replicate the moderation effect three times, using two different products (i.e., a car and a mattress) and employing a set of numbers, which differ not only in precision, but also, more importantly, in the direction of the mathematical difference. By using a smaller but more precise number, Study 2 rules out an alternative explanation that the more positive company perception occurs because the claim presents a larger number. In Study 1b, we explore multiple levels of numeric specificity. The findings suggest that simply adding more decimal digits does not guarantee a linear increase of perceived precision. Perhaps beyond the scope of this paper, it would be interesting to explore the threshold, marginal, or even reversed effect of precision. For instance, does 19.2485% continue the thread of the effect or backfire as unnecessarily precise? We also show that the use of numerical precision can be applied to attributes that differ in the extent of their focus on environmental protection: soy infusion (i.e., higher focus) and foam density (i.e., lower focus) of the mattress.

Finally, we find that high skepticism toward advertising can be overcome in certain conditions. In Study 3, we demonstrate that lack of topic knowledge serves as a boundary condition for the moderating effect of ad skepticism. High skeptics, who were not susceptible to any of our numerical precision manipulations in Study 1a and Study 2, were highly influenced by numerical precision (as much as the low skeptics) when put in a situation of insufficient knowledge about the advertised product attribute (i.e., thermal efficiency). This result resonates with previous research that suggests that scarcity of information enhances the importance and persuasiveness of whatever information is available. In sum, when a company promotes an environmentally friendly attribute of a product that is less familiar to consumers, high skeptics may become susceptible to more precise numerical information in the advertisement.

Theoretical Contribution

Green advertising is often associated with numerical findings, evidence, and projections. The nature of this particular type of advertising served as the basis that motivates this work. The current research attempts to capture the effect of numerical precision in the advertising of environmental product attributes. Providing a possibly more general conclusion regarding precision in advertising, we identify a boundary condition for the impact of ad skepticism on the signaling effect of numerical precision in green advertising. We find that relatively low topic knowledge affects consumers with high skepticism toward advertising: They tend to respond more favorably to precise numerical claims. These findings extend previous research on ad skepticism by introducing a potentially more effective appeal for high skeptics with low topic knowledge.

We use green advertising as a natural context to compare higher and lower knowledge about an advertised product attribute. It is possible that our findings can be extended to nonenvironmental issues. Consumers vary in the degree to which they consider green issues to be important (e.g., Kronrod, Grinstein, and Wathieu 2012; Lord 1994). In comparison, in advertising ordinary utility consumer products, the claims are often not expected to be number-laden. For example, advertising jeans that are sewn using 12.63% more twisted thread may be quite effective because most consumers do not know the significance of thread twisting in sewing jeans. On top of this concern, the numerical precision may be ignored because consumers do not care so much about the degree of twisting of the threads used in their jeans. Thus, predictions for nonenvironmental advertising may be more ambiguous. We speculate, however, that the overarching effect of knowledge on ad skepticism can be generalized to nonenvironmental advertising as well, and we may also see more evidence for higher susceptibility to numerical precision as a result of insufficient knowledge. This theoretical implication is consistent with findings on consumer judgment in cases of information scarcity (e.g., Kivetz and Simonson 2000).

Extending previous research on the effect of complexity on persuasiveness of numerical information, we demonstrate a cognitive account for the salient effect of numerical precision on low skeptics but not on high skeptics—the perceived trustworthiness of the claims. Not surprisingly, our findings suggest that high skeptics do not trust the informational claim as much as low skeptics do. It is important to note that we do not find significant differences between the perceived processing fluency of less versus more precise numbers. This result may also address the mixed findings in the literature regarding the effect of fluency and disfluency, and processing difficulty of complex information. When no computation or number comparison is required, consumers do not necessarily perceive more precise numerical information as more complex or more difficult to process. Therefore, such a signaling effect may be void of complexity and more readily related with the perceived informativeness and scientific-ness of precise numbers in the green claims. In this sense, this research sheds further light on conceptual overlapping, as well as differences between numerical precision and numerical complexity.

Future Research

The current research focuses on percentage ratios and decimals. While the numerical information in all the studies naturally fits such claims of higher or lower carbon emission or fuel efficiency, numbers are not always expressed in percentage ratios. It remains a question for further exploration whether our findings can be generalized to other types of numerical information, such as amounts, fractions, or scales. It is possible, for example, that numerical precision of whole numbers (i.e., a promise of 127 rpm versus 130 rpm) would not be as effective as numbers involving decimal grading because of consumers' general preference for round numbers (e.g., Burson, Larrick, and Lynch 2009; Pandelaere, Briers, and Lembregts 2011; Wertenbroch, Soman, and Chattopadhyay 2007). Another possible reason to find a difference between various measurement units is the relative familiarity of consumers with, say, fractions versus percent units, and the possible levels of ease of computing different units (Thomas and Morwitz 2009). Finally, our findings pertain to a promise of numerical *change*. All the advertising claims were expressed employing percentage of change. It is likely that consumers are less sensitive to numerical precision in fixed numerical information because there is no element of comparison.

These limitations curb the extent to which the findings can be directly generalized across all contexts, but also suggest directions for future research. These situational variations may function as boundary conditions, while the salient effect of numerical precision may persist. Future studies could explore the different types of information, change versus fixed numbers, and the direction of change. It is noteworthy that numerical precision is not always a significant issue in advertising. For example, when an advertisement uses emotional appeals, using numerical precision may backfire, since numerical precision is associated with more rational thinking, which is less congruent with the "state-of-mind" evoked during emotional responses.

To conclude, we demonstrate that in green advertising, which often employs numerical information about issues of varying familiarity to the ordinary consumer, ad skepticism moderates the signaling effect of numerical precision. This effect can be attenuated due to consumers' insufficient topic knowledge. In this regard, the current work echoes the ancient phrase "Knowledge is power" (cf. Proverbs 24:5). More precisely, the findings in this research suggest that in some cases, the *lack* of knowledge is a *weakness*.

REFERENCES

Aiken, Leona S., and Stephen G. West (1991), *Multiple Regression: Testing and Interpreting Interactions,* Thousand Oaks, CA: Sage.

Alter, Adam L., and Daniel M. Oppenheimer (2006), "Predicting Short-Term Stock Fluctuations by Using Processing Fluency," *Proceedings of the National Academy of Sciences,* 103 (24), 9369–9372.

Baron, Reuben M., and David A. Kenny (1986), "The Moderator-Mediator Variable Distinction in Social Psychological Research: Conceptual, Strategic, and Statistical Considerations," *Journal of Personality and Social Psychology,* 51 (6), 1173–1182.

Boulding, William, and Amna Kirmani (1993), "A Consumer-Side Experimental Examination of Signaling Theory: Do Consumers Perceive Warranties as Signals of Quality?" *Journal of Consumer Research,* 20 (1), 111–123.

Boush, Dave M., Marian Friestad, and Gregory M. Rose (1994), "Adolescent Skepticism Toward TV Advertising and Knowledge of Advertiser Tactics," *Journal of Consumer Research,* 21 (1), 165–174.

Burke, Kenneth (1954), *Permanence and Change,* Los Altos, CA: Hermes.

Burson, Katherine A., Richard P. Larrick, and John G. Lynch, Jr. (2009), "Six of One, Half-Dozen of the Other: Expanding and Contracting Numerical Dimensions Produces Preference Reversals," *Psychological Science,* 20 (9), 1074–1078.

Campbell, Margaret C., and Amna Kirmani (2000), "Consumers' Use of Persuasion Knowledge: The Effects of Accessibility and Cognitive Capacity on Perceptions of an Influence Agent," *Journal of Consumer Research,* 27 (1), 69–83.

Carlson, Les, Stephen J. Grove, and Norman Kangun (1993), "A Content Analysis of Environmental Advertising Claims: A Matrix Method Approach," *Journal of Advertising,* 22 (3), 27–39.

Chan, Ricky Y.K. (2000), "The Effectiveness of Environmental Advertising: The Role of Claim Type and the Source Country Green Image," *International Journal of Advertising,* 19 (3), 349–375.

Chernev, Alexander, and Gregory S. Carpenter (2001), "The Role of Market Efficiency Institutions in Consumer Choice: A Case of Compensatory Inferences," *Journal of Marketing Research,* 38 (3), 349–361.

Clark, John M., T. Bettina Cornwell, and Stephen W. Pruitt (2002), "Corporate Stadium Sponsorships, Signaling Theory, Agency Conflicts, and Shareholder Wealth," *Journal of Advertising Research,* 42 (6), 16–32.

Cummins, Chris, Uli Sauerland, and Stephani Solt (2012), "Granularity and Scalar Implicature in Numerical Expressions," *Linguistics and Philosophy,* 35 (2), 135–169.

Darke, Peter R., and Robin J. B. Ritchie (2007), "The Defensive Consumer: Advertising Deception, Defensive Processing, and Distrust," *Journal of Marketing Research,* 44 (1), 114–127.

DeCarlo, Thomas (2005), "The Effects of Sales Message and Suspicion of Ulterior Motives on Salesperson Evaluation," *Journal of Consumer Psychology,* 15 (3), 238–249.

Diemand-Yauman, Connor, Daniel M. Oppenheimer, and Erikka B. Vaughan (2011), "Fortune Favors the Bold (and the Italicized): Effects of Disfluency on Educational Outcomes," *Cognition,* 118 (1), 111–115.

Erdem, Tülin, and Joffre Swait (2004), "Brand Credibility, Brand Consideration, and Choice," *Journal of Consumer Research,* 31 (1), 191–198.

Fagerlin, Angela, Brian J. Zikmund-Fisher, Peter A. Ubel, Aleksandra Jankovic, Holly A. Derry, and Dylan M. Smith (2007), "Measuring Numeracy Without a Math Test: Development of the Subjective Numeracy Scale," *Medical Decision Making,* 27 (5), 672–680.

Federal Trade Commission (FTC) (2012), "Guides for the Use of Environmental Marketing Claims," available at www

.ftc.gov/bcp/grnrule/guides980427.htm (accessed June 15, 2012).

Ford, Garyt T., Darlene B. Smith, and John Swasy (1990), "Consumer Skepticism of Advertising Claims: Testing Hypotheses from Economics of Information," *Journal of Consumer Research,* 16 (4), 433–441.

Forehand, Mark R., and Sonya Grier (2003), "When Is Honesty the Best Policy? The Effect of Stated Company Intent on Consumer Skepticism," *Journal of Consumer Psychology,* 13 (3), 349–356.

Friestad, Marian, and Peter Wright (1994), "The Persuasion Knowledge Model: How People Cope with Persuasion Attempts," *Journal of Consumer Research,* 21 (1), 1–31.

Hardesty, David M., Jay P. Carlson, and William O. Bearden (2002), "Brand Familiarity and Invoice Price Effects on Consumer Evaluations: The Moderating Role of Skepticism Toward Advertising," *Journal of Advertising,* 31 (2), 1–15.

Kangun, Norman, Les Carlson, and Stephen J. Grove (1991), "Environmental Advertising Claims: A Preliminary Investigation," *Journal of Public Policy and Marketing,* 10 (2), 47–58.

Kilbourne, William E. (1995), "Green Advertising: Salvation or Oxymoron?" *Journal of Advertising,* 24 (2), 7–20.

Kim, Hakkyun, Akshay R. Rao, and Angela Y. Lee (2009), "It's Time to Vote: The Effect of Matching Message Orientation and Temporal Frame on Political Persuasion," *Journal of Consumer Research,* 35 (6), 877–889.

King, Dan, and Chris Janiszewski (2011), "The Sources and Consequences of the Fluent Processing of Numbers," *Journal of Marketing Research,* 48 (2), 327–341.

Kinnear, Thomas C., James R. Taylor, and Sadrudin A. Ahmed (1974), "Ecologically Concerned Consumers: Who Are They?" *Journal of Marketing,* 38 (2), 20–24.

Kirmani, Amna (1997), "Advertising Repetition as a Signal of Quality: If It's Advertised So Often, Something Must Be Wrong," *Journal of Advertising,* 26 (3), 77–86.

———, and Akshay R. Rao (2000), "No Pain, No Gain: A Critical Review of the Literature on Signaling Unobservable Product Quality," *Journal of Marketing,* 64 (2), 66–79.

———, and Peter Wright (1989), "Money Talks: Perceived Advertising Expense and Expected Product Quality," *Journal of Consumer Research,* 16 (3), 344–353.

Kivetz, Ran, and Itamar Simonson (2000), "The Effects of Incomplete Information on Consumer Choice," *Journal of Marketing Research,* 37 (4), 427–448.

Kotler, Philip (2011), "Reinventing Marketing to Manage the Environmental Imperative," *Journal of Marketing,* 75 (4), 132–135.

Kronrod, Ann, Amir Grinstein, and Luc Wathieu (2012), "Go Green! Should Environmental Messages Be So Assertive?" *Journal of Marketing,* 76 (1), 95–102.

Laham, Simon M., Peter Koval, and Adam L. Alter (2012), "The Name-Pronunciation Effect: Why People Like Mr. Smith More Than Mr. Colquhoun," *Journal of Experimental Social Psychology,* 48 (3), 752–756.

Lee, Angela Y., and Aparna A. Labroo (2004), "The Effect of Conceptual and Perceptual Fluency on Brand Evaluation," *Journal of Marketing Research,* 41 (2), 151–165.

Lord, Kenneth R. (1994), "Motivating Recycling Behavior: A Quasi-Experimental Investigation of Message and Source Strategies," *Psychology and Marketing,* 11 (4), 341–358.

Luchs, Michael G., Rebecca Walker Naylor, Julie R. Irwin, and Rajagopal Raghunathan (2010), "The Sustainability Liability: Potential Negative Effects of Ethicality on Product Preference," *Journal of Marketing,* 74 (5), 18–31.

Mader, Thomas F. (1973), "On Presence in Rhetoric," *College Composition and Communication,* 24 (5), 375–381.

Main, Kelley J., Darren W. Dahl, and Peter R. Darke (2007), "Deliberative and Automatic Bases of Suspicion: Empirical Evidence of the Sinister Attribution Error," *Journal of Consumer Psychology,* 17 (1), 59–69.

Miles, Morgan P., and Jeffrey G. Covin (2000), "Environmental Marketing: A Source of Reputational, Competitive, and Financial Advantage," *Journal of Business Ethics,* 23 (3), 299–311.

Montoro-Rios, Francisco Javier, Teodoro Luque-Martínez, and Miguel-Angel Rodríguez-Molina (2008), "How Green Should You Be: Can Environmental Associations Enhance Brand Performance?" *Journal of Advertising Research,* 48 (4), 547–563.

Murphy, Patrick E., Norman Kangun, and William B. Locander (1978), "Environmentally Concerned Consumers: Racial Variations," *Journal of Marketing,* 42 (4), 61–66.

Nakajima, Nina (2001), "Green Advertising and Green Public Relations as Integration Propaganda," *Bulletin of Science, Technology and Society,* 21 (5), 334–348.

Obermiller, Carl (1995), "The Baby Is Sick/the Baby Is Well: A Test of Environmental Communication Appeals," *Journal of Advertising,* 24 (2), 55–70.

———, and Eric R. Spangenberg (1998), "Development of a Scale to Measure Consumer Skepticism Toward Advertising," *Journal of Consumer Psychology,* 7 (2), 159–186.

———, ———, and Douglas L. MacLachlan (2005), "Ad Skepticism," *Journal of Advertising,* 34 (3), 7–17.

Pandelaere, Mario, Barbara Briers, and Christophe Lembregts (2011), "How to Make a 29% Increase Look Bigger: The Unit Effect in Option Comparisons," *Journal of Consumer Research,* 38 (2), 308–322.

Peters, E., N.F. Dieckmann, D. Västfjäll, C.K. Mertz, P. Slovic, and J.H. Hibbard (2009), "Bringing Meaning to Numbers: The Impact of Evaluative Categories on Decisions," *Journal of Experimental Psychology: Applied,* 15 (3), 213–227.

———, D. Västfjäll, P. Slovic, C. Mertz, K. Mazzocco, and S. Dickert (2006), "Numeracy and Decision Making," *Psychological Science,* 17 (5), 407–413

Scammon, Debra L., and Robert N. Mayer (1995), "Agency Review of Environmental Marketing Claims: Case-by-Case Decomposition of the Issues," *Journal of Advertising,* 24 (2), 33–43.

Schuhwerk, Melody E., and Roxanne Lefkoff-Hagius (1995), "Green or Non-Green? Does Type of Appeal Matter When Advertising a Green Product?" *Journal of Advertising,* 24 (2), 45–54.

Schwarz, Norbert (2004), "Metacognitive Experiences in Consumer Judgment and Decision Making," *Journal of Consumer Psychology,* 14 (4), 332–348.

Sen, Sankar, and C.B. Bhattacharya (2001), "Does Doing Good Always Lead to Doing Better? Consumer Reactions to Corporate Social Responsibility," *Journal of Marketing Research,* 38 (2), 225–243.

Shah, Anuj K., and Daniel M. Oppenheimer (2007), "Easy Does It: The Role of Fluency in Cue Weighting," *Judgment and Decision Making,* 2 (6), 371–379.

Sheth, Jagdish, Nirmal Sethia, and Shanthi Srinivas (2011), "Mindful Consumption: A Customer-Centric Approach to Sustainability," *Journal of the Academy of Marketing Science,* 39 (1), 21–39.

Shrum, L.J., John A. McCarty, and Tina M. Lowrey (1995), "Buyer Characteristics of the Green Consumer and Their Implications for Advertising Strategy," *Journal of Advertising,* 24 (2), 71–82.

Sigurd, Bengt (1988), "Round Numbers," *Language in Society,* 17 (2), 243–252.

Suau-Jiménez, Francisca (2005), "The Difficult Balance Between Author's and Academic Community's Power over Research Articles in Applied Linguistics," *LSP and Professional Communication,* 5 (2), 59–72.

Stafford, Marla Royne, Thomas F. Stafford, and Jhinuk Chowdhury (1996), "Predispositions Toward Green Issues: The Potential Efficacy of Advertising Appeals," *Journal of Current Issues and Research in Advertising,* 18 (1), 67–79.

Thomas, Manoj, and Vicki G. Morwitz (2009), "The Ease-of-Computation Effect: The Interplay of Metacognitive Experiences and Naive Theories in Judgments of Price Differences," *Journal of Marketing Research,* 46 (1), 81–91.

Viswanathan, Madhubalan (1997), "Individual Differences in Need for Precision," *Personality and Social Psychology Bulletin,* 23 (7), 717–735.

Wei, Jennifer M. Y. (2003), "Codeswitching in Campaigning Discourse: The Case of Taiwanese President Chen Shuibian," *Language and Linguistics,* 4 (1), 139–165.

Wertenbroch, Klaus, Dilip Soman, and Amitava Chattopadhyay (2007), "On the Perceived Value of Money: The Reference Dependence of Currency Numerosity Effects," *Journal of Consumer Research,* 34 (1), 1–10.

Wiener, Joshua Lyle (1985), "Are Warranties Accurate Signals of Product Reliability?" *Journal of Consumer Research,* 12 (2), 245–250.

Zinkhan, George M., and Les Carlson (1995), "Green Advertising and the Reluctant Consumer," *Journal of Advertising,* 24 (2), 1–6.

APPENDIX 1

Study 1 Advertisement Example

APPENDIX 2

Study 2 Advertisement Example

VICTORIA'S *DIRTY* SECRETS

Effectiveness of Green Not-for-Profit Messages Targeting Brands

Marie-Cécile Cervellon

ABSTRACT: "Donna Karan Bunny Butcher," "Bloody Burberry": Not-for-profit (NFP) campaigns regularly take brands hostage. These shock tactics are meant to bring publicity to targeted companies' practices that are deemed socially and environmentally irresponsible. The aim is to coerce such firms into complying with NFPs' demands, for fear of consumers' backlash. Surprisingly, there is scant evidence showing the impact of these messages on consumer behavior. This paper examines consumer response to messages targeting brands in the context of the luxury fashion industry. Two experiments, involving repeated measurement and between-subjects message manipulation (framing and target), were conducted. Results show that eco-involvement and product involvement are moderators of consumer response.

Not-for-profit (NFP) organizations and anticonsumerist media such as Adbuster have a tradition of targeting brands in their communications, often in a controversial way, to promote ideas and actions their proponents believe will improve social welfare (Lenox and Eesley 2009; West and Sargeant 2004). Past campaigns have dealt with a variety of social causes, from the abolition of animal experiments (e.g., the "Forcechange" campaign targeting L'Oréal in 2012) to the eradication of child labor (e.g., the "Clean Clothes" campaign targeting Levi Strauss in 2006). One of the most famous campaigns targeting brands is the series of Absolut Vodka spoof ads ("Absolut Impotent" 1996) by Adbusters.org, aimed at the reduction of alcohol consumption and protesting the influence of brands in society. Recently, People for the Ethical Treatment of Animals (PETA) campaigned against the use of animal furs in fashion collections, targeting Donna Karan New York with the claim "Donna Karan Bunny Butcher" (http://dkbunnybutcher.com 2011) and Burberry with the claim "Bloody Burberry" (http://bloodyburberry.com 2012).

The case that inspires this paper is that of the American lingerie brand Victoria's Secret, which was attacked by the organization ForestEthics for the destruction of endangered forests through the massive printing of catalogues daily. The ad campaign "Victoria's *dirty* Secret" created enormous buzz. Hundreds of women showed their disapproval of the brand by demonstrating dressed in lingerie in front of Victoria's Secret headquarters in New York City. Consequently, Tom Katzenmeyer, senior vice president at Limited Brands holding Victoria's Secret, committed to making his company more sustainable; henceforth, the company would print catalogues only on recycled paper (Hamilton 2007). The campaign "Victoria's *dirty* Secret" can be considered a specific form of green adver-

tising. Following Banerjee, Gulas, and Iyer's definition, green advertising adheres to at least one or more of the following criteria: "1) explicitly or implicitly addresses the relationship between a product/service and the biophysical environment, 2) promotes a green lifestyle with or without highlighting a product/service, 3) presents a corporate image of environmental responsibility" (1995, p. 22). The campaign "Victoria's *dirty* Secret" depicts Victoria's Secret as disregarding the environment, suggesting that the corporation behind the brand is reckless; it accuses the brand of promoting a negligent lifestyle and antienvironmental behaviors by encouraging consumers to read fashion catalogues, and shop through them.

These types of campaigns are part of an arsenal of marketing techniques aimed at achieving "specific behavioral goals, for a social good" (National Social Marketing Center 2006). They pursue several objectives. First, they enhance awareness of particular social causes among consumers with a view to improving social and environmental health and well-being (Lenox and Eesley 2009; West and Sargeant 2004). NFP organizations use the brand targeted as "celebrity endorser," building on its notoriety to catch public attention. In adopting shock tactics, these campaigns "overcome public apathy to good causes" (West and Sargeant 2004, p. 1028). Indeed, organizations such as Friends of the Earth advise their members to build messages with catchy slogans that will "grab the attention in the shortest possible time" (McGrath 2007, p. 272). Second, these types of campaigns motivate consumers to become active players, through overt protests or boycott of the company products (Lenox and Eesley 2009). Thus, these campaigns are used as tactical weapons, threatening corporate reputation unless the firm stops its irresponsible business practices. Within the luxury and fashion industries in particular, reports such as

The author is grateful to the special issue editors and reviewers for helpful comments on previous versions of this article.

the *Deeper Luxury WWF Report* (Bendell and Kleanthous 2007) and the *Style over Substance Report* (Moore 2011) keep pointing toward companies that act in a socially and environmentally irresponsible manner.

Past research investigated the effectiveness of targeting brands on companies' compliance with proenvironmental demands (Lenox and Eesley 2009). Lenox and Eesley indicate that targeting brands is an effective tool to "force firms to internalize negative environmental externalities and motivate firms to comply with their demands absent any intervention by the state" (2009, p. 45). The effectiveness of targeting brands is dependent on the level of harm threatened. Yet the majority of firms comply before their reputation is harmed and before their sales are affected (Lenox and Easley 2009). For this reason, consumer response to these campaigns, aside from activists' overt protests, is difficult to evaluate. To the author's knowledge, no research has been undertaken investigating consumer responses to messages targeting brands. Several questions arise. After seeing the ads, do consumers consider changing their behavior regarding the brand and boycotting its products? Do they consider voicing protests and spreading negative word-of-mouth messages? And last, do these specific types of green messages have a positive influence on consumers' proenvironmental behavior?

These campaigns attack brands for what are deemed negative aspects of their business practices, particularly a disregard for sustainability. Consequently, the paper builds on the literature dealing with both green advertising and negative campaigning. The author proposes that the effectiveness of these "negative" green campaigns is moderated by consumer involvement in eco-purchases and consumer involvement in the target product category. These propositions are tested in the context of two experiments using messages from the organization ForestEthics targeting the brand Victoria's Secret.

CONCEPTUAL FRAMEWORK

The Moderating Role of Involvement on Consumer Response to Messages Targeting Brands

Consumer reaction to persuasive communication has been studied extensively in relation to message involvement (Greenwald and Leavitt 1984; Park and Young 1986). The degree to which the message content is relevant to the consumers' attitudinal position influences the attention devoted to the message and the depth of information processing (Greenwald and Leavitt 1984). Also, the type of ad involvement (affective or cognitive) influences brand attitude formation (Park and Young 1986). Based on this literature, involvement with the message is hypothesized to be a strong determinant of consumer response to green messages (Kronrod, Grinstein, and Wathieu 2012). Yet in the specific context of brands being attacked due to their

environmental misbehaviors, other forms of involvement (for instance, brand involvement, product category involvement, and green purchase involvement) might determine consumer response. Celsi and Olson state, "A consumer's level of involvement with an object, situation or action, is determined by the degree to which s/he perceives the concept to be personally relevant" (1988, p. 211). The involvement literature suggests that consumers might be involved with issues, products, purchase decisions, and advertising messages (Celsi and Olson 1988; O'Cass 2000, 2004; Zaichkowsky 1985). These different forms of involvement lead to different consumer responses (O'Cass 2000, 2004; Zaichkowsky 1985). For instance, in Celsi and Olson's 1988 study, product knowledge has both direct and indirect effects on consumer response to advertisements regardless of message involvement. Also, involvement with purchase decisions increases the search for information in purchasing situations and is a determinant of product choice (O'Cass 2004; Zaichkowsky 1985).

The acceptance or rejection of green claims is partly determined by the involvement and concern of consumers for the protection of the environment (Chan 2000; Chan, Leung, and Wong 2006; Schuhwerk and Lefkoff-Hagius 1995; Shrum, McCarthy, and Lowrey 1996). Environmental concern influences the effectiveness of environmental messages in changing consumer behavior (for a study concerning cars, see Teisl, Rubin, and Noblet 2006; see also Chang 2011). Research shows that environmental concern is a major determinant in the adoption of eco-purchase behaviors (Bamberg 2003; Stanley, Lasonde, and Weiss 1996), as it influences the decision-making process in purchase situations (Roberts and Bacon 1997). Consequently, consumers engaged in eco-conscious behaviors should be more affected by messages communicating brand misbehaviors.

The literature on boycott tends to suggest that when brands are attacked for serious reasons, highly involved consumers become active prosecutors and launch actions to harm the brand image (Cissé-Depardon and N'Goala 2009; Klein, Smith, and John 2004). In line with this reasoning, we propose that highly eco-involved consumers are more affected by communications targeting brands than low eco-involved consumers. In the context of this study, eco-involvement is operationalized as involvement in eco-purchases, the latter being a consequence of environmental concerns (Roberts and Bacon 1997). For highly eco-involved consumers, NFPs' messages are congruent with their concerns. For this reason, they are more likely to "assimilate" the message than low eco-involved consumers. Assimilation has been shown to enhance persuasive effectiveness (Chan 2000; Chan, Leung, and Wong 2006).

In contrast, consumers highly involved with the product category (fashion in the context of our study) are likely to find a message hurting the fashion industry, and in particular, one targeting a brand that embodies fashion, incongruent with their beliefs (O'Cass 2004). Chan (2000) suggests that when highly involved consumers judge a message incongruent with their prior beliefs, they go through a contrast effect, eventually leading to rejection of the message. For this reason, we propose that highly fashion-involved consumers are more resistant to messages targeting fashion brands. Consequently, we propose the following hypotheses:

Hypothesis 1: The more eco-involved the consumer is, the more consumer responses are affected by green messages targeting brands.

Hypothesis 2: The more fashion-involved the consumers is, the less consumer responses are affected by messages targeting fashion brands.

Eco-Involvement and Message Framing: Gain If the Target Complies or Loss If It Does Not?

Numerous studies on operant conditioning investigate the role played by presenting a message through reinforcement of the positive consequences of a change in behavior, compared to the negative consequences of no change in behavior. In the domain of social marketing, and the promotion of healthy behaviors in particular, research findings based on prospect theory (Kahneman and Tversky 1984) indicate that framing a message in terms of costs (loss frame) or benefits (gain frame) affect the behavioral response (Rothman and Salovey 1997). The persuasiveness of the frame is dependent on preexisting perceptions of the issue and on the level of acceptance of the message (Rothman and Salovey 1997). Shiv, Britton, and Payne's findings (2004) also indicate that the persuasive effects of negatively versus positively framed messages depend on the message and the audience, which explains the inconclusive results found in the literature. Also, the literature on pro-boycott messages investigates how framing the message as a gain through highlighting the positive outcomes associated with boycotting, or as a loss through highlighting the negative outcomes in the case of boycott failure, affects consumer perceptions of boycott success. Sen, Gurhan-Canli, and Morwitz (2001) suggest that pro-boycott communication is more effective when highlighting the positive outcomes of a boycott success, over the negative consequences of a failure. Again, a variety of moderators might affect this relationship.

One of the major moderators of framing effects is consumer involvement. Scholars (e.g., Levin and Gaeth 1998; Menon, Block, and Ramanathan 2002) found that the negative framing of advertising messages (loss frame) works better for highly involved consumers, whereas, in contrast, positive framing is more effective for low-involved consumers. Tsai (2007) also found that for individuals highly motivated to process a message and highly involved in the product category, a negative frame provided better responses in terms of attitude toward

the advertisement, attitude toward the brand, and purchase intention than a positive frame. Putrevu (2010) investigates consumer responses to attribute-framed (e.g., 75% lean meat versus 25% fat) and goal-framed messages (i.e., positive and negative goal attainment in performing an act or not performing the act). For goal-framed messages (a frequent framing choice in social and green advertisements), the negative frame induces better responses than the positive frame, a result attributed to a negativity bias that causes the negative information to have a higher perceived diagnosticity than the positive information (Putrevu 2010). Some researchers suggest that the negativity bias is stronger in conditions of high involvement (Meyers-Levy and Maheswaran 2004). In contrast, in line with the Elaboration Likelihood Model (ELM), Dijkstra et al. (2009) propose that for low-involvement consumers, a positive frame would act as a peripheral cue, leading to higher persuasive effects.

The moderating effects of eco-involvement on responses to framed messages have not been studied so far. We propose that framing as a gain or as a loss will not affect the responses of highly eco-involved consumers. Schuhwerk and Lefkoff-Hagius (1995) found that types of green appeals matter only at low levels of involvement. For those highly involved consumers, attitude toward the brand and purchase intent for a green laundry detergent is not affected by the different ad appeals. Based on this reasoning, highly involved consumers should not be affected by different message frames. Yet based on the boycott literature (Sen, Gurhan-Canli, and Morwitz 2001) and research on framing effects in low-involvement conditions (Dijkstra et al. 2009; Maheswaran and Meyers-Levy 1990), we propose that the low eco-involved consumers will be more persuaded toward changing their behavior regarding the environment and in acting against the targeted brand when framing the message as a gain. Consequently, we propose the following hypotheses:

Hypothesis 3a: High eco-involved consumer responses are not affected by framing the message as a loss or as a gain

Hypothesis 3b: Framing the message as a gain affects low eco-involved consumer responses more than framing it as a loss.

Fashion Involvement and Brand Target: The Dark Angel or the Devil Industry?

Not-for-profit campaigns targeting brands can also be considered as special cases of negative campaigning, with the source (the NFP organization) attacking the brand in a direct way. Negative campaigning is a tradition in political advertising, which often takes the candidate's opponent or his or her party as its target. The effect of negative campaigning in politics has been studied at two levels. First, research investigates the effects of negative campaigns on the issues debated and on the willingness of the citizens to vote. Voters might become cynical about the ideas debated in the political campaigns and be reluctant to vote (Pinkleton, Um, and Austin 2002). Yet when negativism is not too extreme, these negative campaigns have a stimulating effect (Pinkleton 1997).

A second line of research investigates the consequences of negative campaigning on the source and on the target of the campaign. Research has found that voters dislike negative campaigns and do not trust negative messages (see Pinkleton, Um, and Austin 2002 for a review). Negative advertising might have backlash effects; voters might defend the candidate who is attacked and develop sympathy for him or her (Merritt 1984). Also, voters might perceive the sponsor of the attack as mean-spirited, unfair, and unethical (Merritt 1984). Nonetheless, when conducted with care, negative campaigns are detrimental to the image of the candidate attacked, more so than to the sponsoring candidate (Pinkleton 1997).

Similarly, the literature on comparative advertisements mentions that attacking a brand is often counterproductive, as consumers are likely to take the defense of the brand "victim." Consequently, several comparative advertisements are considered "offensive, impersonal, less friendly, less pleasant, more aggressive, and more intense, suggesting that negative feelings drive people's unfavorable attitude" (Raju, Rajagopal, and Unnava 2002, p. 480). In addition to negative feelings, attacking a brand might also generate negative perceptions regarding the aggressor, which decreases message believability and leads to higher counterarguing (Raju, Rajagopal, and Unnava 2002).

Based on these two literature domains, we propose that consumers will dislike it when a brand is attacked directly and resist persuasion more so than when the fashion industry (at large) is targeted. Yet fashion involvement should be a moderator of consumer responses to those campaigns. We hypothesize that highly fashion-involved consumers will not be affected by these campaigns, which are incongruent with their beliefs (Chan 2000; O'Cass 2004) and would harm their sense of self (O'Cass 2004).

Hypothesis 4a: Responses of consumers who are highly fashion-involved will not be affected by targeting a fashion brand or the fashion industry in general.

Hypothesis 4b: Targeting the fashion industry in general will affect the responses of consumers who have low fashion involvement more than targeting the brand directly.

Overview of the Experiments

The hypotheses were tested in the context of two experiments. The first experiment investigates responses of high and low eco-involved consumers to a message by ForestEthics targeting the brand Victoria's Secret (VS), manipulating the message frame (gain versus loss) in a between-subjects study. The second experiment investigates the role of fashion involvement in

consumer responses to green communication manipulating the target, comparing responses of messages aimed directly at the brand with those aimed at the industry through the brand.

Each experiment is conducted in two phases in order to classify participants in high- and low-involvement groups and, in addition, to measure attitude and purchase intent before and after exposure to the message. Three weeks separate the testing sessions, a time period long enough to reduce testing effects (or the tendency for participants to seek consistency with their previous answers) and short enough to reduce history bias (or the risk that participants will be exposed to relevant external events such as environmental issues or industry/brand issues) (Kirk 2012). To respect the confidentiality of the answers and reduce the social desirability bias (or the degree to which participants respond in socially acceptable terms to get the approval of the experimenter), questionnaires were self-administered. An external experimenter (a student unknown to the participants) collected the questionnaires. Students' answers were tracked between both phases through ID numbers. The scenario was the same for both experiments: "Victoria's Secret considers operating stores in [*the country*]. This questionnaire is part of a large market research study conducted by the company from the United States. The anonymity of your answers will be preserved." Participation was not compulsory and was not rewarded.

Only women were invited to participate in the experiments, as women are the focal target group of the product category (lingerie; Park and John 2010). Also, O'Cass (2000, p. 562) finds that women have higher involvement with fashion compared to men, whatever the type of fashion involvement (product, consumption, purchase decision, or advertising). In addition, Zelezny, Chua, and Aldrich's meta-analytic review of environmentalism and gender (2000) indicates that women report more environmental concerns and greater participation in proenvironmental behaviors than men. Consequently, women tend to be the focus consumer segment targeted by environmental NFPs organizations, especially when related to fashion (Dobscha and Ozanne 2001).

EXPERIMENT 1

Method

The first experiment uses a between-subject design: 2 message frames (gain, loss) × 2 eco-purchase involvement (high, low).

Sample

Sixty undergraduate and master students completed the first phase of Experiment 1 at the beginning of a regular class in an English-speaking European university. Three students did not show up on the day of the second phase of the experiment. They were not tested individually, as the anonymity of their answers would not be preserved. These drops do not create any selection bias between involvement groups.

The average age in the sample was M_{age} = 22.07 years old (SD = 3.26). All participants stated that they knew of the VS brand. Forty-six participants had purchased a VS item in the past, the vast majority when traveling to the United States. Note that the brand VS is not available in the country of the experiment and cannot be ordered through local Web sites. At the end of the questionnaire, participants declared they had never been exposed to the "Victoria's *dirty* Secret" campaign before answering the questionnaire.

Concerning participants' behavior regarding fashion catalogues, all of them had at least one fashion catalogue at home ($M_{catalogues}$ = 2.05, SD = 1.12). Catalogues are given out free in stores. During the last year, all participants had at least occasionally read fashion catalogues (0% never, 56% occasionally, 26% frequently, 17% regularly). However, no one reported having purchased fashion "directly through catalogues" over the previous year.

Measures

All measures were assessed on seven-point Likert scales. The list of measures and corresponding reliability scores is provided in Table 1.

Phase 1. Taking into account the purpose of the research, eco-involvement was measured through factor 4 of the Eco Conscious Consumer Behavior Scale (ECCB; Roberts and Bacon 1997), which reflects how environmental concerns influence the decision-making process in purchase situations (eco-purchase involvement). In relation to our hypotheses, the subdimension "product involvement" of the fashion involvement scale (O'Cass 2000) was selected. A pretest of the questionnaire (n = 20), including the 16 items of product involvement (O'Cass 2000) and the 12 items of factor 4 of the ECCB Scale (Roberts and Bacon 1997), was conducted prior to the experiment. Results of the pretest indicated that the quality of the data would have been seriously altered due to the length of the questionnaire. Consequently, the three items that had the highest face validity and highest loadings on the factors in the Roberts and Bacon (1997) and O'Cass (2000) studies were selected.

In addition, the phase 1 questionnaire included a measure of the attitude toward VS (two items), and purchase intention if VS were available in the *place of residency* (two items). Issue involvement (protection of the forests; two items) and brand involvement (induced by the scenario of VS launch in the country; two items) were also assessed to control for differences on these variables between groups. Reliability of the measures

was very good (Cronbach's α > .7). Accordingly, multiple item measures were averaged.

Following Zaichkowsky (1985), the distribution derived from the eco-purchase involvement measure was used to divide the sample into two groups (high and low eco-involvement). As data did not depart from a normal distribution, a median split on the measure was adequate to classify participants into high- and low-involvement groups. Note that the use of the mean would have led to the same classification (Median = 3.66, $M_{eco-involvement}$ = 3.74, SD = 1.2). Next, participants high and low in eco-involvement were allocated to one of two conditions (gain versus loss). We controlled for differences between groups on age, issue involvement, fashion involvement, brand involvement, and frequency of reading catalogues. A MANOVA (multivariate analysis of variance) with eco-involvement and framing groups as fixed factors, and age, issue involvement (M = 5.61, SD = 1.38), fashion involvement (M = 5.50, SD = 1.24), and brand involvement (M = 5.42, SD = 1.11) as dependent variables, was carried out. Results show no main effect of eco-involvement; respectively, $F(1, 53)$ = .45, p = .507; $F(1, 53)$ = 2.20, p = .144; $F(1, 53)$ = 1.18, p = .283; $F(1, 53)$ = 2.27, p = .138. Nor was there a main effect of framing: respectively: $F(1, 53)$ = .72, p = .399; $F(1, 53)$ = .82, p = .369; $F(1, 53)$ = .04, p = .835; $F(1, 53)$ = 2.27, p = .138. There were no interaction effects. In addition, the frequency of reading catalogues was not significantly different between involvement groups, $\chi^2(2)$ = .05, p = .976, or between framing groups, $\chi^2(2)$ = 4.05, p = .132.

Phase 2. The second questionnaire started as follows: "On the following page, you will see a draft for a future advertisement by the nonprofit organization ForestEthics that tries to protect endangered forests and the endangered animal species that live in these forests. The campaign is entitled 'Victoria's *dirty* Secret.'" Next, participants were exposed to one of two communication statements: "'Victoria's *dirty* Secret.' If the fashion brand Victoria's Secret stops [does not stop] cutting trees to print one million catalogues a day, some of the world's most endangered forests will be protected [will disappear]. Protect our forests!" Attitude toward VS and intention to purchase VS products when available in the place of residency was assessed postexposure (same items as phase 1). The intention to spread negative word-of-mouth was assessed through two items. The potential behavioral change in reading catalogues was also assessed with two items (see Table 1).

To check for confounding effects, the questionnaire (see Table 1) included an assessment of the message believability (two items) as well as perceived seriousness of the message (deforestation; two items). Two manipulation check questions were meant to assess the success of the framing manipulation ("The message highlights the negative consequences if trees are cut," "The message highlights the positive consequences

TABLE 1
Experiment Measures

Measures	Items	Experiment 1, Cronbach's α	Experiment 2, Cronbach's α
Eco-purchase involvement ECCB factor 4 (three items from Roberts and Bacon 1997)	I normally make a conscious effort to limit my use of products that are made of or use scarce resources. I have switched products for ecological reasons. When I have a choice between two equal products, I always purchase the one that is less harmful to other people and the environment.	.70	.82
Product involvement (three items from O'Cass 2000)	Fashion clothing is an important part of my life. Fashion clothing is important to me. I pay a lot of attention to fashion clothing.	.93	.91
Issue involvement	The protection of endangered forests is an issue that is important to me. The prevention of deforestation is an issue that is important to me.	.93	.95
Brand involvement	It is important to me that VS would consider entering [country]. It is important to me that VS could be purchased in [country].	.89	.93
Attitude toward VS	My attitude toward VS is positive. I have a favorable attitude toward VS.	.94 (phase 1) .92 (phase 2)	.92 (phase 1) .95 (phase 2)
Purchase intention of VS	I have the intention to purchase Victoria's Secret lingerie when available in [country]. I am likely to purchase Victoria's Secret lingerie when available in [country].	.80 (phase 1) .88 (phase 2)	.94 (phase 1) .91 (phase 2)
Intention regarding negative WOM	I consider talking badly about Victoria's Secret. I consider voicing my disapproval toward Victoria's Secret.	.93	.89
Behavioral intention toward reading catalogues	I consider changing my behavior regarding fashion catalogues if not made out of recycled paper. In the future, I will not read catalogues if not made out of recycled paper.	.87	.84
Message believability	The message by ForestEthics is credible. The message by ForestEthics is trustworthy.	.94	.90
Perceived seriousness of message	The message presents a serious issue. Deforestation is not as serious as presented in the message.	.90	.86

Notes: ECCB = Eco Conscious Consumer Behavior Scale; VS = Victoria's Secret; WOM = word of mouth.

if trees are preserved"). Last, participants were exposed to a copy of the original campaign "Victoria's *dirty* Secret." They had to report whether they had been exposed to the campaign before answering the questionnaire.

Results

Manipulation Check

Prior to the analyses, the success of the framing manipulation was evaluated. An ANOVA with the questions on loss and gain as dependent variables and framing as fixed factor shows a main effect of framing groups on both dependent variables. In the loss condition, participants found that the message was highlighting the negative consequences if trees are cut, more so than in the gain condition, $F(1, 55) = 10.13, p = .002, M_{loss} = 5.0, SD = 1.16$ versus $M_{gain} = 3.96, SD = 1.29$. In contrast, in

the gain condition, participants found that the message was highlighting the positive consequences of a change in behavior more so than in the loss condition, $F(1, 55) = 10.43, p = .002, M_{gain} = 5.18, SD = 1.12$ versus $M_{loss} = 4.10, SD = 1.37$. There were no other main effects or interaction effects.

Confound Check

The differences between groups in the perceived credibility of the message and the perceived seriousness of the issue (deforestation as presented in the message) were assessed to rule out confounding effects. The message was perceived as credible ($M_{credible} = 5.39, SD = 1.02$), with no difference between involvement groups, $F(1, 53) = .53, p = .468$, or between framing groups, $F(1, 53) = .22, p = .638$. There was no interaction effect. The issue of deforestation presented in the message was considered moderately serious ($M_{serious} = 4.14, SD = 1.1$

FIGURE 1
Attitude Change Per Eco-Involvement Groups

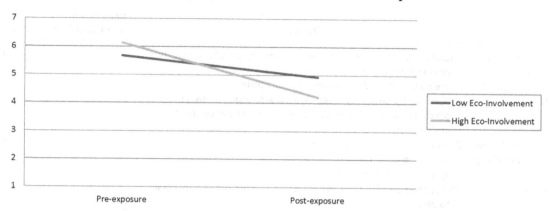

There was no difference between involvement groups, $F(1, 53) = .94$, $p = .337$, or framing groups, $F(1, 53) = .11$, $p = .736$. There was no interaction effect.

Within-Subject Contrasts

Participants' attitudes toward VS were measured at two points in time: before and after exposure to the "Victoria's *dirty* Secret" campaign. A general linear model (GLM) with attitude as repeated factor and framing and involvement groups as between-subject factors was fitted to the data. Results indicate a significant impact of exposure to the message, $F(1, 53) = 22.60$, $p = .000$, $M_{pre} = 5.91$, $SD = 1.00$ versus $M_{post} = 4.57$, $SD = 1.45$, as well as a significant interaction with involvement group, $F(1, 53) = 9.79$, $p = .003$. As indicated in Figure 1, the effect of exposure to the message was stronger for the group that was highly eco-involved than it was for the low eco-involved group. There was no interaction with framing conditions, $F(1, 53) = .62$, $p = .435$.

Results of the GLM model with purchase intention before and after exposure as repeated factor went in the same direction. There was a main effect of exposure to the message, with decrease of purchase intentions postexposure, $F(1, 53) = 24.5$, $p = .000$, $M_{pre} = 6.26$ SD, 1.19 versus $M_{post} = 5.31$, $SD = 1.51$, and an interaction effect with involvement groups, $F(1, 53) = 6.64$, $p = .013$, with the high eco-involved group being more affected than the low eco-involvement group. Framing had no significant effect.

Between-Subject Effects

A multivariate analysis of variance with attitude and purchase intention postexposure as dependent variable and involvement and framing groups as fixed factors indicate a main effect of involvement group on attitude, $F(1, 53) = 3.69$, $p = .05$, as well as a main effect on purchase intention, $F(1, 53) = 12.81$,

$p = .001$. There is no main effect of framing for attitude or for purchase intention ($p > .925$). Yet the interaction framing and involvement is significant for attitude, $F(1, 53) = 5.56$, $p = .022$. As indicated in Figure 2, framing as a gain is more harmful to VS in the low-involvement condition, whereas framing as a loss is more harmful in the high-involvement condition.

The dependent variable word-of-mouth (WOM) is also significantly affected by the level of involvement. A univariate analysis of variance indicates that highly eco-involved consumers are more likely to spread negative WOM than low eco-involved consumers, $F(1, 53) = 5.15$, $p = .027$, $M_{high} = 3.62$, $SD = 1.48$ versus $M_{low} = 2.77$, $SD = 1.24$. Again, there was no framing effect or interaction effect, $F(1, 53) = 2.26$, $p = .139$ and $F(1, 53) = .07$, $p = .792$.

Turning to the effects of green communication targeting brands on changing the behavior of consumers in line with protection of the environment, results of a univariate analysis of variance indicate that the highly eco-involved group is more affected by the message than the low-eco involved group. Highly eco-involved participants reported more likelihood of a future change in their behavior regarding reading catalogues than low eco-involved participants, $F(1, 53) = 9.91$, $p = .003$; $M_{high} = 5.33$ SD, 1.34 versus $M_{low} = 4.24$, $SD = 1.33$. There was no framing effect, $F(1, 53) = .02$, $p = .902$, or interaction effect, $F(1, 53) = 2.37$, $p = .129$.

Conclusion

Results from this first experiment fully support H1. Highly eco-involved participants are more affected by green communications targeting brands than are low eco-involved participants. The effect of exposure to the message is more negative for highly eco-involved participants than for low eco-involved participants. Also, the intention to voice disapproval of the brand (negative WOM) is significantly higher

FIGURE 2
Framing Effect on Attitude

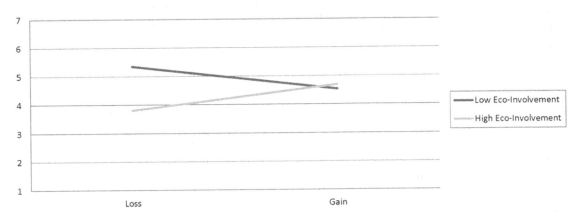

for the high eco-involved consumers. Last, highly eco-involved consumers report higher intentions to change their behaviors regarding the reading of catalogues if they are not made out of recycled paper.

Framing as a gain or loss is quite ineffective, contrary to our expectations (H3). Results indicate an effect only on the attitude toward VS. Framing as a gain is more harmful to VS in the low-involvement condition, whereas framing as a loss is more harmful in the high-involvement condition.

EXPERIMENT 2

The second experiment used an in-between subject design: 2 fashion involvement (high, low) × 2 target focus (brand, industry).

Method

Sample

Forty MBA students and staff members were recruited in an English-speaking European university. Only women were recruited, as in Experiment 1. The average age in the sample was M_{age} = 33.35 years old (SD = 7.15). All participants in the sample had a minimum of three years of working experience. They all knew the VS brand, and 33% had purchased a VS item in the past. At the end of the questionnaire, they stated that they did not know about the campaign "Victoria's *dirty Secret*" before being tested.

Regarding participants' behavior toward fashion catalogues, all participants reported having at least one fashion catalogue at home ($M_{catalogues}$ = 1.9, SD = 1.15). Distribution of the frequency of reading catalogues over the previous year was similar to that in Experiment 1, with at least occasional reading (0% never, 47.5% occasionally, 37.5% frequently,

15% regularly). No one had purchased through catalogues over the previous year.

Data Collection

Data collection proceeded in two phases, as in Experiment 1. The same questionnaires as in Experiment 1 were used (see Table 1 for reliability of the measures). Following Zaichkowsky (1985), two groups (high and low fashion involvement) were created based on a median split on the measure "fashion involvement" (Median = 4.00, $M_{fashion}$ = 4.42, SD = 1.42). Next, participants high and low in involvement were allocated to one of two conditions (brand target versus industry target). Differences between groups on age, issue involvement (protection of forests; M = 5.45, SD = 1.50), eco-purchase involvement (M = 2.87, SD = .95), and brand involvement (M = 5.22, SD = 1.16) were controlled. There was no difference between fashion groups on these variables: respectively, $F(1, 36)$ = .07, p = .785; $F(1, 36)$ = .09, p = .761; $F(1, 36)$ = .01, p = .955; $F(1, 36)$ = .02, p = .895. Nor was there any difference between target groups: respectively, $F(1, 36)$ = .21, p = .650; $F(1, 36)$ = .09, p = .761; $F(1, 36)$ = 1.71, p = .200; $F(1, 36)$ = 1.43, p = .24. The distribution of frequency of reading catalogues was not significantly different between fashion involvement groups, $\chi^2(2)$ = .78, p = .675, or between target groups, $\chi^2(2)$ = 1.20, p = .547.

In the second phase, participants were exposed to one of two communication statements, targeting either the brand or the fashion industry through the brand: "'Victoria's *dirty Secret*.' Victoria's Secret [fashion brands such as Victoria's Secret] mail more than one million catalogues a day, printed on paper made from some of the world's most endangered forests. Protect our forests!" Two manipulation check questions were included in the questionnaire ("The message highlights the role of VS in the destruction of endangered forests," "the message highlights the role of the fashion industry in the destruction of endangered forests"). Message believability and perceived seriousness of the issue presented in the message were also assessed (see Table 1).

Results

Manipulation Check

The successful manipulation of the target focus (VS or the fashion industry) was assessed by comparing between groups the answers to the role of either VS or the fashion industry in the destruction of endangered forests. A one-way analysis of variance was conducted with target focus as a fixed factor. In the VS target condition, participants found that VS was the target of the message more than in the fashion industry target condition: $M_{VS} = 5.05$, $SD = 1.14$ versus $M_{fashion} = 3.95$, $SD = 1.43$, $F(1, 38) = 7.20$, $p = .011$. In contrast, in the fashion condition, participants found that the fashion industry was targeted more than in the VS condition: $M_{fashion} = 5.10$, $SD = 1.11$ versus $M_{VS} = 4.2$, $SD = 1.54$, $F(1, 38) = 4.46$, $p = .04$.

Confound Checks

A MANOVA demonstrates that the message is perceived as credible ($M = 5.30$, $SD = .97$), with no differences between fashion involvement groups, $F(1, 36) = 1.22$, $p = .277$, or between target groups, $F(1, 36) = .02$, $p = .876$. In addition, the issue presented in the message is perceived as moderately serious ($M = 4.2$, $SD = 1.10$), with no difference between fashion involvement groups, $F(1, 36) = .17$, $p = .677$, or between target groups, $F(1, 36) = .70$, $p = .407$. There are no interaction effects.

Within-Subject Contrasts

A GLM with repeated attitude measures was estimated. Exposure to the message has an incidence on the attitude measure, $M_{pre} = 5.76$, $SD = .99$; $M_{post} = 4.52$, $SD = 1.3$; $F(1, 36) = 28.67$, $p = .000$. There is an interaction with fashion group, $F(1, 36) = 9.816$, $p = .004$. As indicated in Figure 3, the attitude in the group that was low in fashion involvement was more affected by exposure to the message than that in the group high in fashion involvement. None of the other effects or interactions were significant.

Exposure to the message also has an effect on purchase intentions, $F(1, 36) = 30.63$, $p = .000$, with a significant decrease in purchase intention ($M_{pre} = 6.52$, $SD = .65$ versus $M_{post} = 5.26$, 1.14). But there is no interaction with target groups or with fashion groups.

Between-Subject Effects

The univariate analyses of variance conducted with WOM and intention to change behavior regarding catalogues as dependent variable and target and involvement groups as fixed factors indicate a significant effect of target group on both variables: respectively, $F(1, 36) = 4.487$, $p = .04$ and $F(1, 36) = 7.978$, $p = .008$. Participants reported higher intention of negative WOM when the target was VS than when it was the fashion industry in general ($M_{Vstarget} = 3.40$, $SD = 1.17$ versus $M_{fashiontarget} = 2.60$, $SD = 1.19$). In contrast, participants were more ready to change their behavior regarding catalogues when the fashion industry in general was the target ($M_{fashiontarget} = 4.90$, $SD = 1.25$ versus $M_{Vstarget} = 3.80$, $SD = 1.15$). Figure 4 presents these results. In both analyses, the effect of fashion involvement was not significant and there was no interaction effect.

Conclusion

In line with H2, our results indicate that highly involved fashion consumers resist better persuasion. After exposure to the message, the attitude toward VS was less affected in the group with high fashion involvement. The attitude toward VS in the group with low fashion involvement was significantly lower after exposure to the message.

H4 is partially supported. Our results show that targeting the industry is more effective in changing consumers' behaviors regarding the cause (reading catalogues). Yet contrary to our expectations, high and low fashion-involved consumers are equally affected. In addition, targeting the brand directly is more detrimental to the brand (negative WOM) than targeting the fashion industry in general, in both high and low fashion-involvement groups.

GENERAL DISCUSSION

Contribution and Findings

This research is, to our knowledge, the first to investigate consumer responses to messages targeting brands. It indicates that brand attitude and purchase intentions are negatively affected by exposure to these types of messages, particularly for consumers high in eco-purchase involvement and for consumers low in product (fashion) involvement. Also, after exposure to these messages, the highly eco-involved consumers reported being more likely to spread negative word-of-mouth and act against the brand. This finding corroborates the literature on consumers' boycotting behaviors (Cissé-Depardon and N'Goala 2009; Klein, Smith, and John 2004). When the company's irresponsible environmental behavior has a personal relevance to the consumer, he or she might engage in actions aimed at damaging the company's reputation.

FIGURE 3
Attitude Change per Fashion Involvement Groups

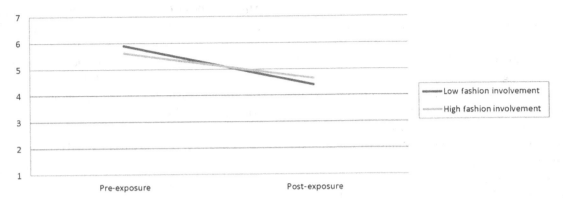

FIGURE 4
Target Effect on Pro-Environmental Behavior and WOM

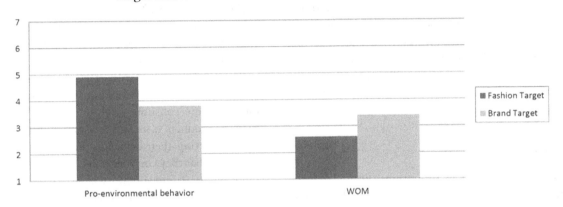

Contrary to our expectations, framing effects did not prove successful in influencing participants (Experiment 1). Our findings indicate that framing the message as a gain is more effective than framing it as a loss in changing the attitude toward the brand for low-involved consumers only. This result is in line with mainstream literature on framing effects (Levin and Gaeth 1998; Menon, Block, and Ramanathan 2002). In particular, Sen, Gurhan-Canli, and Morwitz's 2001 research on individual boycott decision predictors indicates that pro-boycott communication is more effective when framed as a gain (success). Yet, contrary to our expectations, with the exception of attitude toward the brand, no other dependent variables were affected by framing effects. Although the manipulation was successful, it is possible that the framing effects were not strong enough to affect behavioral measures. Future research should investigate framing through messages with higher impact, such as those involving attention-catching images.

The decision to target the brand or the industry through the brand (Experiment 2) has an impact on the effectiveness of these campaigns. Targeting the brand directly is more effective in changing the consumer's attitude and behavioral intentions

toward that brand. In addition, if the objective of the message is creating a consumer movement against the brand (e.g., negative buzz), then targeting the brand directly is more effective. In turn, if the objective is to change the behavior of the consumer in line with the cause, such as encouraging him or her to act to protect the environment (e.g., not reading catalogues if not made out of recycled paper), then targeting the industry in general rather than the brand is more effective.

Implications for Practitioners

This research suggests concrete recommendations to NFP organizations and brands alike. NFP organizations often communicate with very limited budgets. To be cost-effective, NFP communications targeting brands should be directed to those consumers with the highest eco-purchase involvement. They are the most likely to become active and to aim at forcing, through their concrete actions, the brand to comply with the NFP demands. In contrast, targeting those consumers highly involved with the product category might not necessarily be effective. For instance, PETA directed to highly fashion-involved consumers might not be as effective as when the organization communicates through its Web site to the eco-involved community.

The decision to target the brand or the industry is also an important one. It is dependent on the primary objective of the NFP organization: harm the brand image and coerce the firm into complying with the NFP's demands, or encourage consumers to engage in eco-friendly behaviors. Our results indicate that campaigns directed at the brand are more effective in harming brand image and mobilizing consumer actions against the brand. In turn, targeting the industry (through use of the brand name) might be more effective in encouraging proenvironmental behaviors.

Our results also indicate that brand attitude and purchase intentions might be seriously harmed when brands are the target of NFP organizations. Attitudes and purchase intentions decrease postexposure. Consumers are likely to voice their disapproval of the company's irresponsible practices and spread negative WOM. Ultimately, the most eco-involved consumers might become activists and seriously harm the brand's reputation. Companies should be proactive in managing their policies related to corporate social responsibility. When attacked, firms should react as soon as possible through media communications, as VS did via its executives.

Limitations and Future Research

This research has a number of limitations. Future research should draw random samples of subjects from the general population (both men and women) and use brand targets from a variety of industries to deal more successfully with the issue of generalizability of the results. Indeed, only women participated in our research. Although women are both the primary target of environmental messages (Zelezny, Chua, and Aldrich 2000) and the primary target of fashion advertising (O'Cass 2000, 2004), it would be interesting to assess the moderating role of gender on the effectiveness of communications targeting brands. Second, our research is limited to one industry: the fashion industry. Results should be replicated with a variety of brands from industries that are also heavily targeted by NFP organizations, such as the food or car industry.

Concerning the measures, both experiments used intentions to act as proxy. Purchase intentions are weak predictors of sales, although intentions are more correlated to actual purchases when collected for specific brands (here, Victoria's Secret) compared to product categories (Morwitz, Steckel, and Gupta 2007). Yet it is worth mentioning that these NFP campaigns are not meant to affect sales; the objective is to use the negative impact on the brand image, consumer attitude, and purchase intentions as a weapon to effect change. More problematic to our study is the weak link researchers found between intentions and acts in the domain of activism and environmental behavior,

partially due to normative influence and social desirability bias (Cissé-Depardon and N'Goala 2009; Sen, Gurhan-Canli, and Morwitz 2001). Consequently, six months after Experiment 1, a follow-up study was conducted to collect information on behaviors regarding catalogues. Within-subjects, there was a significant decrease in the frequency of reading catalogues for both involvement groups, $F(1, 55) = 22.32, p = .000$, and the effect of involvement was significant: High eco-involved participants reduced their reading of catalogues significantly more, $F(1, 55) = 3.84, p = .055$. In addition, 23% of participants reported that they had refused catalogues in stores over the past six months if not made out of recycled paper. The difference between groups was significant, the high eco-involved participants being more prone to refuse catalogues than the low eco-involved participants, $\chi^2(1) = 2.27, p = .09$. These results, although incomplete, indicate that intentions might indeed be followed by actions in the direction of the protection of the environment. Yet to validate the predictability of the behavioral intention measures and get conclusive results, this study needs to be triangulated with field studies and research collecting eco-behaviors.

The validity of our results might be undermined by the existence of a social desirability bias in our participants' answers. Indeed, some consumers might consider environmentally friendly products a socially desirable choice. Consequently, when reporting their behavior, these consumers might overestimate what they consider to be "desirable behaviors" (Peng and Finn 2010; Sun and Morwitz 2010). To take into account this bias, we considered two paths (see Nederhof 1985). First, we tried to prevent and reduce the bias by putting distance between the target brand, the experimenter, and the participants. For this reason, the research was not presented as academic research, but rather as market research conducted by VS. Also, the anonymity of the answers was ensured across both experimental phases. Second, participants' social desirability levels were assessed on the Social Desirability Scale-17 (SDS-17; Stöber 2001), a shorter validated version of the Marlowe-Crowne Scale, in the context of an experiment unrelated to environmental behaviors. The levels of social desirability are comparable to those obtained by Stöber (2001) on the same population (18–39 years old), both in Experiment 1 ($M_{SDS-17} = 8.51, SD = 3.63$) and Experiment 2 ($M_{SDS-17} = 8.45, SD = 3.73$). There is no difference on the score mean between involvement groups either for Experiment 1, $F(1, 55) = .36, p = .55$, or for Experiment 2, $F(1, 38) = .028, p = .868$. This result indicates that our involvement groups are matched on levels of social desirability.

This research opens fruitful avenues for the future. As mentioned previously, there is a scarcity of research on NFP communications targeting brands. Future research should investigate the type of appeal (transformational [e.g., humor, fear] or informational) that is more effective when targeting brands. In addition, it is important for future work to manipulate different levels of message seriousness and harm threatened, and to assess the consequences on consumer responses. Advertising involvement should also be studied further. In the context of this experiment, we controlled for message/issue involvement. Yet future research should focus on this important aspect of the involvement construct. Last, one of the aspects that has been disregarded so far is how brands should respond and how to frame the most effective message to maintain (or recover) brand reputation. Communicating by targeting brands is likely to become a major weapon of NFP organizations in the future (Lenox and Eesley 2009; West and Sargeant 2004). For this reason, additional research is called for to help both the accusatory and the accused efficiently reach their respective objectives.

REFERENCES

Bamberg, Sebastian (2003), "How Does Environmental Concern Influence Specific Environmentally Related Behaviors? A New Answer to an Old Question," *Journal of Environmental Psychology,* 23 (1), 21–32.

Banerjee, Subhabrata, Charles S. Gulas, and Easwar Iyer (1995), "Shades of Green: A Multidimensional Analysis of Environmental Advertising," *Journal of Advertising,* 24 (2), 21–31.

Bendell, Jern, and Anthony Kleanthous (2007), *Deeper Luxury WWF Report,* available at www.wwf.org.uk/deeperluxury/report.html (accessed March 27, 2012).

Celsi, Richard L., and Jerry C. Olson (1988), "The Role of Involvement in Attention and Comprehension Processes," *Journal of Consumer Research,* 15 (2), 210–224.

Chan, Yee-Kwong Ricky (2000), "The Effectiveness of Environmental Advertising: The Role of Claim Type and the Source Country Green Image," *International Journal of Advertising,* 19 (3), 349–375.

———, T.K.P. Leung, and Y.H. Wong (2006), "The Effectiveness of Environmental Claims for Services Advertising," *Journal of Services Marketing,* 20 (4), 233–250.

Chang, Chingching (2011), "Feeling Ambivalent About Going Green: Implications for Green Advertising Processing," *Journal of Advertising,* 40 (4), 19–31.

Cissé-Depardon, Karin, and Gilles N'Goala (2009), "The Effects of Satisfaction, Trust, and Brand Commitment on Consumers' Decision to Boycott," *Recherche et Application en Marketing,* 24 (1), 44–66.

Dijkstra, Arie, Roos Schakenraas, Karin Menninga, Abraham P. Buunk, and Frans Siero (2009), "Self-Discrepancies and Involvement Moderate the Effects of Positive and Negative Message Framing in Persuasive Communication," *Basic and Applied Social Psychology,* 31 (3), 234–243.

Dobscha, Susan, and Julie L. Ozanne (2001), "An Ecofeminist Analysis of Environmentally Sensitive Women Using Qualitative Methodology: The Emancipatory Potential of an Ecological Life," *Journal of Public Policy and Marketing,* 20 (2), 201–214.

Greenwald, Anthony G., and Clark Leavitt (1984), "Audience Involvement in Advertising: Four Levels," *Journal of Consumer Research,* 11 (1), 581–592.

Hamilton, Gordon (2007), "Victoria's Secret Mends Fences with Eco-Activists," *Vancouver Sun,* available at www.victoriasdirtysecret.net (accessed March 27, 2012).

Kahneman, Daniel, and Amos Tversky (1984), "Choices, Values and Frames," *American Psychologist,* 39 (4), 341–350.

Kirk, Roger E. (2012), *Experimental Design: Procedures for Behavioral Sciences,* 4th ed., London: Sage.

Klein, Jill G., N. Craig Smith, and Andrew John (2004), "Why We Boycott: Consumer Motivations for Boycott Participation," *Journal of Marketing,* 68 (3), 92–109.

Kronrod, Ann, Amir Grinstein, and Luc Wathieu (2012), "Go Green! Should Environmental Messages Be So Assertive?" *Journal of Marketing,* 76 (1), 95–102.

Lenox, Michael J., and Charles E. Eesley (2009), "Private Environmental Activism and the Selection and Response of Firm Targets," *Journal of Economics and Management Strategy,* 18 (1), 45–73.

Levin, Irwin P., and Garry J. Gaeth (1998), "All Frames Are Not Created Equal: A Typology and Critical Analysis of Framing Effects," *Organization Behavior and Human Decision Processes,* 76 (2), 49–188.

Maheswaran, Durairaj, and Joan Meyers-Levy (1990), "The Influence of Message Framing and Issue Involvement," *Journal of Marketing Research,* 27 (3), 361–367.

McGrath, Conor (2007), "Framing Lobbying Messages: Defining and Communicating Political Issues Persuasively," *Journal of Public Affairs,* 7 (3), 269–280.

Menon, Geeta, Lauren Block, and Suresh Ramanathan (2002), "We're at as Much Risk as We're Led to Believe: Effects of Message Cues on Judgments of Health Risk," *Journal of Consumer Research,* 28 (4), 533–549.

Merritt, Sharyne (1984), "Negative Political Advertising: Some Empirical Findings," *Journal of Advertising,* 13 (3), 27–38.

Meyers-Levy, Joan, and Durairaj Maheswaran (2004), "Exploring Message Framing Outcomes When Systematic, Heuristic or Both Types of Processing Occur," *Journal of Consumer Psychology,* 14 (1/2), 159–167.

Moore, Bryoni (2011), *Style over Substance Report,* Ethical Consumer Research Association, available at www.ethicalconsumer.org/ (accessed March 27, 2012).

Morwitz, Vicki G., Joel H. Steckel, and Alok Gupta (2007), "When Do Purchase Intentions Predict Sales?" *International Journal of Forecasting,* 23 (3), 347–364.

Nederhof, Anton J. (1985), "Methods of Coping with Social Desirability Bias," *European Journal of Social Psychology,* 15 (3), 263–280.

O'Cass, Aron (2000), "An Assessment of Consumers' Product, Purchase Decision, Advertising and Consumption Involvement in Fashion Clothing," *Journal of Economic Psychology,* 21 (5), 545–576.

——— (2004), "Fashion Clothing Consumption: Antecedents and Consequences of Fashion Clothing Involvement," *European Journal of Marketing,* 38 (7), 869–880.

Park, C. Whan, and S. Mark Young (1986), "Consumer Response to Television Commercials: The Impact of Involvement and Background Music on Brand Attitude Formation," *Journal of Marketing Research,* 23 (1), 11–24.

Park, Ji K., and Deborah R. John (2010), "Got to Get You into My Life: Do Brand Personalities Rub Off on Consumers?" *Journal of Consumer Research,* 37 (4), 655–669.

Peng, Ling, and Adam Finn (2010), "Whose Crystal Ball to Choose? Individual Difference in the Generalizability of Concept Testing," *Journal of Product Innovation Management,* 27 (5), 690–704.

Pinkleton, Bruce E. (1997), "The Effects of Negative Comparative Political Advertising on Candidate Evaluations and Advertising Evaluation: An Exploration," *Journal of Advertising,* 26 (1), 19–29.

———, Nam-Hyun Um, and Erica Weintraub Austin (2002), "An Exploration of the Effects of Negative Political Advertising on Political Decision Making," *Journal of Advertising,* 31 (1), 13–25.

Putrevu, Sanjay (2010), "An Examination of Consumer Responses Toward Attribute and Goal-Framed Messages," *Journal of Advertising,* 39 (3), 5–24.

Raju, Sekar, Priyali Rajagopal, and H. Rao Unnava (2002), "Attitude Toward a Comparative Advertisement: The Role of an Endorser," in *Advances in Consumer Research,* vol. 29, Susan M. Broniarczyk and Kent Nakamoto, eds., Valdosta, GA: Association for Consumer Research, 480–481.

Roberts, James A., and Donald R. Bacon (1997), "Exploring the Subtle Relationships Between Environmental Concern and Ecologically Conscious Consumer Behavior," *Journal of Business Research,* 40 (1), 79–89.

Rothman, Alexander J., and Peter Salovey (1997), "Shaping Perceptions to Motivate Healthy Behavior: The Role of Message Framing," *Psychological Bulletin,* 121 (1), 3–19.

Schuhwerk, Melody E., and Roxanne Lefkoff-Hagius (1995), "Green or Non-Green? Does Type of Appeal Matter When Advertising a Green Product?" *Journal of Advertising,* 24 (2), 45–54.

Sen, Sankar, Zeynep Gurhan-Canli, and Vicki Morwitz (2001), "Withholding Consumption: A Social Dilemma Perspective on Consumer Boycotts," *Journal of Consumer Research,* 28 (3), 400–417.

Shiv, Baba, Julie A. Edell Britton, and John W. Payne (2004), "Does Elaboration Increase or Decrease the Effectiveness of Negatively Versus Positively Framed Messages," *Journal of Consumer Research,* 31 (1), 199–208.

Shrum, L. J., John A. McCarthy, and Tina M. Lowrey (1996), "Buyer Characteristics of the Green Consumer and Their Implications for Advertising Strategy," *Journal of Advertising,* 24 (2), 71–84.

Stanley, Linda R., Karen M. Lasonde, and John Weiss (1996), "The Relationship Between Environmental Issue Involvement and Environmentally-Conscious Behavior: An Exploratory Study," in *Advances in Consumer Research,* vol. 23, Kim Corfman and John G. Lynch, Jr., eds., Provo, UT: Association for Consumer Research, 183–188.

Stöber, Joachim (2001), "The Social Desirability Scale-17 (SDS-17): Convergent Validity, Discriminant Validity, and Relationship with Age," *European Journal of Psychological Assessment,* 17 (3), 222–232.

Sun, Baohong, and Vicki G. Morwitz (2010), "Stated Intentions and Purchase Behavior: A Unified Model," *International Journal of Research in Marketing,* 27 (4), 356–366.

Teisl, Mario F., Jonathan Rubin, and Caroline L. Noblet (2006), "Do Eco-Communication Strategies Provide a Road to Sustainability? Evidence from the Passenger Vehicle Market," paper presented at the eco-workshop sponsored by Institut National de la Recherche Agronomique, Nancy, France, June 29.

Tsai, Shu-Pei (2007), "Message Framing Strategy for Brand Communication," *Journal of Advertising Research,* 47 (September), 364–377.

West, Douglas C., and Adrian Sargeant (2004), "Taking Risks with Advertising: The Case of the Not-for-Profit Sector," *Journal of Marketing Management,* 20 (9), 1027–1045.

Zaichkowsky, Judith L. (1985), "Measuring the Involvement Construct," *Journal of Consumer Research,* 12 (3), 341–352.

Zelezny, Lynnette C., Poh-Pheng Chua, and Christina Aldrich (2000), "New Ways of Thinking About Environmentalism: Elaborating on Gender Differences in Environmentalism," *Journal of Social Issues,* 56 (3), 443–457.

FACTORS AFFECTING SKEPTICISM TOWARD GREEN ADVERTISING

Arminda Maria Finisterra do Paço and Rosa Reis

ABSTRACT: Despite the growth of green marketing, there is a shortage of studies on green communication. Thus, this research aims to understand whether consumers who are concerned about the environment conserve resources and have environmentally friendly buying habits and whether they are skeptical about the green communications conveyed by companies. Using a proposal of a model about skepticism toward green advertising, several hypotheses are tested. The results indicate that the more environmentally concerned an individual is, the more skepticism he or she will be toward green claims exhibited on packages or featured in ads. In addition, results indicated no significant differences between men and women regarding this skepticism.

During the past few decades, companies' investments in environmental activities have drawn significant attention from the media (Iyer and Banerjee 1993) and society in general (Paço and Raposo 2009). Indeed, the media have played a major role in the widespread dissemination of environmental concerns. The massive media coverage of environmental disasters and conflicts helped to transform many specific problems into major public issues (Qader and Zainuddin 2011).

As a result of the media focus on initiatives related to ecology, environmental protection, environmental degradation, and climate change, individuals are increasingly concerned about the planet. This general concern has increased levels of environmental awareness and changed the way people live and the products they purchase. Green consumers' orientation has thus increased interest in the link between marketing, consumer behavior, and the environment (Awad 2011).

However, despite the growth of green marketing, marketers still do not have the adequate tools for evaluating the success of advertising relative to consumers' attitudes, intentions, and behaviors. This is reinforced by Haytko and Matulich, who state "previous research into consumers' attitudes toward green advertising and the environment has concluded different results over time" (2008, p. 2).

Along with the growth of green communication, the question of skepticism in relation to environmental appeals has arisen. Given that skepticism diminishes the positive impact of communication, its analysis is relevant and may allow companies to design better communications and enhance their effects among consumers (Mohr, Eroglu, and Ellen 1998). Given the importance of this issue, the objective of the present research is to understand whether consumers who are concerned about the environment conserve resources and who have environmentally friendly buying habits are, in fact, skeptical about the communication conveyed by green companies. If skepticism is found, it is necessary to reflect on the best ways to communicate such messages to avoid disappointing current green consumers and alienating other consumers.

Thus, consumer ambivalence about environmental marketing and advertising practices needs to be accessed. To Mohr, Eroglu, and Ellen (1998), consumer reluctance toward environmental claims is of great importance for public policymakers, consumer researchers, and practitioners. The study of this topic could contribute to gaining a better understanding of green consumers.

The present research is based on a sample of Portuguese individuals. In general, Europeans (in the 27 member countries of the European Union) attach great importance to environmental protection (96%), with almost everyone stating that the issue is very or fairly important to them. In Portugal, for instance, this percentage was even higher—97% (European Commission 2008). However, regarding behaviors among the Portuguese population, Paço and Raposo state, "despite their support for policies designed to improve the environment, [they] do not translate their concerns into actions. . . . Their participation is often based on protecting the environment by saving electricity and water, which shows that these concerns may be more closely related with economic factors than with an environmental consciousness" (2009, p. 375). Another study, by Paço and Varejão (2010), about the factors affecting energy-

The NECE—R&D Centre is funded by the Multiannual Funding Programme of the R&D Centres of the FCT (Portuguese Foundation for Science and Technology), Ministry of Science, Technology, and Higher Education, Portugal.

saving behaviors reached the same conclusion. Furthermore, in the Eurobarometer report (European Commission 2008), Portugal presented very low values in the item connected with the purchase of environmentally friendly products. In general, 75% of the respondents said they would buy environmentally friendly products, but only 17% had done so.

This paper is structured as follows. It starts with a brief literature review in which green communication, advertising, and skepticism toward environmental claims is discussed in the context of green marketing. Based on the theoretical foundation, a proposal of a research model of skepticism toward green advertising is presented. The methodology section then follows describing how the research was conducted (sample, methods, variable measurement). Next, the results of the statistical analyses are presented with a commentary. Finally, conclusions, limitations, and implications are discussed.

GREEN ADVERTISING

Companies can show environmental sensitivity by using several strategies; one of these marketing tools can be environmental or green advertising. Haytko and Matulich (2008) have suggested that green advertising started during the 1970s as a result of the recession, caused by high oil prices and the need to deal with environmental problems. Companies trying to follow this green trend began to design and develop environmentally friendly products to achieve a competitive advantage based on this differentiating factor, and started seeking new ways to reach the public (Phau and Ong 2007). This was a way of responding to consumers' and regulators' environmental concerns (Zinkhan and Carlson 1995). As a result, marketing professionals started to integrate the claim "green/environmentally friendly" in communications and green messages also started spreading across various communication platforms, such as word-of-mouth, reference groups, opinion leaders, media activities, advertisements, Internet marketing, and mobile marketing.

Since green advertising makes use of environmental claims, it is necessary to understand what its meaning is. To Scammon and Mayer, "an environmental claim is a statement by a seller regarding the impact of one or more of its brand attributes on the natural environment" (1995, p. 33). Examples of general environmental claims would include terms such as "environmentally friendly," "safe for the environment," and "environmentally responsible."

While traditional advertising has three functions (to inform, remind, and persuade), green advertising aims to create awareness and positive attitudes toward environmentally friendly brands and companies (D'Souza and Taghian 2005). Pranee (2010) simply states that green advertising's aim is to inform clients about the environmental aspects of companies' products and services.

Banerjee, Gulas, and Iyer (1995) indicate that a green advertisement is the one that may clearly or implicitly address the link between a product and the environment; it should be able to encourage green lifestyles and improve the socially responsible corporate image. Furthermore, according to Carlson et al. (1996), green advertising is a way of promoting environmental awareness and stimulating the demand of green products. Awad (2011) suggests that green advertising and producers' claims should be assessed not only in the final product, but also on the resources used in production, packaging, distribution, and disposal.

Green advertising must be legal and honest, and consistent with environmental regulations and policies regarding fair competition (Pranee 2010). Today, however, consumers are not only confused about green advertising claims but also distrustful of them (Iyer and Banerjee 1993; Shrum, McCarty, and Lowrey 1995), becoming increasingly suspicious of everything related to green communication (Carlson, Grove, and Kangun 1993). This situation is aggravated by myths associated with green products, as for example, their perceived inferiority in terms of performance or lower level of scientific research for product development (Grillo, Takarczyk, and Hansen 2008).

Thus, in general terms, the credibility of green advertising is considered to be relatively low and will depend on the particular "type of green" one is. Its nature is much more complex than the existing marketing literature suggests (Kilbourne 1995). With the increase in environmental advertising, some critics have been pointing out that there is great confusion among consumers regarding the green claims of some products. The reasons for this include unclear meanings of claims and no generally accepted definitions of expressions such as "biodegradable," "environmentally friendly," "ozone friendly," and so on. Most of the time, consumers do not have the sufficient technical or scientific knowledge to understand the information underlying the environmental claims (Furlow 2010; Newell, Goldsmith, and Banzhaf 1998). If an environmental ad is perceived as too technical or manipulative, it may hamper the consumer's effort to understand the message, resulting in an advertiser's failure to communicate with its public (Carlson, Grove, and Kangun 1993).

Despite some firms being sincere in their efforts to make environmentally friendly products, others make ambiguous and confusing product claims, or even manufactured claims, to appeal to green consumers (Carlson et al. 1996). Carlson, Grove, and Kangun (1993) call this "greenwashing," that is, advertising in which the green claims are misleading, insignificant, or even false. The potential for confusion and deception may have severe consequences for companies; besides the legal and ethical aspects, misleading communications may damage the brand and the organization, and at the same time, cause consumers to question corporate honesty when saturating them with these kinds of claims (Furlow 2010).

SKEPTICISM TOWARD
GREEN COMMUNICATION

Studies show that green consumers, and even individuals who simply care about the environment, do not give much credence to ads and traditional advertising, which have virtually no impact on the market; therefore, optimal marketing strategy might be to start using unpaid media, because it is considered more credible (Ottman 1998).

However, it may not be easy to integrate a green argument into communication in a way that allows the message to reach the audience. If the message is distorted, green consumers will feel disappointed, may change brands, and as they are usually opinion leaders, may negatively influence other consumers (Shrum, McCarty, and Lowrey 1995). Even if information today is more consistent and less confusing than in the 1980s, the variety of labels, packaging, and environmental appeals is still confusing rather than informative to those who want to join the green consumption movement (Ottman 1998). For instance, consumers are so confused by media terminology that they are unable to distinguish such terms as "energy efficiency," "smart energy," or "energy conservation" (Murphy, Graber, and Stewart 2010).

The difficulty in the determination of the "environmental truth" promoted by companies has created a generalized skepticism around green advertising (Carlson et al. 1996; Mohr, Eroglu, and Ellen 1998; Zinkhan and Carlson 1995). Environmentally friendly brands are facing significant barriers to communicate to this current leery, skeptical, and cynical public and this can discourage the development/production of green products.

Mohr, Eroglu, and Ellen (1998) clarify that skepticism can be defined as a cognitive response that varies depending on the context and the content of communication, and may only reveal itself on certain occasions. Skeptics can be convinced about the veracity of the message through evidence or proof. In contrast, cynicism is a personality characteristic that remains relatively stable through situations and time. Mohr, Eroglu, and Ellen exemplify these differences saying, "an individual with a strong predisposition to doubt the motives for a commercial message (i.e., a cynic) would be more likely to doubt the substance of the message (i.e., skeptical) than a person with a low degree of cynicism" (1998, p. 33). This suggests it would be more difficult to influence a cynical individual than a skeptical one.

In fact, if consumers do not believe in the environmental benefits referred to in the ads and labels, the efforts in developing green communications will be lost; moreover, skeptical consumers may unconsciously give up the chance to help the environment by buying truly environmentally friendly products. As a result, this suspicion on advertising and other forms of marketing communications may diminish marketplace efficiency (Mohr, Eroglu, and Ellen 1998).

Accordingly, Cohen (1991) states that misleading advertising harms more than just the individual who wrongly buys a product he or she believes is green. This purchase may generate considerable harmful cynicism about all environmental claims, including responsible ones. Another very important aspect of green advertising is to ensure that environmental information is available for consumer use. If a consumer has doubts about that information, the market system could collapse.

Due to the difficulty of regulating environmental claims through marketing guidelines, self-regulation is a possible solution. However, differing and ambiguous commitments of private sector industries as well as public sector regulatory authorities have persisted over the years.

RESEARCH MODEL AND HYPOTHESES

Fishbein and Ajzen's (1975) expectancy-value model of attitude theory suggests that consumers will have a better attitude toward products they perceive as more likely to have valued attributes. In turn, in the Theory of Planned Behavior (TPB) (Ajzen 1985), the central idea is that behavioral decisions are not made spontaneously, but are the result of a rational process in which behavior is influenced, although indirectly, by attitudes, norms, and perceptions of control. Smith et al. (2008) state that several researchers have studied the extent to which self-identity might be a useful addition to the TPB, arguing that it is reasonable to assume that there are certain behaviors for which self-identity is a relevant determinant of intentions, and later of the behavior. Thus, the right advertising campaign can help companies better position their brands and influence perceptions and beliefs, which in turn will create among consumers a certain predisposition to think and act.

Based on the stated literature and given the necessity to deepen current knowledge about the existence of a relationship between attitudes (environmental concern [EC]), behaviors (conservation behavior [CB] and buying behavior [BB]), and skepticism toward environmental claims (SCE), a model illustrating those links was established, as can be seen in Figure 1. EC, CB, and BB are considered independent variables and SCE will be treated as a dependent variable.

According to Ajzen (1988), an attitude can be defined as a disposition to respond favorably or unfavorably to an object, person, institution, or event. Hakkert and Kemp (2006) add that an attitude is acquired through information and/or experience with an object, is a predisposition to respond in a certain way, and has to reflect a reliable pattern of positive or negative reactions to that object. In this research, the attitude will be measured through the level of environmental concern.

D'Souza and Taghian (2005) identified the disbelief that consumers sometimes demonstrate toward companies, products, initiatives, or green advertising campaigns. They concluded that in general, consumers who are more environmentally

FIGURE 1
Proposal of a Model About Skepticism Toward Green Advertising

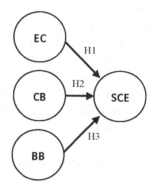

concerned do not consider green advertising as convincing but rather exaggerated, suggesting that advertising should be ethical, legal, true, and honest, and inform the public about the environmental aspects of the products offered.

Newell, Goldsmith, and Banzhaf (1998) tried to prove that the higher the level of a consumer's environmental concern, the more likely it would be that he or she would perceive claims as misleading and false. However, in their specific research, they concluded that the level of environmental concern had little effect on the degree of deception perceived in an ad. By this, the authors suggest the inclusion of the variable environmental knowledge to study the ability to detect misleading claims.

Thus, it seems important to verify whether a positive or negative relationship between environmental concern and skepticism toward green advertising does exist, that is, does it hold that the more environmentally concerned an individual is, the more skeptical he or she will be toward green claims? Hence, we posit our first hypothesis:

Hypothesis 1: Environmentally concerned consumers tend to be more skeptical toward green advertising claims.

The high degree of skepticism demonstrated by consumers toward environmental claims that appear in labels and in ads (influenced by the practice of "green washing" from some organizations that persist in disseminating incomplete or even false information), limits some environmental behaviors related to conservation activities (recycling, energy saving, preservation of resources, etc.) and green product buying (Mohr, Eroglu, and Ellen 1998). Consequently, Shrum, McCarty, and Lowrey (1995) suggest that consumers interested in the purchase of green products are generally skeptical toward advertising in general. Laroche, Bergeron, and Barbaro-Forleo (2001) add that consumers tend to form skeptical attitudes toward green advertising, which can represent a type of risk avoidance in the purchasing of green products. Thus, we would expect that the lack of confidence in environmental claims would reveal itself

in terms of environmental behavior and in the purchasing of green products. Based on these assumptions, two hypotheses were formulated, as follows:

Hypothesis 2: Consumers who demonstrate conservation behaviors tend to be skeptical toward green advertising claims.

Hypothesis 3: Consumers who engage in green buying behaviors tend to be skeptical toward green advertising claims.

Bearing in mind the significance of some demographic variables, the inclusion of gender in this study also seems relevant. Most studies focused in this area tend to point out that women may have different attitudes toward green advertising than men. For instance, Shrum, McCarty, and Lowrey (1995) found that for females, green buying behavior is positively associated with "the belief that advertising is insulting . . . suggesting that women who tend to buy green are more skeptical toward advertising. . . . men's skepticism towards advertising appears to be unrelated to their green buying behavior" (1995, p. 80). Haytko and Matulich's (2008) study indicated that women tend to be more environmentally conscious and have more positive attitudes toward both advertising and products designated as "green." Based on this evidence, it is proposed that:

Hypothesis 4: Women are more skeptical toward green advertising than men.

RESEARCH METHODOLOGY

Data were used from a questionnaire, which had already been designed and implemented for a wider international study. The survey took the form of a structured questionnaire, consisting mainly of closed questions, covering two main sections: attitudes/behaviors and generic variables related to the respondents' milieu and demographics. It was pretested by a group of 20 individuals to identify any language and comprehension problems.   .

A total of 320 questionnaires were randomly distributed to students attending a Portuguese university (the final sample consisted of 301 individuals). The sample comprises university students, not just for a matter of convenience, but also because this target group will play a crucial role in the development of an environmentally conscious population, providing a possible "snapshot" of future society in terms of green behavior. This generation of young people is likely to be better informed about and concerned with social issues, particularly environmentalism. They also represent a significant part of the green market (Furlow and Knott 2009).

The questionnaire was designed to include several scales (see the Appendix), all well established in the literature, to enable information to be gathered about attitudes (New Environmental Paradigm), behaviors (ENVIROCON and

126

Ecologically Conscious Consumer Behavior), and perceptions about green advertising (Skepticism Measure). Finally, some questions to gather demographic information (age, gender, course, and year of frequency) were included.

The scales make reference to four dimensions or constructs:

- *Environmental concern (EC)* includes concerns related to the limits to growth, pollution, steady-state economy, and resource conservation (Dunlap and Van Liere 1978). This scale was used in subsequent research by Van Liere and Dunlap (1980) and Straughan and Roberts (1999).
- *Conservation behavior (CB)* is related to conservation activity and comprises a broad range of items: dispositional activity, recycling of nondurable goods and packaging, preservation of resources, attitude toward packaging, and so forth (Pickett, Kangun, and Grove 1995).
- *Buying behavior (BB)* covers topics such as purchasing green products, the attention given to packaging, energy-efficient equipment, polluting or recycled products (Schuhwerk and Lefkokk-Hagius 1995; Straughan and Roberts 1999).
- *Skepticism (SCE)* measures skepticism toward environmental claims in marketers' communications regarding perceived exaggerations, misleading/confusing information, and the perception of truth in ads and packages (Mohr, Eroglu, and Ellen 1998).

The data was statistically analyzed and interpreted using the statistical software SPSS, version 19.0. Descriptive analysis, variance analysis, multiple regression, and correlation analysis were used.

RESULTS

The sample had an age average of 22 years (mode 20; standard deviation 4.731; minimum 17; maximum 50). Half were male, and the majority studied business and economics (29.6%), sports (16.9%), and engineering (16.6%). About 28.9% were attending the first year in university, 38.2% the second, and 30.2% the third, mainly at the undergraduate level (85.7%).

To test the first three research hypotheses, multiple regression was used to analyze the effect of environmental concern (EC), conservation behavior (CB), and buying behavior (BB) on skepticism toward environmental claims (SCE). To check the reliability of the scales, Cronbach's α coefficient was estimated. The usual threshold level is .7 for newly developed measures (Nunnally 1978). In our case, values ranged from .70 to .90: EC = .807, CB = .712, BB = .895, and SCE = .707. Therefore, the scales may be considered as reliable and have a good level of internal consistency.

Multiple regression analysis was carried out in addition to the study of the determining coefficients and simple correlation. To see whether functional relationships could be inferred between the dependent variable (SCE) and the independent variables (EC, CB, and BB), it was necessary to ensure that the model assumptions were valid. Hence, verification was performed to see whether the errors reported an average null measurement and constant variance, whether they followed a normal pattern of distribution (by the Kolmogorov-Smirnov test), and whether there was error independence (using the Durbin-Watson test). As the model assumptions were verified, the model was deemed valid across all variables analyzed. The analysis performed is shown in Table 1.

Analysis of the determining coefficient, R^2, in which $R^2 = .141$, enabled us to affirm that 14.1% of the variation in the dependent SCE variable was explained by the EC, CB, and BB independent variables, with the remaining variation explained by factors beyond the scope of the model. The simple correlation coefficient ($R = .375$) demonstrated that there was a positive, but low correlation between the variables; that is, they tended to vary in the same direction, meaning that, on average, any rise in the independent variables caused a rise in the dependent SCE variable.

To undertake analysis of model variance, an F test was applied with its associated determined p-value of .000. Testing of the regression coefficient β_1 was provided by the t-student test, which generated a p-value of .000 for EC, .216 for CB, and .149 for BB. These results indicated that the independent EC variable only significantly affected the dependent SCE variable. The value of the regression coefficient was negative ($\beta_1 = -.352$) and represents a unit of variation in the EC variation estimated for the SCE variation as 35.2%.

To test the last research hypothesis, an analysis of variance was performed to see whether there were significant differences between men and women concerning skepticism toward environmental claims (see Table 2).

The results indicated that there are no significant differences between men and women regarding their skepticism of environmental claims exhibited in packages or ads. This was evidenced not only in each item of the scale individually, but also in the total construct. If we simply consider the analysis of the means, however, it is possible to see that men are slightly more skeptical than women.

DISCUSSION AND CONCLUSION

This research sought out to analyze the relationship between environmental concern (EC), conservation behavior CB, buying behavior (BB), and the skepticism toward environmental claims present in adverting (SCE).

The findings demonstrated that only 14.1% of the skepticism can be explained by the three variables of the model

TABLE 1
Multiple Regression Analysis (EC, CB, BB, and SCE)

Model	R	R^2	R^2_{adj}	$\hat{\sigma}$
	.375[a]	.141	.132	1.04114

Analysis of variance				
	SQ	df	QM	F	Significance
Regression	52.824	3	17.608	16.244	.000[b]
Error	321.940	297	1.084	—	—
Total	374.764	300	—	—	—

Coefficients				
	Coefficient	σ	t	Significance
Constant	6.153	.454	13.539	.000
EC	−.352	.077	−6.325	.000
CB	−.090	.082	−1.239	.216
BB	.104	.067	1.478	.140

Notes: EC = environmental concern; CB = conservation behavior; BB = buying behavior; SCE = skepticism toward environmental claims.

[a] Predictors: (Constant), BB, EC, CB.

[b] Dependent variable: SCE.

$\alpha = .05$.

TABLE 2
ANOVA (Skepticism Versus Gender)

Scale of SCE	Mean/SD	Sum of squares	Mean square	F	Significance
Most environmental claims on package labels or presented in advertising are true. (R)	M(3.326, 1.278) F(3.369, 1.388)	.139	.139	.078	.780
Because environmental claims are exaggerated, consumers would be better off if such claims on package labels or in advertising were eliminated.	M(2.993, 1.580) F(2.847, 1.524)	1.611	1.611	.669	.414
Most environmental claims on package labels or in advertising are intended to mislead rather than inform consumers.	M(4.306, 1.548) F(4.052, 1.679)	4.825	4.825	1.844	.175
I do not believe most environmental claims on package labels or presented in advertising.	M(3.556, 1.594) F(3.532, 1.595)	.041	.041	.016	.899
Skepticism (total scale).	M(3.545, 1.104) F(3.450, 1.131)	.679	.679	.542	.462

Notes: ANOVA = analysis of variance; R = reverse; M = male; F = female.

(EC, CB, and BB). This allows us to attest to the existence of a relationship between the variables EC, CB and BB, and SCE. However, variations in SCE are not entirely explainable by EC, CB, and BB, which may represent a limitation of this study, and at the same time, a future line of investigation whose aim would be to discover other variables that could better explain skepticism toward green adverting in order to improve our proposed model. In fact, the more significant and higher correlation was between conservation behavior and buying behavior (.640), followed by the correlation between skepticism and environmental concern (−.366).

The results of the multiple regression analysis point to the acceptance of the first hypothesis formulated and to the rejection of H2 and H3. For H1, the statistical test was significant, which indicates that the most concerned consumers are, in fact, the most skeptical toward green communication. This is in line with D'Souza and Taghian's (2005) results: Consumers who are more environmentally concerned do not consider green advertising convincing. This contrasts with Newell, Goldsmith, and Banzhaf's (1998) finding that a consumer's level of environmental concern has little effect on the degree of deception perceived in an ad.

The nonsignificance of the statistical tests performed to test H2 and H3 lead us to reject these. Thus, it seems that behaviors related to environmental conservation activities and buying behaviors are not good predictors of SCE. It would be expected that the skepticism toward environmental claims would be related to environmental behaviors and the buying of green products, which did not happen in this research. However, Shrum, McCarty, and Lowrey (1995) and Laroche, Bergeron, and Barbaro-Forleo (2001) found opposite results. Thus, this nonsignificant result of the relationship between environmental behaviors and skepticism toward green advertising may indicate that consumers who are skeptical of such claims can, even so, perform and participate in green activities and buy environmentally friendly products. Mohr, Eroglu, and Ellen (1998) state that many consumers are by nature skeptical of advertising claims unless they have reliable bases for evaluating the claims. In some cases, what seems to happen is that consumers are not entirely influenced by companies' communication claims.

To check the significance of gender in relation to skepticism toward green advertising, an analysis of variance was carried out and the results point to the rejection of H4. In contrast to Shrum, McCarty, and Lowrey (1995) and Haytko and Matulich (2008), this research found no significant differences between men and women. Nevertheless, according to Shrum, McCarty, and Lowrey (1995), green advertising should pay attention to detail, since green consumers do so. Advertisements should display a true and accurate message, with plausible arguments, using print media more than audiovisual media to better target women, the group most likely to buy "green." Females usually believe that audiovisual media, in general, and television, in particular, are less credible than other media.

Related to the issue of type of media is media exposure. Qader and Zainuddin (2011) found that the repetition of a message, its consistency over time, and congruence can help shift public opinion over the long term. In this way, all tactical processes can help to change attitudes and behaviors in a variety of contexts, including one related to the environment. Thus, it can be argued that media exposure is an important predictor of purchase intention, and therefore, communication should be carefully planned to avoid causing skepticism and reluctance among consumers.

While green consumers may be more receptive to green marketing and advertising than others, managers should be careful not to push them away by using ambiguous, confusing, or even false messages. However, Mohr, Eroglu, and Ellen (1998) state that skepticism is healthy to a certain point, that is, the consumer should be skeptical about those areas where there is a potential to mislead. In this case, public policy action in the form of additional regulation or consumer education may be called for. Global governmental institutions should continue to be involved in regulating misleading advertising, and in the development of more creative and effective solutions to the market dysfunction that may characterize this type of environmental regulation. This is also a wonderful opportunity for companies, together with nonprofit organizations, to educate and train consumers in order to provide them with the tools that will allow them to distinguish between real and false environmental claims.

Because this research is exploratory in nature, there are some limitations that should be considered that may affect the generalization of the findings. The first is the use of a convenience sample of university students. This comes with the usual set of caveats, particularly in the study of the relationship between environmental attitudes and buying behaviors. Another possible limitation was the choice of the specific scales used to measure the constructs of our research model.

In terms of future lines of investigation, we recommend investigating the development of a structural equation model that could reflect the relationships and interdependencies among different constructs, as well as the study of skepticism in greater detail. Specifically, future research should seek to understand how skepticism might change according to the type of media used in green communication.

All these results reinforce the importance of marketers' understanding of the issue. They should ask: Why is there still skepticism? Why are so many people still suspicious of green claims?

REFERENCES

Ajzen, I. (1985), "From Intentions to Actions: A Theory of Planned Behavior," in *Action Control: From Cognition to Behavior,* J. Kuhl and J. Beckman, eds., Heidelberg: Springer, 11–39.

——— (1988), *Attitudes, Personality and Behavior,* Stony Stradford: Open University Press.

Awad, T. A. (2011), "Environmental Segmentation Alternatives: Buyers' Profiles and Implications," *Journal of Islamic Marketing,* 2 (1), 55–73.

Banerjee, S., C. Gulas, and E. Iyer (1995), "Shades of Green: A Multidimensional Analysis of Environmental Advertising," *Journal of Advertising,* 24 (2), 21–32.

Carlson, L., S.J. Grove, and N. Kangun (1993), "A Content Analysis of Environmental Advertising Claims: A Matrix Method Approach," *Journal of Advertising,* 22 (3), 27–39.

———, ———, ———, and J. M. Polonsky (1996), "An International Comparison of Environmental Advertising: Substantive Versus Associative Claims," *Journal of Macromarketing,* 16 (2), 57–68.

Cohen, D.S. (1991), "The Regulation of Green Advertising: The State, the Market and the Environmental Good," Pace Law Faculty Publications, paper no. 421, available at http://digitalcommons.pace.edu/lawfaculty/421/ (accessed June 5, 2012).

D'Souza, C., and M. Taghian (2005), "Green Advertising Effects on Attitude and Choice of Advertising Themes," *Asia Pacific Journal of Marketing and Logistics,* 17 (3), 51–66.

Dunlap, R.E., and K.D. Van Liere (1978), "The New Environmental Paradigm," *Journal of Environmental Education,* 9 (4), 10–19.

European Commission (2008), "Attitudes of European Citizens Towards the Environment Report," Special Eurobarometer 295/Wave 68.2—TNS Opinion & Social, Brussels, March.

Fishbein, M., and I. Ajzen (1975), *Belief, Attitude, Intention, and Behavior: An Introduction to Theory and Research,* Reading, MA: Addison-Wesley.

Furlow, E.N. (2010), "Greenwashing in the New Millennium," *Journal of Applied Business and Economics,* 10 (6), 22–25.

Furlow, N., and C. Knott (2009), "Who's Reading the Label? Millennials' Use of Environmental Product Labels," *Journal of Applied Business and Economics,* 10 (3), 1–12.

Grillo, N., J. Takarczyk, and E. Hansen (2008), "Green Advertising Developments in the U.S. Forest Sector: A Follow-up," *Forest Products Journal,* 58 (5), 40–46.

Hakkert, R., and R.G.M. Kemp (2006), "An Ambition to Grow a Multidisciplinary Perspective on the Antecedents of Growth Ambitions," SCALES report, Zoetermeer, June.

Haytko, D.L., and E. Matulich (2008), "Green Advertising and Environmentally Responsible Consumer Behaviors: Linkages Examined," *Journal of Management and Marketing Research,* 7 (1), 2–11.

Iyer, E., and B. Banerjee (1993), "Anatomy of Green Advertising," in *Advances in Consumer Research,* vol. 20, Leigh McAlister and Michael L. Rothschild, eds., Provo, UT: Association for Consumer Research, 494–501.

Kilbourne, W.E. (1995), "Green Advertising: Salvation or Oxymoron," *Journal of Advertising,* 24 (2), 7–19.

Laroche, M., J. Bergeron, and G. Barbaro-Forleo (2001), "Targeting Consumers Who Are Willing to Pay More for Environmentally Friendly Products," *Journal of Consumer Marketing,* 18 (6), 503–520.

Mohr, L.A., D. Eroglu, and P.S. Ellen (1998), "The Development and Testing of a Measure of Skepticism Towards Environmental Claims in Marketers' Communications," *Journal of Consumer Affairs,* 32 (1), 30–55.

Murphy, R., M. Graber, and A. Stewart (2010), "Green Marketing: A Study of the Impact of Green Marketing on Consumer Behavior in a Period of Recession," *Business Review,* 16 (1), 134–140.

Newell, S.J., R.E. Goldsmith, and E.J. Banzhaf (1998), "The Effect of Misleading Environmental Claims on Consumer Perceptions of Advertisements," *Journal of Marketing Theory and Practice,* 6 (2), 48–59.

Nunnally, Jum C. (1978), *Psychometric Theory,* New York: McGraw-Hill.

Ottman, J.A. (1998), *Green Marketing: Opportunity for Innovation,* 2d ed., Chicago: NTC Business Books.

Paço, A., and M. Raposo (2009), "'Green' Segmentation: An Application to the Portuguese Consumer Market," *Marketing Intelligence and Planning,* 27 (3), 364–379.

———, and L. Varejão (2010), "Factors Affecting Energy Saving Behaviour: A Prospective Research," *Journal of Environmental Planning and Management,* 53 (8), 963–976.

Phau, I., and D. Ong (2007), "An Investigation of the Effects of Environmental Claims in Promoting Messages for Clothing Brands," *Marketing Intelligence and Planning,* 25 (7), 772–788.

Pickett, G.M., N. Kangun, and S. J. Grove (1995), "An Examination of the Conservative Consumer: Implications for Public Formation Policy in Promoting Conservation Behavior," in *Environmental Marketing: Strategies, Practice, Theory and Research,* Michael J. Polonsky and Alma T. Mintu-Wimsatt, eds., New York: Haworth Press, 77–99.

Pranee, C. (2010), "Marketing Ethical Implication and Social Responsibility," *International Journal of Organizational Innovation,* 2 (3), 6–21.

Qader, I.K.A., and Y.B. Zainuddin (2011), "The Impact of Media Exposure on Intention to Purchase Green Electronic Products Amongst Lecturers," *International Journal of Business and Management,* 6 (3), 240–248.

Scammon, D., and R. Mayer (1995), "Agency Review of Environmental Marketing Claims: Case-by-Case Decomposition of the Issues," *Journal of Advertising,* 24 (2), 33–43.

Schuhwerk, M., and R. Lefkokk-Hagius (1995), "Green or Not-Green? Does Type of Appeal Matter When Advertising a Green Product?" *Journal of Advertising,* 24 (Summer), 45–55.

Shrum, L.J., J.A. McCarty, and T.M. Lowrey (1995), "Buyer Characteristics of Green Consumers and Their Implications for Advertising Strategy," *Journal of Advertising,* 24 (2), 71–82.

Smith, J., D. Terry, A. Manstead, L. Winnifred, and D. Kotterman (2008), "The Attitude-Behavior Relationship in Consumer Conduct: The Role of Norms, Past Behavior, and Self-Identity," *Journal of Social Psychology,* 148 (3), 311–333.

Straughan, R.D., and J.A. Roberts (1999), "Environmental Segmentation Alternatives: A Look at Green Consumer Behavior in the New Millennium," *Journal of Consumer Marketing,* 16 (6), 558–575.

Van Liere, K.D., and R.E. Dunlap (1980), "The Social Bases of Environmental Concern: A Review of Hypotheses, Explanations and Empirical Evidence," *Public Opinion Quarterly,* 44 (2), 181–197.

Zinkhan, G.M., and L. Carlson (1995), "Green Advertising and the Reluctant Consumer," *Journal of Advertising,* 24 (2), 1–5.

APPENDIX

Environmental concern (EC)

Plants and animals exist primarily to be used by humans. (R)
We are approaching the limit of the number of people that the earth can support.
To maintain a healthy economy, we will have to develop a steady-state economy where industrial growth is controlled.
The earth is like a spaceship with only limited room and resources.
Humans need not adapt to the natural environment because they can model it to suit their needs. (R)
There are limits to growth beyond which our industrialized society cannot expand.
The balance of nature is delicate and easily upset.
When humans interfere with nature, it often produces disastrous consequences.
Humans must live in harmony with nature in order to survive.
Mankind is severely abusing the environment.
Humans have the right to modify the natural environment to suit their needs. (R)
Humankind was created to rule over the rest of nature.

Conservation behavior (CB)

How often do you separate your household garbage (i.e., glass, papers) for either curbside pickup or to take to the nearest recycling center?
How often do you use reusable containers to store food in your refrigerator rather than wrapping food in aluminum foil or plastic wrap?
How often do you conserve water while washing dishes?
How often do you conserve energy by turning off light switches when leaving a room, turning down the thermostat when leaving home, and so forth?
How often do you conserve water while brushing your teeth, shaving, washing your hands, bathing, and so forth?
When disposing of durables such as appliances, furniture, clothing, linens, and so forth, how often do you either give that item to someone else, sell it to someone else, or donate the item to a charitable organization?
How often do you refuse to buy products that you feel have extensive packaging?

Buying behavior (BB)

I try to buy energy-efficient products and appliances.
I avoid buying products that have excessive packaging.
When there is a choice, I choose the product that causes the least pollution.
I have switched products/brands for ecological reasons.
I make every effort to buy paper products made from recycled paper.
I use environmentally friendly soaps and detergents.
I have convinced members of my family or friends not to buy some products that are harmful to the environment.
Whenever possible, I buy products packaged in reusable containers.
I try to buy products that can be recycled.
I buy high-efficiency light bulbs to save energy.

Skepticism (SCE)

Most environmental claims on package labels or presented in advertising are true.
Because environmental claims are exaggerated, consumers would be better off if such claims on package labels or in advertising were eliminated.
Most environmental claims on package labels or in advertising are intended to mislead rather than inform consumers.
I do not believe most environmental claims on package labels or presented in advertising.

Index

Page numbers in **bold** type refer to **figures**
Page numbers in *italic* type refer to *tables*
Page numbers followed by 'n' refer to notes

Absolut Vodka: *Absolut Impotent* 110
Adbuster 110
affective response: electronic media 62
age: differences 62; environmental message importance 88
Ajzen, I. 125
Amazon.com: Mechanical Turk 65
analytic response: print media 62
anger: prevention-focus 56
animal experimentation 110
anti-materialism 72
anxiety: prevention-focus 56
appeals: advertising 78–9
assimilation 111
assurance *see* eco-seals
attitude: behavior disconnect 62; brand 5–7, 51, 111; definition 125; Eastern 21
attitude commitment 62–3; social media survey 65–8, *66, 67, 68, 69*
attitude theory: expectancy-value model 125
attitude-behavior gap: consumer behavior 1; consumer behavior eco-seals 2
automobiles 6

backlash 5; negative campaigns 113
behavior: buying 127; conservation 127; consumer 1, 2, 41; disconnect with attitudes 62
belief scale 31n
believability: credibility 5–7
benefit claims: process-orientated 5; product-orientated 5; response model 7; strength 6; types and consumer response 5–7
benefit type: and price endings 77–94
benefits: gentle 41; health 88
bias 50
biodegradable definition 124
Bloody Burberry campaign 110
Blue Ocean Institute 63
boycott 110; literature 111
brand: fashion 112–13
brand attitudes *26,* **26, 28,** 111; credibility 5–7; eco-seals 51, 54
brand familiarity: eco-seals 48
brand reputation: eco-seals 50
buying behavior: skepticism 127

campaigning: negative 112–13
Celsi, R.L. 111
certification 88
charitable donations 72
charities 74
child labor 110

China: sustainability 1; willingness to pay more for green 61
classification programs *see* eco-seals
Clorox: GreenWorks 44
Coca-Cola: environmental sustainability 44
commons dilemma 21
communication: green 125
compact fluorescent light bulbs (CFL): mercury 85
company competence 99, **100,** 101, **102,** 103–4, *104*
concern: ecological 8
conservation behavior: skepticism 127
consumer behavior: attitude-behavior gap 1; regulatory focus 41
consumer receptivity: literature review 5–8
consumer receptivity study: correlations of latent constructs *13;* demographic profile 9; design and data collection 8; effect of ad claims on consumer response 10–11; measures 9; measures and scale reliabilities *10;* proposed model *13;* results 9–12; results of confirmatory factor analysis *12;* results of the model *14;* sample 8; stimulus ad copy *18;* stimulus materials 9; test of model of consumer response 11–12
consumer response: benefit claim type 5–7
consumers: environmental 79; expertise 89, 95, 97–109; green 61, 63; self-regulatory focus 35; spending power 61; USA 1
country differences: social media survey 70–2
credibility: brand attitudes 5–7; defined 6
cross-country analysis 61–76
culture: social media 61

decision making strategy 35
desirability 120
disbelief 125
donations: charitable 72
Donna Karan Bunny Butcher campaign 110

eager strategists 35
eagerness: association with strength 41
Earth Day 78
Eastern attitudes: self-construal 21
Eco Conscious Consumer Behavior Scale (ECCB) 114
eco-involvement: message framing 112
eco-seals: advertising attitude to 51–2; ambiguous 50; bias 50; brand familiarity 48; brand reputation 50; future research 55–6; impact on persuasion model 46; impact varies by HEC/LEC 54–5; implications for advertising 55; measures and reliabilities *59;* persuasion 44–60; testing manipulation 47; third-party 44, 50
eco-seals study 1: background 46; known brand with eco-seal 58; mean intentions and attitudes by condition *47;* purchase intentions X environmental concern, brand

familiarity and seal 49; regression results *48*; results 47–50; unknown brand without eco-seal **58**

eco-seals study 2: ad attitude 51–2; background 50–1; brand attitudes 51; brand attitudes X eco-seal source, environmental concern and message appeal 54; manipulation checks 51; mean intentions and attitudes by condition *52*; prevention appeal and government agency eco-seal **60**; promotion appeal and manufacturer eco-seal **60**; purchase intentions 51; purchase intentions X environmental concern and seal source 53; regression results *52*; results 51–3

Ecologically Conscious Consumer Behavior scale 127

effectiveness: green products 56

Elaboration Likelihood Model (ELM) 6, 112

electronic media: emotional response 62

electronic word of mouth (eWOM) 63

emotional response 62

emotions: prevention-focus 56

energy: efficiency 125; smart 125

environmental appeals: message framing 19–33

environmental benefits: context 89

environmental claims 124; persuasion 45–6

environmental concern: attitude and behavior 7–8; growth in 78

environmental consumer 79

Environmental Leader 61

Environmental Protection Agency (EPA): EnergyStar program 44

environmental skepticism 83, 85, 89

environmentally friendly term 124

ethical products 36

Eurobarometer 124

Europe: environmental protection 123

expectancy-value model: attitude theory 125

expertise: consumers 89, 95, 97–109; power 106

EZ Survey 65

Facebook 61–76; differences with Twitter 72; unique characteristics 64

fashion involvement: brand target 112–13

Federal Trade Commission (FTC) 1, 85

Fishbein, M. 125

food: organic 31n , 72, 74; sea 63

ForestEthics 110, 111

framing: negative 112; positive 112, *see also* message framing

Friends of the Earth (FoE) 110

gender 113; differences 62; skepticism research 126–9, *128*

gentle benefits 41

Germany: sustainability and social media 64–76

global issues 20

goal compatibility 19, 20

goal pursuits theory 19

goal-framed messages 112

green advertising: aims 124; background 124; definition 1, 78, 110; growth in 77

Green Bands Study: WPP Brands 61

green communication: skepticism 125

green consumers: characteristics 63; spending power 61

green gap 2

green issues 8

green marketing: spending plans 61

green message: definition 124; signaling effect 95–6

green products: effectiveness 56; inferiority 77, 79

Green Seal Certified 45

Greenlist classification: SC Johnson 44, 45

greenwashing 44, 124

GreenWorks: Clorox 44

guilt 63

health: appeal for personal 19–33; benefits 88

high environmental concern (HEC) 45; eco-seal attitude 49–50, 54–5

independent self-construal 19

Indonesia: time spent on social media 62

inferiority: green products 77, 79

information: sources for green products 61

interactivity: social media 63

interdependent self-construal 19

internet: information source 61; usage 72–3

involvement: consumer response to targeting brands 111–12

issues of concern 8

Katzenmeyer, T. 110

Keller, K.L. 34

Kilbourne, W.E. 1

knowledge: expertise 89, 95, 97–109

Korea: South 64–76, 72

labeling: organic 53

labor: child 110

Levi Strauss: *Clean Clothes* 110

Liebowitz, J. 1

light bulbs: compact fluorescent (CFL) 55

low environmental concern (LEC) 45, 54–5

low price appeal: 99p ending 80

Luchs, M. 89

McLuhan, M. 64

manipulation checks: eco-seals 51

marketing: green 61

Marlowe-Crowne Scale 120

Mechanical Turk: Amazon.com 65

media: exposure 129; print 62, *see also* social media

mediation analysis 99–100

Mental Accounting Theory 78, 80

mercury 85

message: green 95–6, 124; not for profit (NFP) 110–22

message framing 78–9; eco-involvement 112; future research 30; goal compatibility findings and extensions 30; regulatory focus and self-view 19–33

message framing study 1: brand attitude by treatment condition *26*; brand attitudes as function of self-view and regulatory focus *26*; manipulation checks *24*; participants, measures and procedures 22–3; results 23–4; two-way ANOVA results *25*

message framing study 2: brand attitudes as function of self-view and regulatory focus *28*; manipulation checks *24*; messages corresponding to ad treatment conditions *33*; participants, measures and procedures 25–6; results *26, 27*; three-way ANOVA results *25*; two-way ANOVA results *25*

metapersonal self-view 21

milk cartons 85

misleading advertising: harms 125; regulation 129

Model of Consumer Response: analyzing structural relationships 11–12; measurement validity 11

Monterey Bay Aquarium 63

Montoro Rios, F. 34

motivation 62–3

National Social Marketing Center 110
negative advertising 111
negative campaigning 112–13
negative framing 112
Never-Greens 85
non-product-related appeals 36–7
norms: social 63
not for profit (NFP) messages: effectiveness 110–22
not for profit (NFP) organizations: tactics 110–11
numerical precision 96–7; advertising skepticism 95–109; conceptual model 98; future research 105–6; high ad skeptics 95; low ad skeptics 95; signaling effect 95–109; studies results 104–5; testing effectiveness 97; theoretical contribution 105
numerical precision study 1: advertisement 109; company competence 100
numerical precision study 1a: competence 99; manipulation check 99; measures 98–9; mediation analysis 99–100; procedure 98; stimuli 98
numerical precision study 1b: competence result 101; importance of precision 101–2; mediation analysis 101; numerical precision result 101; procedures and measures 101; stimuli and manipulation 101
numerical precision study 2: advertisement 109; competence 102; manipulation check 102; procedure and measures 102; stimuli and manipulation 102
numerical precision study 3: company's competence with low knowledge 104; competence 103–4; manipulation check 103; procedures and measures 103; stimuli and manipulation 103

odd-ending pricing 88
Olson, J.C. 111
organic food 31n , 72, 74
organic labeling: USA 53
ozone friendly expression 124

People for the Ethical Treatment of Animals (PETA) 110
perceived consumer effectiveness (PCE) 7, 14
personal health appeals: message framing 19–33
personal perspectives 20
persuasion: eco-seals 44–60; environmental claims 45–6; regulatory focus 35–6
Persuasion Knowledge Model (PKM) 2, 45–60, 85, 89
political regulation 62
Portugal: environmental protection 123
positive framing 112
power: expertise 106; spending 61
prevention: versus promotion 34–43
prevention focus 20; consumer behavior 41; emotions 56; safety motivations 41
price: quality 79–80
price endings: .00 perception 80; and benefit type 77–94; experimental advertisements 94; further study 89–90; just below .99 - low price appeal 80; Prospect Theory 80, 89; psychological 79–81; quality perception 88; value assessment 80
price endings study 1&2: descriptive statistics *83*; MANCOVA results *82*; means for main effects *86*
price endings study 1: analysis and results 82–3; interaction effects on price and quality 84; manipulation check 81; measures 82; method 81–2; sample and procedure 81–2
price endings study 2: analysis and results 86–7; environmental skepticism 83, 85, 89; interaction effects on price and quality 87; sample and procedure 85–6
pricing: green products 1; odd-ending 88

priming techniques: self-view 21
print media: rational response 62
process-orientated benefit claims 5
product attractiveness: indicators 43; self-regulatory focus 38, 39, 40
product attribute framing 79
product knowledge 111
product-orientated benefit claims 5
product-related appeals 36
product-related attributes 34
products: green 56, 77, 79
promotion: orientation 20; versus prevention 34–43
promotion focus 41; non-green message preference 41
Prospect Theory 78–9; price endings 80, 89
psychological price endings 79–81
purchase intentions: eco-seals 49, 51, **53**; indicators 43; self-regulatory focus 38, 39, 40

quality: price endings 79–80, 88

rational response: print media 62
recycling 74; social pressure 63
red-rated seafood 63
regulation 62
regulatory focus: consumer behavior 41; goal pursuits theory 19; persuasion 35–6; relation to self-construal 21–2; and self-view in message framing 19–33; theoretical development 20; theory 35, *see also* self-regulatory focus
regulatory-fit 20
reputation: eco-seals 50
risk: and reward matching 79
Roper's Green Gauge Report 79
Russia: social media 62

safety motivations: prevention focus 41
SC Johnson: Greenlist classification 44, 45
seafood: red-rated 63
self-construal: relation to regulatory focus 21–2; theoretical development 21; Western and Eastern attitudes 21, *see also* self-view
Self-Construal Scale 21
self-regulatory focus 34–43; consumer 35; future research 42; tailoring green advertising 42, *see also* regulatory focus
self-regulatory focus study 1: design and sample 37; independent variable 37–8; interaction effects on product attractiveness **39**; interaction effects on purchase intentions **39**; product attractiveness 38; purchase intention 38, 39; results 38; stimuli and procedure 37
self-regulatory focus study 2: dependent variables 39–40; design and sample 38–9; independent variables 39; interaction effects on product attractiveness 40; interaction effects on purchase intentions 40; results 40; stimuli and procedure 39
self-view: metapersonal 21; priming techniques 21; and regulatory focus in message framing 19–33; Self-Construal Scale 21, *see also* self-construal
signaling effect: green message 95–6
skepticism 2, 45, 85, 89, 123–31; buying behavior 127; conservation behavior 127; definition 125; environmental 83, 85, 89; environmental concern 127; gender 126–9; green backlash 5; green communication 125; numerical precision 95–109
skepticism research: gender 126–9, *128*; methodology 126–7; multiple regression analysis *128*; proposed model 126; results 127
smart energy 125

smoking 20

Social Desirability scale 120

social media: culture 61; Russia 62; and sustainability 64–76; and sustainable marketing 61–76; targeting 63; time spent on 62

social media survey: attitude commitment 65–8, *66*, *68*, *69*; attitude commitment and sustainable behaviors 67; conceptual model *70*; country differences 70–2; demographic profiles by country *65*; measurement model results *68*; measurement model results and sustainable behaviors *69*; measures 65–6; media differences 72; respondents and procedures 64–5; results 68–72; structural model results: Facebook and Twitter comparison *73*; structural model results and country comparison *71*; sustainable behavior survey items *66*

social norms 63

South Korea: consumer characteristics 72; sustainability and social media 64–76

spending power: green consumers 61

strategists: eager 35

strength: association with eagerness 41

sustainability: China 1; definition 62; environmental 44; measurement 62; and social media 64–76

sustainability index: Wal-Mart 44

sustainable behavior: reluctance to participate 62; social media survey *66*, *69*

sustainable marketing: and social media 61–76

targeting: social media 63

terminology confusion 125

Theory of Planned Behavior (TPB) 125

Toyota Prius 85

transportation: green 72, 74

trust 61

Twitter 61–76; differences with Facebook 72; unique characteristics 64

UniPark (surveys) 65

United Kingdom (UK): willingness to pay for green 61

United States of America (USA): consumer 1; organic labeling 53; sustainability and social media 64–76; time spent on social media 62; willingness to pay for green 61

universal focus 21

value: assessing 80; green goods 61

Victoria's dirty Secret campaign 110–11

Victoria's Secret: experiments overview 113; future research 120–1; implications for practitioners 119–20

Victoria's Secret experiment 1: attitude change per eco-involvement groups 116; between-subject contrasts 116; confound check 115–16; framing effect on attitude 117; manipulation check 115; measures 114–15, *115*; sample 113–14; within-subject contrasts 116

Victoria's Secret experiment 2: attitude change per fashion involvement 119; between-subject effects 118; confound checks 118; data collection 117–18; manipulation check 118; sample 117; target effect on pro-environmental behavior and WOM 119; within-subject contrasts 118

vigilant strategists 35

vouchers 74

Wal-Mart: sustainability index 44

Western attitudes: self-construal 21

Whole Food Market 63

word-of-mouth (WOM) 116

WPP Brands: Green Bands Study 61